MANX MURDERS

This book is dedicated to all
the victims of serious crime.

MANX MURDERS

150 Years of Island Madness, Mayhem and Manslaughter

KEITH WILKINSON

MAINSTREAM
PUBLISHING

EDINBURGH AND LONDON

For every copy of this book sold the author will make a donation to the NSPCC (National Society for the Prevention of Cruelty to Children).

First published in Great Britain in 2003 by
MAINSTREAM PUBLISHING COMPANY (EDINBURGH) LTD
7 Albany Street
Edinburgh EH1 3UG

Reprinted 2003, 2004

ISBN 1 84018 692 5

A catalogue record for this book is available from the British Library

Typeset in Allise and Van Djick
Printed and bound in Great Britain by Mackays of Chatham

ACKNOWLEDGEMENTS

Many people assisted me in the preparation of this book.

Mr Michael Moyle, the High Bailiff of the Isle of Man gave assistance, as did members of the Manx Constabulary, and I am very grateful to Mr Moyle for writing the Foreword. Mr Mike Culverhouse, the Chief Constable, kindly gave permission for me to use relevant photographs in the possession of the constabulary.

Invaluable advice was given by Irene Teare, Tina Challenor and John Lee who helped to proofread the manuscript. I would like to thank Mike Blayney for his helpful suggestions for the cover design.

The staff of the library in the Manx Museum in Douglas were always helpful and courteous and in particular the Senior Archivist, Roger Sims, deserves a special mention for his encouragement and invaluable advice. I am equally grateful to the staff of the Public Records Office for their help with Chapter 8.

I would especially like to draw attention to the efforts of my secretary, Diane Butler, who kindly typed the manuscript and never complained about the never-ending changes made to it. Thank you, Diane, for encouraging me to carry on when it seemed that the book would never be published!

Finally I would like to thank my wife, Kerry, and daughters, Emma, Katie and Cara, for their love and support.

CONTENTS

FOREWORD

When I was recently asked by Dr Keith Wilkinson to write a few lines about his book, I was delighted to accept. Up to that point, I had been totally unaware of his somewhat unusual interest in violent crime. Those readers in the Isle of Man may be familiar with the more recent cases. However, the author's thorough and painstaking research has unearthed many more cases than one might have ever imagined. Students of Manx criminal history will find the various cases fascinating, while others will simply find them very interesting reading.

I have also been asked by the author to provide simple guidelines as to the court procedure in the Isle of Man. Before embarking upon such a task, I feel it might be important to ensure the reader is familiar with the geography and the constitutional position of the Isle of Man. Geographically it is 227 square miles in area and measures 32 miles from its northernmost tip at the Point of Ayre, to the Chicken Rock in the south and its widest point is 13 miles from east to west coast. It is found in the Irish Sea and its nearest point to Scotland is 16 miles, to England 34 miles, to Northern Ireland 40 miles and to Wales 55 miles. Constitutionally the Isle of Man is a dependency of the British Crown. It is neither part of the United Kingdom nor a colony. It has its own independent government and passes its own laws.

The criminal laws of the United Kingdom do not apply to the Isle of Man. Having said that, however, it would be idle to pretend that there are not considerable similarities between the two systems. I would venture to suggest that if a law student in the United Kingdom were somehow whisked into Court Number 3 in Douglas and were present throughout a murder trial, he or she would be hard pressed fully to appreciate all the differences. If the student arrived early enough, he or she would notice one obvious difference as the Coroner (a court official – *not* to be confused with the Coroner of

Inquests) proceeded to 'fence' the court. The Coroner does this by charging 'that no person shall quarrel, brawl or make any disturbance and that all persons shall answer their names when called'. The Coroner then (three times) calls upon all persons present 'to bear witness this court is now fenced'. The court then commences 'officially' to sit and the trial begins.

On looking around, a law student would see the defendant in the dock, a jury of 12 men and women trying the case, lawyers dressed in their familiar garb of black gowns and horsehair wigs and a judge presiding over proceedings. It might strike the student that the judge – known in the Isle of Man as a 'deemster' – is soberly dressed in a black gown, as opposed to the exotic 'livery' worn by his United Kingdom counterparts. He or she might also observe that the familiar coat of arms of lion and unicorn do not adorn the court but have been replaced by a coat of arms peculiar to the Isle of Man: a peregrine falcon and a raven.

The student might possibly, albeit after some considerable time, appreciate that behind what he or she believes to be the barristers in their wigs and gowns, there are no instructing solicitors to be found. This is because in the Island the professions of barristers and solicitors have been fused into one and all such practitioners are known as 'advocates'. I might also add at this point that at the Manx Bar there are no Queen's Counsel (that is not to say QCs never appear in the Isle of Man. There is provision in Manx law for English Counsel to be specifically licensed to conduct cases here).

Our hypothetical student would find the laws of evidence, definition of murder and the court procedure adopted to be indistinguishable from those adopted in a United Kingdom court. The only real difference that might register is that the deemster, in summing up to the jury, would direct the members that their verdict must be unanimous. There is no provision in Manx law for any majority verdict.

After summing up, the deemster would put the jury in charge of the Coroner. The members of the jury would then retire until they returned to deliver their collective verdict. Until the passing of the Death Penalty Abolition Act 1993, the only lawful sentence that could be imposed for an offence of murder was to order that the defendant 'suffer death as a felon'. Until its repeal, Section 368 of the Criminal Code 1872 provided:

> the judgment sentence and punishment shall be, that the person convicted shall be hanged by the neck until he be dead, and that the dead body of such person shall be buried within the precincts of the gaol or such other place as shall be ordered by the Court.

MANX MURDERS

Incidentally, I might point out that the Isle of Man still theoretically recognises the distinctions between felonies and misdemeanours although the reasons for those historical differences have, by and large, vanished.

Although the death sentence was actually pronounced in several recent cases until 1993, the actual penalty itself had not been carried out in the Island for well over 100 years and the death sentence in recent years would invariably be commuted to life imprisonment by the United Kingdom Home Secretary.

The Island has its own laws but there are distinct similarities as regards the two systems. For example, summary matters (in other words the less serious offences) are heard in the United Kingdom before lay magistrates or a district judge. In the Isle of Man, whilst we have lay magistrates, we do not have a district judge but we do have a High Bailiff, who sits alone when hearing and determining summary matters. The office of High Bailiff is an ancient and well-respected one and in addition to his duties as a stipendiary magistrate, the High Bailiff also acts as Coroner of Inquests and in various other capacities too lengthy to detail here.

The very serious matters (for example murder, manslaughter, rape, robbery) cannot be dealt with by the magistrates or the High Bailiff. These matters must eventually be heard before a deemster sitting in the Court of General Gaol Delivery. However, once a defendant has been arrested by the police in respect of such serious matters, he or she makes an initial appearance before the High Bailiff or the magistrates. Once the prosecution has completed its enquiries and all witness statements are taken, the defendant, if the circumstances warrant it, is then committed (or 'sent') to the Court of General Gaol Delivery either on bail or in custody to be dealt with there. The defendant at such a court will enter his or her plea to the formal written charge known as 'an Information' (the equivalent to the United Kingdom indictment) and if the defendant pleads 'not guilty' then a trial date will be fixed and the case will be heard before a jury of twelve in murder cases (but generally seven in the other serious cases such as rape, robbery etc.) selected by ballot from a panel itself selected at random.

I will add a historical note at this juncture. As indicated nowadays a defendant will almost invariably have to be committed by a magistrates court or by the High Bailiff to answer a charge of murder at the Court of General Gaol Delivery. This was not always the case. In Dr Wilkinson's book, you will find several examples of defendants finding their way to General Gaol via the finding of a Coroner of Inquests' jury. In cases such as murder or manslaughter, the jury would name the person(s) alleged to have committed the offence and the inquest operated as an indictment of the person(s) so charged, who would be committed to stand trial at the next convenient Court of General Gaol Delivery. Manx law was changed in 1987 (so as to bring it in line with its UK counterpart) and specifically by Section 12 (3): 'no such inquisition shall charge a person with murder, manslaughter or infanticide'. It would appear that Janice McCallum's death (Chapter 9) was the last time a particular person was named by a jury as being responsible for a death.

Furthermore, up until 1918 there was also a procedure by which an inquiry could be held before a deemster and a small jury of 'six good and lawful men', composed of jurors from the 'Special Jury List of Jurors from the Sheading' (district) in which the defendant resided. The Attorney General appeared either in person (or through a local advocate) to conduct what was in effect committal proceedings. The duty of the jury was not to find whether the accused was guilty or not but to say what charges, if any, should be preferred against the accused. If the Jury found there was a prima facie case of murder or manslaughter, the defendant was then committed to stand trial at a Court of General Gaol Delivery before a deemster and a jury of 12 who would determine whether or not he or she was guilty.

Nowadays, whilst the very serious cases must go to a Court of General Gaol Delivery, there are a number of matters which can either be heard summarily or before a Court of General Gaol Delivery. These offences consist of such matters as theft, obtaining by deception, causing actual bodily harm, 'simple' criminal damage etc. Unlike in the United Kingdom, the defendant does not have an automatic right to apply for his case to be heard before a jury. He may seek to persuade a summary court that a jury trial is appropriate but the final decision rests with the court itself.

If a defendant is convicted by a summary court and wishes to appeal, then there is no provision, as there is in the United Kingdom, for the case to be re-heard before a Crown judge and two magistrates. Appeals from the summary courts and from the Court of General Gaol Delivery are heard by the Manx Appeal Court (Staff of Government Division). In exceptional cases a defendant can appeal through the Staff of the Government Division to the Judicial Committee of the Privy Council. In recent times one defendant convicted of murder was able to persuade the Privy Council to overturn that verdict and substitute a conviction for manslaughter in place thereof. The other defendant, whose case was heard at the same time by the Privy Council, was not so successful and his conviction was upheld (*see* Chapter 4).

There is no Crown Prosecution Service in the Isle of Man. Uniformed police officers holding the rank of Sergeant and above prosecute the vast majority of criminal matters before the magistrates or the High Bailiff. If the complainant (i.e. body bringing the charge) is a government department, then the prosecution is generally conducted by a professional member of staff of the Island's Attorney General. All matters prosecuted at the Court of General Gaol Delivery are generally conducted by such professional members of the Attorney General's staff, although in certain cases they may do so with the assistance of English Counsel specially licensed for the purpose.

I hope I have not bored the reader overmuch and I have endeavoured merely to give a flavour of the law and procedures of the Isle of Man. I do not pretend that the aforementioned is comprehensive and, it should also be remembered, there will inevitably be exceptions to the various general rules.

On a personal note, I can clearly remember what is commonly called the 'Golden Egg Murder'. Indeed, even though it is nearly 30 years ago, certain parts are fresh in my memory, as if the event had only occurred last week. On the day that the body was discovered, I was by chance speaking to the Island's Attorney General, Arthur Christian Luft (later to become a most distinguished and universally respected second deemster and then first deemster), in his room at his chambers, which were then at the Tromode Drill Hall. He was telephoned by a senior officer of police and advised that the bound and bloody body of Nigel Neal had been found at the Golden Egg restaurant when a member of staff had gone in to open up for business that morning. The reaction of the Attorney General (which was the general one in the Island) was one of complete and utter disbelief. There had been no murder committed in the Isle of Man within most people's living memory and indeed a considerable number of police officers had joined the police force, completed their service and retired, without ever having encountered such a case. 'Such things do not happen on the Isle of Man' was quite a common cry to be heard throughout the Island.

Lunney was arrested within a few days of the offence and brought back to the Isle of Man. He was defended by two well-known and prominent local advocates and throughout the hearings was remanded in custody. Also it was not possible for there to be a 'paper' committal (that is a committal where the defendant is sent to the Court of General Gaol Delivery without the lower court even having to consider the evidence against him). It was necessary for the prosecution to conduct what is colloquially known as an 'old fashioned' committal. In other words, all the witnesses the prosecution were seeking to call at the eventual trial of the defendant were initially required to attend before His Worship the High Bailiff, who would take their sworn depositions. The defendant was allowed, if he so wished, to cross-examine the witnesses.

After committal proceedings had been completed (which from memory took some three days) the then High Bailiff, Henry William Callow (subsequently to become a distinguished Second Deemster some years later) determined that there was a prima facie case for Lunney to answer and accordingly committed him in custody to stand his trial at the next convenient Court of General Gaol Delivery. Although my memory may be at fault, I have it firmly fixed in my mind that the usual legal aid rate at that time was the princely sum of £3 2s 6d per hour. (It was also widely rumoured that the Defence Advocate had prevailed upon the authorities and had managed to achieve an uplift to somewhere in the region of £5 per hour!)

As the author has indicated, Lunney, having pleaded not guilty at an earlier court, then stood his trial in December 1973. It is quite interesting to note that the time between the murder and the actual hearing took only some four months. Regrettably the Isle of Man seems to be following the United Kingdom in that cases of this nature appear to be taking ever longer before the matter is finally determined. Such is progress!

As you might appreciate, the trial was the main subject of conversation throughout the Island and when the hearing did actually take place, I distinctly recall that the public galleries were packed. The jury consisted of 12 men (it was not until 1980 that the 'progressive' Isle of Man government decided that women might also be trusted to sit on a jury!), chosen at random and by ballot. Following his trial, Lunney was convicted and the rest, as they say, is history. (A complete account of the murder is contained within Chapter 1.)

I might also add that following Lunney's case it appeared to me that if the flood gates had not actually opened wide, then they had at least parted a little, because there were a considerable number of homicide matters (murder, manslaughter and infanticide) regularly coming before the Island's courts thereafter. In fact, I also clearly remember, on or about the third trial for murder following Lunney's case, looking around the back of the court to find that the public gallery consisted of only two or three people in it. These people were obviously friends or relatives of the defendant and there appeared to be no 'ordinary' members of the public interested in the proceedings. It was in stark contrast to what had occurred in the Lunney case but perhaps the novelty had worn off!

Up until the early 1970s the Isle of Man prided itself upon being a law-abiding community with very little crime and certainly very little violent crime. With the case of Lunney these misconceptions were banished and the age of innocence (if it ever really existed) had been lost forever. (At the time of writing, there are several defendants before the courts, two alleged to have committed murder and three alleged to have committed manslaughter.)

T. M. Moyle
High Bailiff

INTRODUCTION

Murder is a fascinating subject. Fictional murder stories have been popular for many years, but more recently there has been a dramatic increase in the number of books detailing true murders, which often become bestsellers. There is also the steadily increasing number of fictional television detectives who investigate murder cases. At the same time the number of television programmes dealing with the subject of true crime, particularly those on some of the satellite channels, seems to be increasing at an exponential rate.

The Isle of Man, with a current population of around 80,000, is often thought of as an island with a relatively low serious crime rate and as we shall see, this certainly was the case in the past. For example, apart from a case during the Second World War where the defendant was acquitted, a murder trial in 1973 was the first on the Island for 43 years.

Since 1973 up until 2003 there has been a dramatic change with at least 11 murder trials resulting in a conviction either for murder or manslaughter. In one case a man who had committed suicide was found guilty by a jury of murdering a young woman. In another murder trial in the 1970s a man who killed his wife was acquitted of all charges and walked free from the court. At the present time there is an ongoing investigation into the double murder of two teenagers.

Advances in techniques of crime detection and in particular the role of DNA profiling, as well as recent developments in the field of psychological profiling, have stimulated considerable interest in the subject of murder.

In this book I will endeavour to give the reader an account of some of those murders on the Isle of Man which have occurred over the last 150 years. Much of the information used in the book has been obtained from newspapers of the time, original inquest transcripts and trial transcripts, when it has been possible to obtain these.

MANX MURDERS

I know there will be some who would rather not hear about such events; they might consider that it would be best if they were forgotten forever and not 'dragged up from the past'. This may well be an understandable reaction, but there will be others who will be interested in reading about what is, after all, part of Manx history. All of these cases are *real*, they all *happened*, and nothing can ever change that. Perhaps by learning from them we may prevent similar tragedies occurring in the future – we might learn from our mistakes. If this book is a record of a part of Manx history of which many were unaware, I will have achieved many of my aims in writing the book.

One very serious concern I have had during the preparation of this book is the possibility of causing distress and heartache to any of those who were intimately involved in any of the cases I have described. If I have failed in my efforts to avoid this I can only offer my most sincere apologies. I have always attempted to describe only the facts of a case and have taken every precaution to minimise this risk. I have thought long and hard about even mentioning certain cases but feel that for the sake of completeness they should be included, if only in the briefest of details concerning the crime. Any errors are my own.

(Note: The chapters containing individual murders are not in chronological order.)

LIST OF MURDER CONVICTIONS ON THE ISLE OF MAN

VICTIM	MURDERER	DATE OF MURDER	DATE OF CONVICTION	LOCATION OF CRIME
Keith Kirby (45)	Andrew Dickson (29)	January 2000	March 2001	Douglas
Margaret Dobson (25)	Darren Christopher Dobson (29)	July 1997	November 1998[1]	Douglas
Steven Helwich (18)	Charles McCluskey (28)	October 1994	November 1995	Douglas
Corinne Bentley (22)	Anthony Robin Teare (22)	July 1991	July 1992[2]	Druidale
Brian Battista (1)	Stephen Philip Moore (19)	April 1982	November 1982	Douglas
Richard Ormrod Lindesay (79)	Michael John Pate (21)	April 1981	October 1981[3]	Ballasalla
Jack Bridson (67)	Graham Ralph Frankland (27)	October 1979	April 1980[4]	Castletown
Nigel Neal (26)	James Richard Lunney (21)	August 1973	December 1973	Douglas
Sgt William H. Malings (47)	Sgt John Williams (46)	May 1916	August 1916[5]	Knockaloe Camp
Percy W. Brooke (62)	Thomas Edward Kissack (43)	October 1930	November 1930[6]	Sulby Glen
John Kewish (69)	John Kewish (son) (40)	March 1872	July 1872[7]	Sulby Glen

[1] Reduced to manslaughter on appeal, December 1999. March 2000 given life sentence (minimum ten years).

[2] This was his first trial. Teare appealed and the conviction was quashed in November 1993. At the end of his trial in April 1994 he was again found guilty of murder and given a life sentence.

[3] Reduced to seven years for manslaughter on appeal, December 1981.

[4] Initial appeal of July 1980: dismissed. Privy Council March 1987: conviction for murder quashed. Reduced to nine years for manslaughter.

[5] Found guilty of murder but insane.

[6] Found guilty of murder but insane. Sent to Broadmoor.

[7] The last execution on the Isle of Man, 1 August 1872.

1

NIGEL NEAL: THE GOLDEN EGG MURDER (1973)

The Summerland indoor leisure centre opened on 25 May 1971. The first phase of the complex, the adjoining Aquadrome building containing two swimming pools, had been up and running for two years. Situated at the northern end of Douglas Promenade, the centre was a large building with a capacity for approximately 5,000 people and was designed to have a controlled 'tropical' climate. There were several upper floors arranged in open-faced terraces and the centre offered a variety of entertainments, including music, dancing, sunbathing, eating and drinking, bingo and table tennis. The building was enclosed by a steel framework, clad mostly in a transparent acrylic sheeting material known as 'Oroglas'.

A booklet entitled *The Summerland Story* explained the background to the complex and described Summerland as 'the biggest entertainment complex under one roof in the world and without doubt the finest'. In the section detailing the many problems encountered during its planning and construction, the reader was told that:

> With an entertainment centre of such a size, the question of fire-proofing was another major problem. Nothing could be left to chance. The main structure was ideal – solid concrete and non-combustible acrylic sheets. Any outbreak of fire in the future had to be one which could be localised to one room or one machine without any risk of spreading. Again the problems were overcome.

Within a year of those words being written, any illusions of safety that those involved in the creation of Summerland may have had would be shattered by a tragedy which made headlines around the world.

On the evening of Thursday, 2 August 1973, approximately 3,000 people were in Summerland. At around 7.40 p.m., three Liverpool schoolboys who were holidaying on the Island caused a partly dismantled yellow fibreglass kiosk to catch fire in the area of the mini-golf course on the terrace outside the main building. The schoolboys later told police that a discarded cigarette end accidentally started the fire, but at a subsequent inquiry into the events of that night it was revealed that the fire was started by a lighted match. Summerland staff were alerted and several tried unsuccessfully to extinguish the fire, which rapidly spread to an adjacent outer wall of the main building. In a very short space of time the entire building was engulfed in flames and all the floors at or above the entrance level were completely destroyed. Fifty men, women and children lost their lives in what was then the worst peacetime fire disaster in the British Isles since 1929.

The official public inquiry into the tragedy severely criticised almost all aspects of the design and operation of the centre, including the lack of fire resistance in the external wall of the building, some of the materials used in its construction – such as Oroglas – the lack of any proper preparation for the evacuation of the building and inadequate provision for means of escape. Before listing 34 recommendations which they hoped might help prevent a similar tragedy occurring again, the Commission stated:

> In all the above inadequacies and failings, it seems to the Commission that there were no villains. Within a certain climate of euphoria at the development of this interesting concept, there were many human errors and failures and it was the accumulation of these, too much reliance upon an 'old boy network', and some very ill-defined and poor communications, which led to the disaster.

Assistance was requested from the Lancashire Police Force in the subsequent investigation into the tragedy. People were still trying to come to terms with the Summerland disaster when, two weeks later, they were stunned to hear the news of the discovery of a body in suspicious circumstances in a restaurant in central Douglas.

Nigel Neal, aged 26, was married with two young children. After leaving school he had trained to be a chef in Coventry, later working as joint manager of a restaurant in Bowness, Cumbria, before moving with his family to Great Harwood in Lancashire where he worked as a night chef in a nearby hospital. He had left his home in Lancashire in May 1973 to take up a position as manager in the Golden Egg Restaurant at 10 Strand Street (now Boots Opticians), Douglas and lived in a flat above it. His bound and gagged body was discovered in the kitchen area of the restaurant on the morning of Wednesday, 15 August 1973, by the cleaner, Jean Cowell. She summoned the aid of a window cleaner, George Cawte, who then informed the police. Staff arriving for work were interviewed and taken to Douglas Police Station for questioning. The body lay in a pool of blood with a blood-stained frying-pan found nearby and, two days later, a blood-stained fire-extinguisher was also discovered. It was soon found that more than £1,000 was missing from the restaurant. Some CID officers from Lancashire were still on the Island investigating the Summerland fire and they were transferred to the new case. Others, who had only just returned home, were hastily recalled to assist in the murder investigation.

James Richard Lunney, aged 21 and single, came to live and work in the Isle of Man in June 1973. He had left school in Surrey at the age of 16, having obtained several O levels, and later worked in various casual jobs in different parts of England and in Guernsey. These included being a builder's labourer, farm worker, chef and trainee barman. By August 1973 he had several convictions for burglary and theft and was sought by police for fraud offences and the theft of a car. Although initially unemployed after arriving on the Island, he had soon obtained work as a lorry driver in Douglas but he left this position after five weeks. He stayed at several addresses before moving into lodgings at 14 Christian Road, Douglas on 22 July using the name Richard Harris. He started work as a grill chef at the Golden Egg Restaurant one week before Neal's body was found but he fell behind with his rent payments and on 14 August he was ordered to leave the house in Christian Road by his landlady, Mrs Ada Elizabeth Taylor. From statements taken from staff at the Golden Egg it soon became clear that Lunney was the last person to see Neal alive. Although it had been reported that the two men appeared to be on good terms, Lunney quickly became the main suspect in the murder investigation. It was never clearly established, but subsequently suspected by police, that Neal and Lunney may have known each other before they came to the Island. There was also later to be a suggestion of some ill-feeling between the two men over their relationship with a young waitress at the restaurant.

A search for Lunney was instigated and a description of the chief suspect in the inquiry was released by police the day after the discovery of the body. They named the man as James Richard Lunney, who also used the aliases Richard Harris, J. R. Harris and John Sandrey. Born on 27 July 1952, he came from Wimbledon and was 5 ft 11 in. tall with a 'fresh' complexion. Described as 'well spoken', he had short, light brown hair and blue eyes. He was last known to have been wearing a navy blue rally coat. It was quickly established that he had checked into the nearby Athol Hotel under the name John Sandrey at around 10.00 p.m. on the night of the 14 August. The police soon discovered that between midnight on Tuesday, 14 August and 12.30 a.m. Wednesday, 15 August, a part-time taxi driver, Geoffrey Walmsley, was driving his taxi along Douglas Promenade. He was hailed by a man who ran from between cars parked on the sea side of the Promenade, close to what at that time was the Athol Hotel. The man told Walmsley that his wife was seriously ill in Newcastle and he had to get off the Island as soon as possible so that he could be with her. The taxi driver suggested that he should contact the airport about flights and said that it might be possible to get a boat to take him to England. The man got into the taxi and was taken up Victoria Street but asked to be let out near the top of the street. The taxi driver thought no more of the incident until he later heard a description of the wanted man.

Lunney returned to the Athol Hotel around 12.30 a.m. on the morning of 15 August and was at that time noted to be sweating. He told the manageress of the hotel that he had received a telegram informing him that his wife had been in a car crash in Newcastle and that he had to get off the Island as soon as possible. He asked her how he could charter a plane and after she made some enquiries for him, he was told that the airport was closed until 7.00 a.m. Lunney also asked her about boats leaving the Island. He left the bar at 12.45 a.m. and at approximately 1.00 a.m. the hotel porter saw him leave the hotel with a black suitcase. At 1.50 a.m. he booked a room at the Palace Hotel on Douglas Promenade about half a mile away, also under the name of John Sandrey, paying for this with a £5 note. He was later observed several times in the hotel and was seen to take a taxi from in front of it.

When he heard the description of the wanted man, the driver of that taxi, George Pyatt, aged 57 years, came forward to tell police that he may have valuable information. He explained how he had been driving along a deserted Douglas Promenade at around 6.00 a.m. on Wednesday, 15 August and as he passed the Palace Hotel he heard a shout and a whistle. He saw that a man on the first floor balcony was signalling for him to stop and went on to describe how the man asked to be taken to Ronaldsway, the Island's airport near Castletown. The only luggage he was carrying was a small 'executive-type' briefcase. During the journey to the airport he told Pyatt that he had earlier 'made a killing' in the casino, clearing a gambling table of £300. Pyatt added that there was nothing unusual in the man's behaviour and that he had told him he needed to get off the Island as soon as possible as either his mother or sister was ill. When they arrived at Ronaldsway, about eight miles from

Douglas, at around 6.15 a.m. the man had paid the £1.50 fare with two £1 notes from a large roll of banknotes. The airport was closed at that time but when a member of the airport police emerged from a nearby hut, Pyatt suggested that his passenger speak to him. The taxi driver thought no more about his early morning trip to the airport until he heard about the man the police wished to question and he felt sure that his passenger was Lunney. The airport policeman, Ronald Ian Ludgate, told detectives that he had contacted John Lewis, a pilot with the Manx Flyers Aero Club, on Lunney's behalf and he had agreed to take the man to Blackpool. Ludgate was with the man for about an hour and five minutes and made him a cup of coffee while they waited for the pilot. The passenger filled in a form using the name John Sandrey of 38 Hauteville Street, St Peter's Port, Guernsey, but strangely he had dated the form 12 October, although Lewis did not notice this until later. The pair left Ronaldsway at approximately 7.35 a.m. in a two-seater plane, arriving in Blackpool about thirty minutes later, around the time that Neal's body was being discovered in Douglas. Ten minutes later Lewis was on his way back to the Island while Lunney, having paid for the trip with £15 from a roll of banknotes, continued in his attempt to escape justice and left the airport in a taxi, on the next leg of his journey.

Police acting on this information then switched what the press described as 'the biggest manhunt the Island has ever known', to Blackpool and a description of Lunney was circulated to police throughout the country. The taxi driver who picked him up from Blackpool airport was soon located. He described how he had taken Lunney to a garage at Clayton-le-Woods near Chorley where he paid £510 cash for a car: a white MGB Roadster, registration number JFV 465F. Enquiries revealed that he had also purchased three road maps for northern England and southern and central Scotland.

After a brief stay at a hotel near Ulverston, Cumbria, Lunney made his way to Edinburgh. Information about his vehicle had by now been circulated, requesting that all public and hotel car parks be visited that night in an effort to trace the car. At 12.30 a.m. on Friday, 17 August, Police Constable David Berry located the vehicle in the car park of the Post House Hotel in Edinburgh and after surveillance during the night, Lunney was arrested at 6.05 a.m. that same morning, when he emerged from the hotel and got into the car. He was taken to the Central Police Station in Parliament Square, Edinburgh.

When searched by police, he was found to have in his possession £331.02 and, amongst other things, a bunch of keys which were later found to belong to the lock of the front door of the Golden Egg Restaurant. Also found in

Lunney's suitcase was an anorak belonging to the owner of the Golden Egg, Royston Knight, which was later shown to have been taken from the restaurant.

On the day Lunney was arrested, the Head of CID on the Isle of Man, Haydn Fitzsimmons and Detective Sergeant Alan Jones, travelled to Edinburgh to interview him. He told them that he wished to make a written statement and following this he was taken back to the Island. At 7.40 p.m. the following day, Saturday, he was charged with Neal's murder. In answer to the charge he replied 'Just as I said before, I didn't do it with malice aforethought.' On 7 September Lunney was also charged at Douglas Police Station with robbery with violence.

An inquest was held in Douglas the day after the body was found. The dead man's wife, Mrs Hilary Neal, from Great Harwood, Lancashire, gave identification evidence. She told the inquiry that she had identified her husband's body in the mortuary of Noble's hospital and she stated that she had last seen her husband alive on 11 July when he had returned home for the day. She had spoken to him regularly on the telephone, the last time being Tuesday, 14 August, the day before his body was discovered. She explained how she had rung her husband at 12.25 a.m. on the morning of 15 August but there was no answer. She rang several more times, until 2.25 a.m., but there was still no answer.

Dr Joesph H. Ferguson, police surgeon to Douglas District, gave evidence. He described how he had been called to the scene of the crime at 8.45 a.m. on the morning the body was discovered. It was lying face upwards on the floor of the small scullery on the ground floor at the rear of the premises. The body was dressed in a shirt, trousers, butcher's apron and boots. The legs were tied together at the ankles by a cloth and piece of rope. The hands were tied together across the front of the body with a neck-tie, which was also secured to the metal leg of a sink unit and the mouth was gagged with a cloth, which was knotted into it. The face and head were covered in blood and bloodstained footmarks were seen around the body, on the stairs and on the floor above. A pathologist, Dr Stephen Baker from Noble's Hospital, was present at a post-mortem carried out by a forensic pathologist from Chorley. He stated that death was caused by a cerebral haemorrhage due to skull fracture.

Lunney's trial opened in the Douglas Courthouse on 6 December 1973 in front of a packed courtroom. It was the first murder trial to be heard on the Island for 43 years. (The murder trial in 1943 of a Finnish POW who was acquitted of a charge of killing another Finnish internee in a fight, was held *in camera* for security reasons and most of the details of that case were not heard by the general public; *see* Chapter 3.) The prosecution team was led by the Attorney General, Mr Arthur Luft, and government advocate Michael Moyle. The defence team was led by Edwyn Garside and Eric Teare and the trial was heard before Deemster R. K. Eason.

Evidence was given that although he was not on duty on the evening in question, Lunney had gone to the Golden Egg Restaurant. He had spoken to Mr Neal between 9.00 p.m. and 10.15 p.m. and had then left the restaurant before returning after 11.00 p.m. when he told other members of staff present that he and Neal planned to visit the casino later. Mrs Joan Benson of Foxdale was the night cashier at the Golden Egg on 14 August. She described being given a note by Lunney for Neal, who was working in the kitchen at the back of the restaurant. When Mr Neal opened the note at about 8.30 p.m. she saw that it started with something about 'Annette and Chris' and she added that Neal seemed 'a bit annoyed' by it. Sergeant Ralph Kewley, stationed at Douglas, told the court of the discovery in the victim's wallet of this note. The note said: 'Nigel, have seen Annette and Chris is back. We'll be in the lounge bar at the casino if you're interested at 12.30. Richard.' Mrs Benson left the restaurant shortly before midnight, when her husband arrived to take her home. Three waitresses left the restaurant shortly after this, leaving Neal and Lunney alone in the building. Mrs Benson said that apart from the note she had not heard any argument between the two, and so far as she was aware they seemed to be on good terms that evening.

Lunney himself gave evidence at the trial. He described coming to the Island in June 1973 and taking up employment at the restaurant the week before Neal was killed. On the evening in question he described how he left the Athol Hotel some time before 10.00 p.m., going along Strand Street to a Chinese restaurant where he had a meal before returning to the Golden Egg to wait for Nigel Neal to finish work. He said that he arrived back at the Golden Egg at about 11.00 p.m. or maybe a little after and the restaurant had already closed. The staff were by now busy cleaning up and he sat inside the restaurant and spoke to several of them, chatting to Mrs Benson's husband for about five minutes while he was waiting for his wife. After they had left the restaurant, Lunney said he spoke to the other staff who left shortly afterwards in a taxi at approximately 11.45 p.m.

Lunney then spoke to Nigel Neal and they had a drink together in the restaurant. He stated that Neal then went to the kitchen at the back of the restaurant to finish off cleaning up and after Lunney went to join him there, the topic of conversation had soon turned to the subject of women. Lunney claimed that Neal wanted an introduction to a friend of his called Annette whom he had met shortly after coming to the Island. An argument then started and he claimed that he had told Neal he did not agree with things he was saying and reminded him that he, Neal, was married. He felt that Neal had wanted to 'get Annette into bed', adding that Neal then took a wild swing at him and a fight broke out between the two, and they fell to the floor. Neal had then, according to Lunney, tried to hit him with a pan which he took from a rack above the sinks. Lunney explained that he then grabbed a fire extinguisher and described how he hit Neal two or three times with it on the head. Neal fell to the floor and Lunney found that his shirt was covered in blood. He said that he removed his shirt and left it in the kitchen before going upstairs where he found a sweatshirt, which he then put on. He washed the blood off his hands and arms, went downstairs again and out of the front door. Having locked the door behind him he left the restaurant for about 10–15 minutes whilst he considered his predicament. He then returned to the Golden Egg, unlocked the door, and went back inside. He found a brown paper bag with money in it next to the cash desk, which Neal had not put in the safe and also found the safe keys next to the money. After going upstairs and opening the safe, he found a pile of banknotes but then heard noises coming from the kitchen below and returned to find Neal groaning on the floor. Neal looked as though he was trying to get up but was unable to do so. Lunney claimed that he thought Neal would be all right until the morning and he then tied his legs and hands with cloth and gagged him but tried to ensure that he would be able to breathe adequately. Lunney said, 'He looked bloody but he didn't look like he was going to die.'

After leaving the Golden Egg Restaurant Lunney took a taxi along Douglas promenade to the Palace Hotel where he rented a room, giving his name as John Sandrey of St Peter's Port, Guernsey. He also declared in the hotel register that he was a Canadian national and gave his occupation as pilot. He told the court that he and Neal had been good friends. He then referred to the note that he had written to Neal, explaining that this was an invitation for the manager to join him and Annette in the lounge bar of the casino.

Dr Stephen Garratt, a pathologist attached to the Home Office, gave his evidence. He said that death had been caused by several hard blows with a heavy blunt instrument and was not instantaneous. He estimated the time of death to be approximately 1.00 a.m. on 15 August, plus or minus one hour.

Another griddle chef in the restaurant, Kevin Paul Carey from Dublin, said that he was cleaning up in the griddle area on 17 August when he found a fire extinguisher under the chip fryers. This was later given to the chief fingerprint officer from the Lancashire Constabulary. Bloodstained fingerprints on the extinguisher were found to be identical to Lunney's right thumb and fore-fingerprints.

Police Constable Kelly told the court that he had gone to the Golden Egg at 10.00 a.m. on 15 August. He described the state of the body and also described bloody footprints on the floor.

At the end of the six-day trial, the jury brought in a verdict of guilty on both counts. The only possible sentence under Manx law at that time was death, under Section 18 of the Criminal Code, although it was fully expected that the Home Secretary, Mr Robert Carr, would reprieve the prisoner and commute the sentence to one of life imprisonment. However, as one of the reporters from a local newspaper said:

> It was a breathtaking moment when he [Lunney] was sentenced to death by Deemster Eason at the end of the trial. It was a unanimous verdict from the 12-man jury (which it had to be) after a retirement of one hour.

When he was found guilty of murder and robbery with violence Lunney showed no emotion. Details of his criminal record were then read by Haydn Fitzsimmons, head of the Manx CID. Asked if he had anything to say, Lunney replied, 'No, Sir.'

The deemster then told him: 'The sentence of this court is that you should be hanged by the neck until you are dead.' No black cap was donned by the deemster and, as expected, the sentence was later commuted to one of life imprisonment.

Deemster Eason complimented the Manx Police Force on the way the investigation had been carried out and the evidence brought before the court.

2

FRANCES ALICE QUAYLE (1914)

Murder is a devastating event, one which affects the victim's family and friends, as well as those close to the person who has committed the crime. When the victim of a murder is discovered and the identity of the killer is not known, people living in the surrounding area can experience many different emotions. They often feel fear, either for themselves or members of their family or friends and although this can diminish with time, it often lasts until the perpetrator has been arrested. For example if a small child had been abducted and later murdered, all parents would fear for the safety of their children. If an elderly person was murdered during a burglary people would become frightened of a similar fate befalling their elderly relatives or neighbours.

Certainly, most people will also feel a sense of shock and horror that such an awful crime could occur in their community and may find that they are unable to sleep properly. People's sense of security and safety is often shattered when such a serious crime is committed and their whole outlook on life can change. They sometimes feel intense anger towards the person who has perpetrated a crime in their midst, a crime they hoped they would never personally encounter. In the aftermath of a murder committed locally, their daily routines may change. Some people might decide that they will not go out alone after dark; they may install burglar alarms or buy personal attack alarms; or they may learn the basics of self-defence. Others might stop visiting certain areas where they perceive the risk of harm to be greatest and police warnings in the local press and information given on posters, billboards and walls are a constant reminder to them of the danger they may face from a faceless, nameless killer.

Those close to the victim often have even more intense feelings. They can feel guilt, hatred, an intense desire for revenge and, in some cases, suicidal thoughts. Many experience simple raw pain over their loss, which is worse than anything they have previously experienced and which shows no sign of going away and is not eased by their attempts to relieve it.

If the suspected murderer is apprehended some of these fears may diminish and once that person has been charged with the crime and remanded in custody people may begin to return to some semblance of normality. If the murderer is convicted at the subsequent trial and imprisoned for many years the vast majority of people will put the awful events behind them and move on with their lives. Of course, this does not always happen for the unfortunate few who have lost loved ones, who may never recover from their loss and find that they are constantly thinking about what has happened and what might have been. Birthdays, anniversaries, Christmas and any number of other occasions can bring the sad memories flooding back and make it seem as if there is no end in sight and no hope of any improvement in the situation.

In the situation where such a crime occurs and police do not find the perpetrator, the fear can persist indefinitely. It is a well-recognised fact that the best chance of identifying the murderer is in the early days after the crime and the chances of finding the person responsible then diminish with increasing duration of time following the event. In a small island community such as the Isle of Man the suspicion that a killer is on the loose is a very frightening proposition indeed, but this was precisely the situation for the people of Douglas in 1914, when a brutal murder occurred which remains unsolved to this day.

Mrs Frances Alice Quayle was 55 years old and lived alone at 40 Bucks Road in central Douglas. It was reported in newspapers of the day that her husband, Thomas Henry, had been a steward on one of the Isle of Man Steam Packet Company's boats and had died when Mrs Quayle was 26. Described as quite a well-built lady, probably about 6 ft tall, she kept a small grocery and wine and spirits shop in Bucks Road that was attached to her house and it seems that this was apparently quite a successful business and one her father had before her. She had one daughter, Maud, who was married to John D. Cowley and lived with him in Douglas. Mrs Quayle had a brother who lived in Ballaugh and another who had gone to Australia. Well known and respected in the area, she was known to be fond of animals and had a small garden behind Fairfield Terrace at the end of Tynwald Street, again close to her house, where she kept rabbits. She sometimes went to the garden in the morning and on most nights fed the rabbits after her shop closed in the evening. Every day she fed corn to the pigeons that constantly roosted outside her shop on Bucks Road.

After closing her shop on the evening of Saturday, 25 April 1914, Mrs Quayle called at a sweetshop opposite at 43 Bucks Road, and spoke to a Miss Catherine Isobel Quayle after buying some sweets there. Miss Quayle had asked her if she was not afraid of going to the garden at such a late hour. She replied that she had been to the garden at all hours and had 'never been molested and had no fear'. The two women had spoken around 10.30 p.m. for about five minutes and then she had left the shop and set off for her little garden at the rear of Finch Hill Congregational Church to feed the rabbits. She must have first called at her house, as the sweets she had just bought would be later found on a table there.

There were no reported sightings of her on the Sunday and a young boy was later to describe how he called at her house and found a door open but she had not been in. The following morning, Monday 27 April, a neighbour, John Kelly, a car showroom proprietor whose premises were opposite Mrs Quayle's shop, noticed that it was not open for business at its usual time. Feeling uneasy when he found that the blinds were still down and the door was locked, he then spoke to Miss Quayle at the sweetshop. The pair of them went back to Mrs Quayle's shop and Miss Quayle found that the side door was open. Letting herself in, she found that the gas was still burning in the kitchen and called out to Mrs Quayle several times but received no response. Kelly then decided to try to contact Mrs Quayle's son-in-law, John D. Cowley and telephoned his place of work, Heron and Brearley's. Kelly soon met up with Cowley in Albert Street and explained his concerns to Cowley who then made a fruitless search of the house. With still no sign of his mother-in-law, Cowley, accompanied by Kelly, went to the garden. After walking up the narrow lane joining Tynwald Street to Clarke Street they reached the door in the high wall surrounding the garden and tried it but found it locked. Cowley then, assisted by Kelly, climbed with difficulty to the top of the wall from where he saw his mother-in-law's body. Dropping down into the garden whilst Kelly ran to summon medical aid, Cowley found that there was no key in the lock on the inside of the door, and using a spade to force the lock, he opened the door and awaited the arrival of the doctor. Kelly soon returned with Dr Henry Caird. The men saw that the body lay in a small passageway between a shed and a greenhouse. The recess in which it was found was approximately 6 ft long. The body was discovered in a huddled-up sitting position with the face towards the ground and the top of the head beaten in; a lot of blood lay around the body. Three of the victim's fingers had been broken in the attack and splashes of blood were found on the shed, the rabbit hutch and the greenhouse. It was discovered that blood had flowed 10 to 12 ft from the body along the ground. Dr Caird found that the blows to Mrs Quayle's head were so severe that she had suffered skull fractures and bone had been driven into her brain.

The body was removed to the mortuary. The police were called and subsequent enquiries revealed that several neighbours had heard a scream at approximately 11.00 p.m. on the Saturday night. No one, however, had witnessed the crime but quite a few people came forward to report that they had been in and around the lane on the night in question. Although there was no definite motive, it was felt that the murderer had followed Mrs Quayle into the garden with the intention of attacking her. It appeared that after attacking Mrs Quayle the killer had locked the door to the garden behind him or her before fleeing the scene. The blood-stained keys were found by a young boy in a lane near Princes Street, about 100 yards from the garden gate, and they included one which fitted the lock to the gate. After searching the properties belonging to the murdered woman it was found that there did not appear to be anything missing from either Mrs Quayle's house or shop and police later found approximately £79 in cash in her house.

Assistance was requested from Scotland Yard and Chief Inspector Ward and Sergeant Cooper arrived on the Island to conduct the enquiries. An extensive search for the murder weapon ended with the discovery by a policeman of a large eye-bolt – a tool used for tightening the wire supports on telegraph poles. This too was blood stained and also had traces of human hair on it which proved to be the victim's. The murder weapon was found several hundred yards from the murder scene on land near Noble's Hall. It was made of iron and described as being approximately 13 in. in length and 2.75 in. in width.

An inquest was opened on the Tuesday following the discovery of the body and a 13-man jury was sworn in. They first viewed the body at the mortuary and then visited the scene of the crime before returning to the courthouse. Coroner Gell outlined the case to the jury and they heard about the circumstances surrounding the discovery of Mrs Quayle's body and a description of the victim's terrible injuries. Several witnesses then gave evidence about events of the night of 25 April before the Coroner adjourned the inquest and released the body, which was buried at Braddan on Thursday, 30 April.

The inquest resumed on Friday, 22 May. Albert Skillicorn was 13 years old and he gave his evidence. His statement as told to the jury went as follows:

Since August last, I have been in Mrs Quayle's employ as an errand boy after school hours. On the evening of Saturday, 25 April, I left the shop at quarter past ten. The shop was then closed and the gates put up outside. About nine o'clock I went on a message to Mr Kneale's in Peveril Street. I went from Peveril Street through the lane to Tynwald Street. I saw a man standing in the lane. He was standing against the wall. He looked a young man. He had what looked like a blue suit of clothes on and a grey cap. I thought he was drunk and was frightened. I returned to Mrs Quayle's but not by the lane.

On Sunday morning I took Mr Cowley's little boy, aged three years, for a walk and we called at Mrs Quayle's. I knocked at the back door and got no answer. I found the door was not locked and I went in the kitchen door, which was open. The little boy called his grandmother but there was no answer.

We went again in the evening about half-past six o'clock. We went to the kitchen door and called to Mrs Quayle but there was no reply. I noticed that the gas was burning in the kitchen and the hall. I did not tell anyone that Mrs Quayle was not in.

Another witness, Thomas Crennell, stated that he had known Mrs Quayle 'all his life'. He said that he had often seen her going from her home across Princes Street and up the lane leading to her garden, explaining that this would generally be from 10.30 p.m. to 11 p.m. He had been to the Strand Cinema earlier on the evening of the murder and left about 10.15 p.m. before going straight home. After ten minutes he had gone out again to go to the sweetshop and on his way there he had seen Mrs Quayle in Princes Street. She was just entering the lane leading in the direction of her garden and he estimated the time to be about 10.40 p.m. She had a basket under her arm and was alone. He had looked up the lane but saw no one in it and no one following her.

Joseph Bucknall recalled that he had gone into Miss Quayle's sweetshop as Mrs Quayle was coming out. The time would then have been between 10.30 p.m. and 10.35 p.m.

Mrs Quayle's son-in-law, Cowley, said that she often had 'hundreds of pounds' in the house. He could not see that anything had been disturbed when he had searched it. He had no suspicion of anyone who might have been involved in the murder of his wife's mother.

Dr Caird described the severe head injuries which he found on examination of the body. In the doctor's opinion, the injuries were caused by repeated heavy blows. There were skull fractures, lacerations and bruising to the face and further bruising to the arms. He stated that the head injuries could not possibly have been self-inflicted, nor could they have resulted from an 'ordinary fall'. He said that 'the injury to the head could perfectly well have been caused by the eye-bolt' and felt that it would be impossible for the murderer to have 'escaped without being splattered with blood'. There was bruising to all the fingers of both hands and several were broken and there was a great deal of blood on and around the body.

Catherine Quayle of 43 Bucks Road, Douglas, said that Mrs Quayle had come into her sweetshop at about 10.20 p.m. and stayed about five minutes, but did not notice which way she went as she left. She knew that Mrs Quayle was in the habit of going to her garden after closing time to feed her rabbits. When she had arrived at her shop at 8.30 a.m. on the Monday morning she noticed that Mrs Quayle's shop was still closed and this, she said, was very unusual as the shop was generally open before hers. She described going to the house, finding it empty and then informing Mr Kelly of this. She was not aware of anyone who had threatened Mrs Quayle or had 'any grievances against her'.

Alice Dobson had also seen Mrs Quayle at about 11.00 p.m. as she went for chips at Kelly's shop in Tynwald Street. She saw her cross Tynwald Street then go up the lane towards her garden. She too had not seen anyone else in the lane. She said that she knew a man called Thomas Hall but did not see him that night.

Ridgeway Quirk was also out and about that evening, and he told how he had seen Mrs Quayle about 10.45 p.m. at the bottom of Finch Hill Lane. She was going up the lane towards her garden and he followed a yard or two behind. He too recalled that she was carrying a basket and was alone. He thought he heard her unlock the door before she went in and close it behind her. He did not hear her lock it on the inside. He then continued on his way and went home. After five minutes he went back down the lane and later went back up it. He saw no one in the lane and heard no noises from the garden as he passed it on these latter two occasions.

James Bridson and his brother walked through the lane about 10.20 p.m. that night. James said he saw a shadow of someone in the lane near the door to Mrs Quayle's garden but could not say if it was a man or a woman. He heard the door being closed and locked on the inside and added: 'By the jingle, I thought it was by a key on a bunch. I was right abreast of the door when it was closed and locked.' His brother, Alfred, also heard the keys jingle but saw no one in the lane.

Mary Jane Canipa described how she was on her way to church at 7.30 a.m. with her children on the Sunday morning, 26 April, when her little boy had found a bunch of keys in a lane near Princes Street. She told her son to put them down and met a police constable later and told him about the keys. The police officer made enquiries about the keys but was unable to trace the owner. He then took them to the police station. They were subsequently found to belong to the murdered lady and one of the keys fitted the lock in the door to the garden.

Another policeman, Philip Watterson, described how he was searching the area near the murder scene on Monday, 27 April when he found the eye-bolt in the garden at the rear of Noble's Hall. The garden was surrounded by a 7 ft-high wall with barbed wire on top of it. The eye-bolt had blood and hairs on it.

Thomas Hall, a butcher living in Tynwald Street, also spoke at the inquest. He had gone out that evening to buy some meat. Walking along Tynwald Street to Bucks Road, he met a man called Thomas Angus Moore and briefly saw Moore's wife. He also saw Mrs Quayle. She had walked from Bucks Road into Tynwald Street. Moore asked him for tobacco then a match. As she passed them he asked Mrs Quayle if she was going to feed her pets and asked her for a match, which she gave him. She was carrying a basket and continued on her way but Hall said she did not go up the lane by her garden. After Mrs Quayle passed by, Hall claimed that Moore had said to him that he would 'knock her bloody head off' as he claimed she had refused to serve him with something in her shop. Hall said that he had seen Moore with something like an eye-bolt that night.

Moore said that he 'had no fixed home'. He had been out with his wife that Saturday. He denied seeing Hall and had slept rough both during that night and also on the Sunday. This man was questioned by police but emphatically denied any involvement in the murder and was later released.

A local newspaper published a plan showing the murder scene and surrounding area which jogged the memory of one potential witness. He was a motorcyclist who had returned home through Allan Street on the night in question between midnight and 1.00 a.m. He had seen a man close to where the weapon was later found. The man was standing under the light of a street lamp but had quickly retreated into the shadows when he heard the cyclist approaching, as if not wanting to be seen. As he was not really acquainted with that part of Douglas, the motorcyclist had not initially come forward, until seeing the plan in the *Daily Times*. He gave a description of the man to police investigating the case. The case aroused great interest in England, with reporters from several national newspapers travelling to the Island, including reporters from the *Daily News*, *Daily Mail* and *Daily Despatch*.

The murdered lady's brother, Campbell Stewart Cubbon, aged 50 years, of Ballaugh, told a reporter with the *Isle of Man Weekly Times*, a week after his sister's death, 'Hanging is too good for the man who has done this deed; he ought to be cut into pieces and flung into the sea. He is not fit to be on God's Acre among other men and women, and not fit to be buried with other people.' He also felt that the murderer had climbed over the garden wall and had lain in wait for his sister. He added that in his opinion more than one person was involved in the crime and that whoever had committed it must have been aware that his sister went to the garden at the same time each night. Mr Cubbon later offered a reward of £50 for information leading to the conviction of the killer.

The Grand Theatre in Victoria Street had been the venue for two weeks for a show billed as 'The Event of the Year'. An advertisement in a local newspaper informed the reader that the 'World Renowned Author, Scientist and Entertainer, The Famous Bloodless Surgeon and Electric Wizard, assisted by the gifted and beautiful La Belle Electra' were giving daily performances. An article in the newspaper described how, on 1 May, Dr Walford Bodie had placed the clairvoyant 'La Belle Electra' in a hypnotic trance in private and subsequently read out to the audience what he claimed was a description given by her of the murder. He reported that:

> The murder took place on Saturday night at 11.25 p.m. The murderer is a tall, fair man with a short stubbly moustache, wearing a cap and dark grey suit. After leaving her shop, Mrs Quayle was followed by the man who had a bar of iron under his jacket, up a lane near the shop. After she opened the garden gate, the murderer followed her in. She was making towards the rabbit hutch when she heard the sound of the murderer's footsteps. She turned round sharply and said 'Who is there? What do you want here?' The man immediately felled her to the ground by a blow from his fist, smashing a pair of glasses she wore and cutting her face with the blow. He then delivered two very severe blows with the bar of iron on his victim's head, took the keys from her and locked the garden gate. He then made for the shop. Coming down a lane at the end of the street, he saw a policeman standing not far from the shop and as he was bespattered with blood, he got alarmed, turned up a side street, placed the keys on a window sill, then crossed

the street, passed down a narrow lane near some stables, got out into a wide street and made off towards the country. At this stage Mademoiselle La Belle Electra collapsed.

In his summing up, the Coroner told the jury that in his view the statement given by Hall was untrue. He said, 'The only evidence to implicate anyone in this matter is the evidence of Hall and he states that Thomas Angus Moore threatened Mrs Quayle.' His said he felt Moore and his wife had told the truth, adding, 'I am very much inclined to suggest to you that Hall's story is fictitious.'

Despite all the efforts of the police they were unable to solve the mystery of who had killed Mrs Quayle. Many vagrants were questioned without any light being shed on the mystery. The verdict of the inquest jury was: 'Wilful murder by a person or persons unknown'. The murder remains unsolved to this day.

3

NESTOR HUPPUNEN: SECOND WORLD WAR CASE (1943)

In the early stages of the Second World War it became clear that internment was required for those who might pose a threat to national security. Internment camps were set up in the Isle of Man by Home Office officials in co-operation with the Manx government. Camps were established in Douglas, Ramsey, Peel and Port Erin. By 1940 there were around 14,000 enemy aliens interned on the Island. In 1943 the Mooragh Camp in Ramsey held men of three nationalities – German, Finnish and Italian. The three groups of men were held in separate parts of the main camp divided by wire fences.

Among the men in the Finnish camp were Karlo Albin Salminen and Nestor Huppunen. In April that year their paths were to cross in circumstances which would leave one dead and the other to face trial for murder.

Salminen had been born in Michigan, USA on 30 March 1907 but was of Finnish nationality. He was a merchant seaman and first arrived in the UK in March 1941. He had registered at the Aliens Office in Liverpool and was given an Aliens Registration Certificate and an ID card by the National Registration Office.

While in Liverpool he lived at the Sailors' Home and made two trips to sea as a ship's fireman until he arrived back in Liverpool on 5 October 1941 on a Canadian steamer. He failed to rejoin the vessel and was therefore arrested on 18 October and taken to HM Immigration Office in Liverpool, where a detention order was issued for deserting his ship. He was then detained in prison in Liverpool while arrangements could be made by the Cunard White Star Line to have him removed from the country. However, before this could be done the Home Secretary ordered the internment of all Finnish subjects and he was sent directly from the prison in Liverpool on 8 December 1941 to the Mooragh internment camp in Ramsey on the Isle of Man.

MANX MURDERS

Huppunen had been born on 26 February 1916 in Finland. He had also been a seaman and was unmarried. He had arrived in Hull and was detained under the Aliens Order 1920, Section 1 (1A). Initially he had been transferred to the Palace camp in Douglas on 2 May 1942 and later was interned in the Mooragh Camp in Ramsey on 3 November 1942.

It is important to consider the situation which existed in the camp in the weeks and months leading up to the fatal meeting between the two men. The Finns in the camp were in a peculiar situation. The USSR and Finland had previously had a war of their own which resulted in great antagonism between the countries. When the USSR came into the war against Germany, Finland allied with the Germans against the Russians. Relations between Britain and Finland had until then been very friendly but after Finland sided with Germany, Britain was forced to declare war on Finland. To confuse matters, whilst the Finnish government was pro-Germany (and hence many of the Finns in the Mooragh Camp were pro-Germany) some prisoners were pro-Russia and supported the Allied cause. Initially some 400 Finns had been interned and the majority were pro-Russia, or to put it another way pro-Ally. If it became clear that a man was pro-Ally and he signed a form (1LB/A) promising continuing loyalty to the Allied war effort and his case was felt to be genuine, he would then be released to serve on the mainland. One paragraph of this form bore the words 'I hereby declare that I am willing to assist the war effort of the UN in due course'.

The UN here refers to the Allied forces, rather than the organization that came into being in 1945. Included within the umbrella of the 'United Nations' was the USSR. This was of great importance to the anti-Allied section of the camp, which, in some unknown manner, had obtained a copy of the form with the names of the pro-Allied prisoners. To the anti-Allied section of the camp, every man named on that list was a traitor to Finland – a pro-Russian.

The majority of the pro-Allied men in the Finnish camp had been gradually released from internment to serve on mainland UK. Therefore, although initially most of the Finns were pro-Allied in the camp, because of this gradual release the majority became anti-allied.

By April 1943 there were only about 30–40 pro-Allied men and 90–100 who were anti-Allied in the camp. About 30 pro-Allied had signed the form in March and April 1943 and there was friction between these and the 'non-signers'. Some of the anti-Allied men were fanatical in their beliefs and were considered trouble-makers by the guards in the camp. They were extremists and resented other Finns signing the form and being released from the camp.

MANX MURDERS

In accordance with government policy of making living conditions as bearable as possible under the circumstances, the Finns were allowed moderate rations of beer. On Sunday, 18 April some men broke into the canteen where the small stock of beer was kept and stole it. The beer was subsequently hidden under the floorboards in one of the houses in the camp. Despite strenuous efforts by the guards, some of the Finns also manufactured their own alcohol from potatoes, potato skins, bread, lemonade and yeast. There were reports of rowdy behaviour caused by drunkenness in the camp, and this worsened the friction already existing between the two groups of men (those who had signed the form and those who had not). There was constant bickering and arguing and the scene was set for serious trouble.

It was later revealed that in the early hours of 20 April 1943 there were several attacks on men who were sleeping, carried out by anti-allied men. Karl Erik Tefke was to admit that although he had been drinking earlier he was not drunk and had gone into several men's rooms 'to teach them not to inform on other internees'. He and some friends beat the other men and one was beaten so badly he remained in the hospital for three days. Several pro-allied men were abused and called 'Bloody Communists' during the early hours of 20 April. Later that morning a state of tension was evident in the camp.

Salminen was one of the men who wanted to sign the form, being pro-allied, while Huppunen was one of the leaders of those who were anti-allied; the bad feeling between the two groups saturated the atmosphere. On the morning of 20 April, Salminen put on his best suit – he had planned to go to the camp office and ask if he could get out of the camp. It would have been clear to those who saw him dressed in his best clothes that this was his intention as the prisoners usually wore dungarees and overclothes. It is probable that this would have angered some of the other prisoners. He could not have slept much the previous evening, as he was later to describe how he had heard men running up and down the corridor outside his bedroom threatening both himself and others. He had also witnessed one man, Rinar Otto Rosquist, being beaten outside his room by several men who had run away when a guard approached. He had earlier that morning spoken to a friend who was very frightened of being attacked. Other men had verbally abused him as they passed. He described how several of these men, including Huppunen, were drinking beer at around 11.30 a.m. on 20 April, and how he was again verbally abused by the men.

The events which followed were later described by several witnesses, including a German doctor, Dr Martin Scholtz, who was also an internee in the camp. Around 12.10 p.m. Salminen was standing outside House 9 of F camp, which housed all of the Finnish men. Huppunen emerged from House 8 and was carrying a bucket containing dirty water in his right hand. As he approached Salminen, Huppunen suddenly gripped the bucket with both hands and threw the contents over him. Salminen was surprised by what had happened and a scuffle ensued. Salminen put his hand into his right-hand trouser pocket, took out a knife and with an upward thrust stabbed Huppunen, who staggered back several steps and then collapsed. The shirt below his chest was then seen to become rapidly saturated with blood. This whole episode was witnessed by Scholtz, who lived in the German camp adjoining the Finnish enclosure. Although he did not see the knife, the doctor realised immediately that Huppunen had been stabbed and he ran to the camp hospital to get help and a stretcher. He then contacted the camp doctor, Dr Templeton, and the pair went to the gate of F camp. As they arrived they saw that Salminen was being given a severe beating by other Finns and was lying on the ground being kicked and bleeding from his nose and mouth. Meanwhile, Huppunen had been placed on a hand cart by other internees and was being wheeled to the camp gate – but he was already dead. The men who had been attacking Salminen were restrained by the guards and he escaped through the gate and walked ahead of the doctors and internees pushing the hand cart. Dr Scholtz attended to Salminen's injuries at the hospital. Salminen was fully conscious and asked, 'Is this man finished?'

Scholtz replied, 'Yes.'

The doctor noted that Salminen did not smell of intoxicating liquor.

Another Finn, Veikko Anteroinen, also witnessed the stabbing. He would later describe how he was sitting in his room in House 8 when he heard Salminen shouting outside. Looking out, he saw that Salminen's clothes were wet, while Huppunen was 'guarding himself with the bucket in front of him'. He saw Salminen, the knife in his right hand, stab Huppunen – he made an 'upward movement' and then withdrew the knife and wiped it on a handkerchief. Huppunen then staggered forwards before falling onto his back. Anteroinen then went downstairs and left the building, where he saw Salminen surrounded by other inmates. Salminen then ran off, chased by a 'crowd' of men.

It emerged that Salminen had made the knife some time earlier at his previous internment camp. It was a table knife, which he had sharpened on cement.

After being examined at the camp hospital Salminen was transferred to Noble's Hospital, Douglas, for further treatment and whilst there remained under police guard. Police Constable R. J. Kermeen removed the dead body of Huppunen from the camp hospital and had it transferred to Ramsey mortuary. Dr John McAlister carried out the post-mortem later that day in the presence of Dr Henry H. S. Templeton, the camp doctor, in the Public Mortuary, Queen's Drive, Ramsey. He found a wound three-quarters of an inch long between the fifth and sixth ribs, half an inch from the edge of the sternum on the right-hand side. The wound extended upwards, backwards and towards the midline to a depth of about three inches and had penetrated muscles, pleura, right lung, pericardium and then ended at the right ventricle and atrium of the heart. Death had resulted from haemorrhage due to this injury.

At Noble's Hospital, Salminen was found to have severe contusions of his face and head, a broken nose, a cut upper lip and laceration to a finger. He also had several loosened teeth. He remained in hospital for several weeks until at 9.30 a.m. on 13 May 1943 he was arrested there and taken to Douglas police station. At 10.00 a.m. Salminen was charged and cautioned for the murder of Huppunen. He replied: 'It was not wilful or malicious but in self-defence as I was afraid that nearly 100 men would attack me. I am not guilty.'

The trial started on 15 June before Deemster Cowley and a 12-man jury. Attorney General Mr Ramsay D. Moore prosecuted the case and Mr R. K. Eason represented the defendant. The case was held almost entirely in camera for what the Home Office described as 'security reasons'. The men were not identified in court by name and only the charge and a description of the killing itself were heard by members of the press and public. Salminen admitted stabbing Huppunen but claimed that he had only meant to frighten him. He had felt threatened by the events of the previous evening, the verbal abuse and the friction which existed between the two groups of men. He told the court that he had never intended the knife that he had made ever being used as a weapon, but merely as a penknife. He appeared to be genuinely remorseful. He said, 'I am extremely sorry. I never thought I would be the cause of a man's death.' Various witnesses described events leading up to the incident in Mooragh Camp.

The trial ended on 19 June and the jury retired at 3.30 p.m. after being told by the deemster that there were three possible verdicts. These were: guilty of murder, guilty of manslaughter or an acquittal following upon a successful plea of self defence. They returned to deliver their verdict at 4.45 p.m. They found Salminen not guilty of murder and not guilty of manslaughter and he was discharged. After the trial he was taken to jail pending further internment arrangements.

On 21 June he left Douglas on the 9.15 a.m. passenger steamer en route to Fleetwood, under military escort.

It is thought that Salminen subsequently became resident in a YMCA hostel in Newcastle-upon-Tyne and eventually made his way back to Finland.

4

BRIAN BATTISTA (1982)

The murder of a child is fortunately a very rare event. When it does occur it is usually carried out by a person known to the child. The crime that all parents fear and dread is extremely rare indeed – that which is committed by a paedophile who is also a sadistic sexual psychopath and a complete stranger to the child. In December 2001 in a well-publicised case heard at Lewes Crown Court, in which Roy Whiting was found guilty of the horrific abduction and murder of eight-year-old Sarah Payne, the trial judge rightly described him as 'truly evil – a menace to little girls and every parent's and grandparent's worst nightmare come true'. I was in the public gallery of the court at the end of the trial and I closely studied Whiting's face for any sign of emotion when a young lady on the jury delivered the guilty verdict. There was not even a flicker. When the judge ordered Whiting to stand, before delivering his withering condemnation and sentencing the defendant to spend the rest of his life behind bars, Whiting again appeared to be totally unconcerned. It was clear to everyone in the court that there was not the slightest hint of any remorse for his dreadful crime.

In contrast is the all too common scenario where the child is killed after a period of physical abuse, usually by a parent or step-parent or both. The first such case to make national headlines and shock the whole country out of its complacency occurred in 1973 and it involved the murder of Maria Colwell, aged seven years, by her step-father, in Brighton. In her case the abuse had escalated and culminated in her tragic death. When she died, she had weighed only 2.5 st. and among her injuries were two black eyes, brain damage, internal injuries and extensive bruising all over her body. Warning signs were missed by social workers, teachers, neighbours, police, doctors and other professionals. Since that time there have been numerous formal inquiries into the deaths of children under the care and/or supervision of social workers.

The tragic list of little victims includes Jasmine Beckford (1984), Tyra Henry (1984), Kimberly Carlisle (1986) and more recently Leanne White and Victoria Climbie.

It has been estimated that approximately 150–200 children die each year in England and Wales, often after a period of abuse, at the hands of their parents or carers. A recent study carried out by a detective revealed that 476 children in England and Wales were either unlawfully killed or seriously injured by their parents/carers during a three-year period up until the end of 2000. In many of these cases police are unable to prove which of the parents/carers are responsible as they often blame each other. As a result, neither is brought to justice. The NSPCC have stated that they are extremely concerned and frustrated by the problem and it seems that a change in the law will be required to rectify this awful situation.

Editorials in the national press of the day usually express the wish that we all share, namely that the lessons learned from the subsequent inquiries into these cases will prevent similar tragedies occurring in the future; that the warning signs will not be ignored; that we will listen to the child; that we will act and that the death from child abuse about which we have just read will be the last one ever. Of course it never happens. We never seem to learn.

Brian Marcus Battista was born on the Isle of Man on 30 November 1980. His father left the Island shortly after the birth and was not seen again by the child's mother. His Italian mother, Clodi Battista, aged 21 years became friendly with a young man called Stephen Moore who was 18 years of age. The boy's mother worked as a barmaid in a local public house and Moore was unemployed. The couple moved into a first-floor flat in Bucks Road, Douglas, a busy main road close to the centre of the town. Miss Battista became pregnant again, to Moore, and the pair decided to get married on 29 April 1982.

The relationship, however, was not a happy one and there were frequent rows between the pair. It was to be revealed later that the child did not like Moore, who on occasions had been seen to lose his temper and smack the boy violently. The child's mother had called the police on one occasion after Moore had hit Brian so hard that the blow had left bruises on his buttocks. She had wanted him to leave the flat and had put his clothes at the front door. Moore, however, later returned. Clodi Battista, who was described in court by the prosecuting counsel as a caring and loving mother, although not very happy about the situation, had to leave the child in the care of Moore while she worked.

On 20 April 1982 Clodi Battista left for work around noon. After her shift, she left the public house around 5.00 p.m., taking about ten minutes to return to the flat. When she arrived Moore was watching television and Brian was apparently sleeping in bed. She checked on the child and noted that he felt cold but did not realise at that time that anything was amiss. Another row soon erupted and she threw a book and a clock at Moore. She later stated that he had attacked her and she then threw him out of the flat. Moore left saying he was 'going for good'. After he had gone Miss Battista spent about half an hour carrying out various tasks and left the flat for a few minutes to visit a local shop. When she returned she went to feed Brian but when she tried to wake him there was no response. She began to panic and became hysterical. A friend, Elaine Gordon, who had been sitting on the front doorstep of the building waiting for her boyfriend and who lived on the third floor, heard screams and ran upstairs to find Miss Battista holding Brian. She was hysterical, believing her child to be dead. Both women then carried the baby to nearby Noble's Hospital but Miss Battista's neighbour realised before they arrived there that Brian was indeed dead. When they reached the A&E department, attempts at resuscitation were unsuccessful and Dr Fay Rennie informed Brian's mother that he was dead. After receiving the awful news, Miss Battista viewed the body and saw bruising over much of it. She later returned to the flat.

Meanwhile Moore had gone into town and met up with a friend, Forbes Ivor Donnan, at around 7.30 p.m. They decided they would have a game of snooker, but first had gone to the public house where Miss Battista worked. When they arrived they found that she was not there and were informed that she was at the hospital. Donnan would later describe how Moore showed no interest in hearing this news and they later played their planned game of snooker. Donnan was also to state later that during the evening Moore was quiet and did not seem his usual self. He had been told by Moore that he had been thrown out of the house. Donnan also recalled Moore having said that Brian was 'really good' and that he 'loved him'.

Around 10.30 p.m. that night Moore returned to the flat. Miss Battista said that he was shaking but he had sworn that he had not harmed Brian in any way. Shortly afterwards police arrived and took Moore away for questioning. The following morning he returned to the flat again. He was further accused by the child's mother of beating Brian and again denied this.

Dr Joe Deguara, consultant pathologist at Noble's Hospital, started a post-mortem examination on the body of the child. When it became apparent that the death was not due to natural causes he contacted Dr Brian Beeson, a forensic pathologist from Chorley, who came to the Island to complete the post-mortem. He found there were bruises on the abdomen which were compatible with blows from a fist and which were probably caused by the knuckles. The pathologist gave the opinion that the blows must have been delivered with terrific force as they had caused a split in the liver. He also stated that they must have been delivered whilst the child's back was up against a hard surface. The child had bled to death from this injury.

Moore was charged with the murder of the young boy and his trial started on 30 November 1982 before Deemster Jack W. Corrin. Michael Moyle, prosecuting, outlined the case for the jury. Moore was defended by Robert Jelski. The various allegations made by witnesses claiming to have seen the boy mistreated by Moore were heard. Moore often frequented an amusement arcade in Strand Street, Douglas, sometimes taking Brian with him. The court heard from the manager of the arcade, Hugh Oliver, that he had spoken to Moore on several occasions because he felt that the child was being mistreated. On one occasion, for example, Moore was seen to be holding the baby under the pool table with his foot on the child's head and on another he was seen to strike the child violently. A friend of both Miss Battista and Moore also said that he had seen Moore mistreat Brian and had also noticed bruising.

Clodi Battista told the court that Moore had admitted to her at the police station that he had 'thumped' Brian. During interviews with police Moore had made three statements. In the first one he denied all responsibility for the child's injuries and this was the story he adhered to when giving his evidence at the trial, on what would have been Brian's second birthday, 30 November 1982. In his second statement, Moore claimed the injury to Brian's abdomen may have been caused accidentally during play. In the third and final statement he admitted losing his temper and punching the baby three times in the abdomen. He explained that he had been trying to put a nappy on the boy, who was resisting his efforts. He then lost his temper. The prosecution also alleged that he had orally confessed to Sergeant Dudley Butt. Moore denied this in court.

It was clear throughout the case that nobody but Moore could have caused the injuries between noon and 5.10 p.m., when Miss Battista returned to the flat. After that time only his mother could have harmed him as Moore had by now left. She was asked by Mr Jelski, 'Did you do it, Miss Battista?' She replied, 'Certainly I did not.' Moore claimed in court that he had only signed the second statement because police promised that he would then be able to see a lawyer. With regard to the final damning statement, he said that he only signed this after he was 'beaten up by three police officers'. The police officers strenuously denied these allegations. Their version of events was supported by two senior detectives who were outside the interview room when the third written statement was made. Neither heard anything which would suggest an assault was taking place within the interview room.

On Wednesday, 1 December 1982, after a retirement of one hour, the jury of ten men and two women returned to give their verdict. They found Moore guilty of the murder of Brian Battista. Deemster Corrin told Moore he had acted in a brutal manner towards the little child saying, 'You are a strong 18 year old, punching and killing a 17 month old.' He then sentenced Moore to death, although it was clear that the Home Secretary would later commute the sentence to one of life imprisonment.

Moore immediately said that he would appeal against the sentence. This appeal against his conviction was rejected in February 1983 and a subsequent appeal to the Privy Council in March 1987 was also dismissed.

5

JOHN KEWISH: LAST HANGING ON THE ISLE OF MAN
(1872)

The last executions in Great Britain took place on 13 August 1964. Two men, Peter Anthony Allen, 21, and Gwynne Owen Evans, 24, were found guilty of the murder of John Alan West, 57, during a burglary. The victim had been stabbed and battered to death at his home in Seaton, Cumberland. The murder was committed on 6 April 1964. The trial started in June of the same year and their appeal against the death sentence was dismissed by three Appeal Court judges on 21 July. The two hangings took place simultaneously at 8.00 a.m. on 13 August, one in Walton Prison, Liverpool and the other at Strangeways Prison, Manchester. In Great Britain, The Murder (Abolition of the Death Penalty) Act became law on 9 November 1965, abolishing the death penalty for the offence of murder.

The Isle of Man is separate from the UK and has its own legal system and laws. On the Island, hanging remained on the statute books until it was abolished in 1993. Until 1993, by law a person found guilty of murder was sentenced to death. Five men were sentenced to death on the Island between 1973 and 1992. These were: James Richard Lunney, 21, convicted in 1973; Graham Ralph Frankland, 27, convicted in 1980; Michael John Pate, 21, convicted in 1981; Stephen Philip Moore, 19 (at the time of his trial), convicted in 1982; and Anthony Robin Teare, aged 22, convicted in 1992. Teare went into the history books as the last man to be sentenced to death when hanging was abolished the year after his conviction. In all of these cases the death sentence was subsequently commuted to a life sentence. Following the abolition of the death penalty in England the passing of the death sentence upon a person found guilty of murder became a purely ritual process. It was debated by the local press and in Tynwald, being variously described as, among other things, 'nonsense', 'farcical' and 'pointless'. Many of the Manx people were horrified that the death sentence should remain on the statute books when there was no intention to carry it out.

The last conviction for murder prior to 1973 was in 1930. The man who committed that murder had escaped from a psychiatric hospital and was found to be insane and sent to Broadmoor. Going back further, there were several unsolved murders and cases where the killer had committed suicide. The last murder conviction before the 1973 case which led to a hanging was in 1872 and the man convicted of that murder was called John Kewish.

The Kewish family lived in Glen Moar, Sulby Glen. There was John (senior), aged about 69 years, his wife Mary, his son John and his daughter, who was described as an imbecile and was subsequently sent to live in a lunatic asylum (her name is not recorded). Lower down the glen was a house where John Crane and his wife Marg lived and higher up the glen was another house occupied by another son, Thomas Kewish. There were therefore three houses in the glen – the house where the Kewish family lived and one on each side of it. It was common knowledge that there was a lot of friction between members of the Kewish family. Some four or five months earlier Mr Kewish (senior) and his wife had fallen out over some matter or other and lived in separate areas of the house – John Kewish lived alone in one part of the house, whilst his wife, son and daughter occupied the other. There were frequent altercations. For example, several months earlier John (junior) had owed his father money. He had apparently paid some money and the dispute between the two had been settled by the son promising to give the father a cow in May. There were also accusations made by the son that his father had stolen sheep and fowl belonging to him and John had threatened to give his father 'a good licking'. In fact, it is clear that John (junior) was a well-known sheep stealer in the area in which he lived.

Early on the evening of Monday, 28 March 1872 three people came up the glen in the direction of Thomas Kewish's house: Marg Crane, Hugh Kneen and John Kewish (junior). As the trio passed the Kewish family house they left John, who went inside. Mrs Crane and Mr Kneen carried on and heard John Kewish (senior) and his wife talking as they went past the house. At that time there were only three people in the house: the Kewish parents and their son, John.

Marg Crane and Hugh Kneen continued on to Thomas Kewish's house and approximately ten minutes later Mary Kewish also came to the house, leaving John alone with his father. About an hour later John arrived at Thomas's house. He was asked why he had not come sooner to help his brother, who was killing a pig, but did not give any reply to the question. He appeared quiet and sullen. After they had assisted Thomas with the pig, Mary Kewish asked John if she should go home to get supper. He told her to go and Mrs Crane and Mr Kneen left at the same time.

On reaching the house, Mrs Crane and Mr Kneen carried on. Mary Kewish went inside to her own room and lit the fire and cooked supper. All of this took roughly an hour. She then came out of her room and noticed that the door of her husband's room was open. She went inside and saw that the old man was dead. He was kneeling down in front of a chair and leaning on it. She immediately went to Mr Crane's house for help, then Marg Crane accompanied her to Thomas's house. They then returned to the Kewish house with William Kneale, whom Thomas had asked for help, and on arrival they got a light and went into the kitchen. Shortly afterwards another man, John Crane, arrived. He also had been summoned by Thomas Kewish.

Crane and Kneale examined the body. They noticed four fresh wounds on the man's back and two on his chest, from which blood had been flowing. They noticed a pitchfork leaning against a partition in the room and both men wondered whether the holes in his back and chest had been caused by the pitchfork. John and his mother were in the kitchen whilst the two men were examining the body and Kneale heard Mrs Kewish say, 'I hope Johnny has not done anything to him.' Crane stayed in the house all night. He noticed that the man's wife and his son John appeared to be unconcerned by his death. Several people made a comment that in view of the man's injuries an inquest would need to be held, but both Mrs Kewish and John appeared not to be interested in this. They had intended to bury the man without any inquiry!

On the Saturday following the death the authorities received information that John Kewish, aged 69 years, had died in suspicious circumstances. The High Bailiff of Ramsey, accompanied by Mr William Boyd, Chief Constable, Dr Tellett and the Coroner of the Sheading, went to the house of the deceased. When they arrived the body was laid out as if ready for a funeral, which was to have been held on the Sunday morning, and all the preparations had been made for a reception for those who were to attend. A jury was summoned and an inquest opened. After a few witnesses had been examined the inquest was adjourned until the following Monday.

At noon on Sunday, 3 April, Dr Clucas and Dr Tellett made a post-mortem examination of the body. They observed two wounds on the right side of the chest. The upper one was about 2 in. from the midline between the first and second ribs; the other was 3 in. directly below it. This wound had penetrated the cartilage of the third rib. Both were puncture wounds and the lower wound was found to have penetrated about 6 in. Examining the man's back, the doctors found there were four more puncture wounds on the lower part of his chest. On opening the chest they found that the right lung had collapsed and the pleural cavity on that side was filled with blood. They found a large laceration, passing right through the ascending part of the aorta and they noted that this last wound would have caused instantaneous death. The doctors felt that the wounds had been caused by a two-pronged instrument and thought it impossible that they could have been self-inflicted as considerable force must have been used.

Thomas Kneale, a policeman from Ramsey (unrelated to William Kneale), told the inquest that he had been outside the house about 11.00 a.m. earlier that day and he heard Mrs Kewish, the dead man's wife and her son John talking in Manx. He heard John tell his mother to be 'steady on her oath' and he had said that if they got over today, there 'would be no more about it'. The policeman said that John had told him his father had 'deserved what he had got'. He had been stealing John's sheep and fowl and often beat his wife. It was clear that there was no love lost between John and his father and John had been the last person in the house with his father before the body was found. He had appeared unconcerned when told about his father's death, and since that time had told several people of the friction between the two of them.

The High Bailiff told the jury that the murder was one of the most diabolical he had ever known and he argued that the evidence pointed to the son John as the murderer. The jury retired and returned about five minutes later with their verdict.

Mr T. Christian, the foreman, said, 'We find that John Kewish ought to stand trial for the murder of his father.' The prisoner was then brought into court and placed in the dock. The High Bailiff informed him of the jury's verdict and cautioned him.

John Kewish said, 'I never laid a hand on him. I was not there when it was done.' He was then taken into custody and sent to Castle Rushen Gaol that evening. On Tuesday, 16 April, John Kewish junior was taken from the gaol to Ramsey Courthouse to face a charge of sheep stealing. He was found guilty of this offence and was returned to Castle Rushen to await trial for the murder of his father.

It was later revealed that during the search of the house by the police a young woman about 30 years of age was found in one of the upper rooms – the Kewish daughter. The woman was in a disgraceful state and very distressed. It was felt she was insane. On the night of the murder she had been at her brother's house with Thomas's wife. Certificates of insanity were given by Dr Clucas and Dr Tellett and the same vehicle which took her brother to gaol also took the woman to the lunatic asylum.

MANX MURDERS

On Tuesday, 11 June 1872, John Kewish's trial started at Castle Rushen. The Attorney General prosecuted the case and Mr Steven and Mr G. H. Quayle represented the prisoner, who pleaded not guilty to the charge of murdering his father. The Attorney General outlined the case for the jury and said that on 28 March, John Kewish (senior) had been found dead in his own house. He was discovered in a kneeling position, down before a chair and had two wounds in his chest and four in his back. These wounds had evidently been inflicted by a two-pronged instrument, probably a pitchfork, and had led to his death. He described the events of that night and told the jury of the ill-feeling between the son and father. The Attorney General said that one of the son's defences may be that the mother might have killed her husband. He said this was unlikely as when the body was discovered the blood was almost dry. If the mother had murdered her husband this would not have been the case. He also felt that considerable force would have been needed to inflict the injuries, and the murder would have been more likely to have been committed by the son. He also told the jury that inquiries had shown that on the day of the murder John Kewish, the son, had been wearing a pair of russet-coloured trousers which had not been seen for several days after the murder. It was possible that the trousers had been cleaned during this time.

He did admit to the jury that the facts of the case were few. It was clear, he said, that there had been a murder but the question was: was the prisoner guilty of this offence? He admitted that his entire case depended upon circumstantial evidence. He reminded the jury that the prisoner and his father were alone together on the premises, and it was very unlikely in such a scarcely populated area that the crime was committed by a passer-by and there was no evidence the victim was on unfriendly terms with anyone else. He was, though, not on friendly terms with his son who was with him alone for about an hour – during which it was thought he was murdered. The Attorney General thought the likely motive for the murder was the fact that the son had to give his father a cow.

The accused's mother, Mary, told the court that she had heard her son threaten his father. The Ramsey constable gave his evidence about the conversation he had heard between mother and son, and the doctors gave their evidence, informing the jury of the terrible injuries Mr Kewish had sustained. William Kermode, the gaoler at Castle Rushen, said that when John arrived in the gaol he had told him that his father had been in a fight with a man in which he had taken off his coat and waistcoat. The man with whom he was fighting, John said, had then stabbed him in the chest with a pitchfork. When Mr Kewish had fallen to his knees, the man had then stabbed him twice in the back. Daniel Cowley, a police constable of Lezayre, described how when he was searching the house of the dead man for any clothes on which there might be marks of blood he found a pair of russet-coloured trousers belonging to the accused on which there were several blood stains. The trousers were found in the room occupied by John, his mother and his sister. Whilst carrying on the search however he had left the trousers in another room but when he returned they had gone. He never saw them again until several days later when they were given to him by John's mother and the blood stains by this time were not as visible as they had been earlier.

Mr Quayle, for the accused, addressed the jury and pointed out that this was a case of circumstantial evidence and warned them that as such it must be received with great caution. He said there was no evidence whatsoever that would justify the jury convicting the prisoner. He said that after the murder had been committed, the son had appeared to several people to be his normal self and he did not appear to be flustered or upset. He told the jury that the case was so full of doubt that they should return a verdict of acquittal. No one had seen the murder and there did not appear to be any real motive for the son killing his father. Certainly, the son had to give his father a cow in May, which was hardly sufficient motive for murder. He said that there was as much opportunity for the man's wife to have killed her husband as there was for the son to carry out the murder.

The deemster then summed up to the jury for an hour and a half. He felt that there was not an obvious motive for a third party to have committed the offence. He reminded them that the case was one of circumstantial evidence only and he reiterated the lack of real motive for the son to have killed his father. There had been a lawsuit between the two but this had been settled by an agreement whereby the prisoner would give his father a cow and was also to give up possession of a small field of about one acre. There was also no obvious motive for the man's wife to have killed him. The deemster told the jury he felt there was no question of a manslaughter verdict in this case and that they must consider whether the man's wife could have committed the crime.

The jury retired at 8.55 p.m. and returned to court at 9.55 p.m. The deemster asked if the jury had reached a verdict and Mr Black, the foreman, said, 'We have not, Your Honour, and we are unlikely to do so'. The deemster then told the jury that they must be locked up all night and the jurors were allowed to have the use of the courtroom. The case was adjourned until the following day, Wednesday, 12 June.

When the court was reconvened at 10.00 a.m., the foreman of the jury informed the deemster that they had still not reached a verdict. They were then sent out again to consider the matter further. At 11.00 a.m. they were again called and said they could not agree and there was no chance whatever of their doing so. It was then proposed to discharge the jury. One of them, a man from Port St Mary, said that he had been ill during the night. Mr Steven, representing John Kewish, said that if the jury could not, after a reasonable time, agree to convict the prisoner, it should be considered equivalent to a verdict of acquittal as it was clear there must be strong doubt. He contended that the prisoner was entitled to have a verdict. Dr Johns from Castletown was sent for and examined the man who was ill. The doctor certified that he was not well enough to remain on the jury and the jurors were then discharged, without agreeing on a verdict. Seven jurors had voted for the acquittal of the prisoner and five for finding him guilty. John Kewish then had to face a new trial with a new jury.

A retrial was ordered to be held on Wednesday, 3 July. The same evidence which had been heard at the first trial was given again during Wednesday and into Thursday. After the summing up by the deemster, the jury retired at 2.30 p.m. on Thursday, 4 July. They returned at 3.04 p.m. to deliver their verdict. The jury found Kewish guilty of the murder of his father. The deemster told Kewish: 'You have been found guilty of the crime of the murder of your own father. The jury of your countrymen, who have patiently heard the whole of the evidence, have come to this unanimous verdict, a verdict in which the whole court agrees. I do not know whether you have manifested any remorse for having committed so dreadful a crime. What have you to say why sentence should not be passed upon you for the crime which you have committed?' The prisoner made no reply. The deemster then continued, 'The sentence of this court is that you, John Kewish, for the crime of murder, of which this jury have brought you guilty, be hanged by the neck until you are dead; and in the meantime you are to be taken back into Castle Rushen, where you have been imprisoned, and there to await Her Majesty's pleasure.' As the prisoner was removed, he appeared indifferent to his fate.

For the first few days after being sentenced Kewish protested his innocence. He was visited by his brother Thomas a few days later, who urged him to make a full confession of his guilt, telling John that he believed he had murdered his father. Thomas hoped John would confess so as to clear his mother, whom, he said, many people felt may had something to do with the murder. John however refused to confess. Kewish was watched night and day while he was in the condemned cell at Castle Rushen. PC Thomas Kneale was responsible for guarding him every night for the three weeks prior to the execution.

MANX MURDERS

On 9 July a memorial pleading for clemency was sent by John's lawyer, Mr Steven, to Lieutenant Governor Loch. This consisted of a number of sworn statements, which, it was hoped, might encourage leniency. The advocate asked the Lieutenant Governor to pass this on to the Home Secretary and the Queen (Victoria) and hoped that the Queen would use her royal prerogative to commute the death sentence. On 13 July the advocate again wrote to the Lieutenant Governor, as he had not received an acknowledgement to his previous communication. The Lieutenant Governor was off the Island and the letter and telegram were sent to Macclesfield post office. He also enclosed a report of the prisoner's mental status made by Dr Ring, who apparently felt that John Kewish's physical appearance was of a kind sometimes associated with insanity. Dr Ring stated that 'his jaw bones are like those of a carnivorous animal – his body short, his gait awkward', believing these characteristics were signs of an unsound mind and idiocy. Dr Ring did feel, however, that Kewish was capable of understanding questions put to him at the trial, but the doctor was vague in his views as to whether Kewish was responsible for his actions.

On Sunday, 14 July an entry was made into the 'gaoler's journal', a daily record kept by the gaolers. John Kewish had on that day spoken to John Kneale, a turnkey, whilst exercising in the yard. Kewish had told Kneale that there was something on his mind he wished to discuss, explaining that on the night his father died he had gone into the kitchen where his father was lying on two chairs. He had asked his father to take a gun down from where it was kept over the fire, which he did. In doing so the hammer must have caught on something and it went off. The shot resulted in a chest wound to his father. He said the gun had been loaded with five or six slugs and some number-one shot. When the gun went off his father had fallen on his side, made an exclamation and died immediately. The prisoner admitted that he had then hidden the gun in the thatch of an outhouse.

An article appeared in the *Mona's Herald* in which a reporter described how he had spoken to some of the prison officers at Castle Rushen the night before the execution. PC Thomas Kneale told the paper that Kewish had confessed to him saying:

'My father was ready to go to bed with his jacket and waistcoat off and sitting at the fire on a stool smoking, when the devil tempted me to shoot him. I came out of my room and struck my father in the back. The gun was charged with four slugs. I fired the gun at his back and my father fell saying, 'Shee Creest' [which in English means 'The peace of Christ be with you']. I think from his using that word he has gone to Heaven. My father has one hundred pounds and therefore Satan led me to do this; and I had no schooling, and I knew no better.'

The last execution on the Island prior to 1872 had been in 1832, when two men from Peel had been hanged at Castle Rushen for attempted murder. Therefore there were many arrangements to be made in organising the construction of the gallows and obtaining a hangman who would visit the Island. The Home Office was contacted and they informed the Manx authorities that they should speak to a hangman called William Calcraft. A hand-written letter was sent to him requesting his services on the Isle of Man on 1 August at 8.00 a.m. An article in a Manx newspaper on Saturday, 3 August described Calcraft's arrival on the Island. Two days before the execution was due to take place, Calcraft boarded the steamer *Tynwald* which left Liverpool for Douglas. He was described in the paper as 'This notorious public official, who has become almost white with age and manifests somewhat of the feebleness of advancing years'. This was Calcraft's first visit to the Island but when he landed at the red pier in Douglas he was recognised and a crowd of people followed him as he left the ship. He was met off the boat by Police Inspector Cashen and taken to Castle Rushen where a room had been specially prepared for him.

On 27 July a telegram was sent by the High Bailiff of Castletown, Mr H. B. Jeffcott, to the Lieutenant Governor: 'No carpenter in Castletown or Douglas will make gallows. Will ask Governor of Kirkdale to send carpenter today.' It appeared that local craftsmen did not wish to have anything to do with the impending execution.

The following day another telegram was sent: 'I beg to say I did not get men from England. Boys and Coopers of this town have agreed to make gallows for prisoner's execution.' A firm of joiners, Messrs Cooper of Castletown, subsequently constructed gallows during the three days leading up to the execution (the old scaffold had lain unused for forty years and was found to be useless). The drop was 18 in. and it appears that Calcraft was pleased with the new construction.

On 29 July a further telegram was sent from the High Bailiff to the Lieutenant Governor. In this one the High Bailiff explained that he had spoken to John Kewish's family, who requested the body after the execution. John's brother Thomas had asked the High Bailiff to discuss this with the Lieutenant Governor, who had then contacted the Home Office. This return telegram read: 'Bodies of executed criminals must by law be buried within the prison perimeter and are therefore never delivered to friends.' It was clear to everyone concerned that John's body would be buried in the grounds of Castle Rushen.

On 29 July an entry was made into the 'Visiting Magistrate's Minute Book': 'July 29th I I visited John Kewish. Mr Ferrier accompanied me. John Kewish declared he shot his father and that the charge in the gun was four slugs – two of which had gone through his father's body. He persisted that he only fired at him once.'

On 31 July, the day before the execution, an entry in the gaoler's register read: 'No visitors to be allowed into gaol on this day, Wednesday, Thursday and Friday, by order of His Excellency the Governor.' The entry was signed by the gaoler, Kermode.

Over the few weeks Kewish had been in prison since his sentence he had never been alone. He had been watched day and night by Thomas Kneale, the constable from Ramsey, and the turnkeys. During this time he often had the Bible read to him. John himself was apparently very anxious the day before his execution that his body should be given up to his relatives. However his family were by now aware of the Home Office ruling. It was reported that he had slept fairly well the night before his execution. The execution was witnessed by several people, including the High Bailiff of Castletown, W. B. Stephenson, several gaolers and officers of the gaol. Also present were the Head Constable and several members of the police, the Coroners of Glenfaba and Rushen, reporters from the various Manx newspapers (*Isle of Man Times*, *Manx Sun* and *Manx Times*) and also a reporter from Liverpool.

The press were admitted to the Castle at 7.30 a.m. and were taken to the Debtor's Yard where the gallows stood. Shortly after this Calcraft, dressed in black, arrived to prepare for the execution. Meanwhile Rev. M. E. Ferrier was saying prayers with John in his cell.

An article in the *Mona's Herald* on 7 August described the execution of Kewish:

A few minutes before eight, Calcraft went into Kewish's cell and shook hands with the prisoner, who allowed himself to be pinioned so that he was unable to move his arms. As he left the cell John said, 'God bless all my good neighbours around me.' These were the last words he said. The procession, led by Rev. Ferrier, then Kewish, then Calcraft, made their way to the gallows, which was only about eighty feet away. A black flag was raised immediately after the Castle clock struck eight o'clock. Kewish walked firmly to the gallows, up the steps and to the spot under the rope. Calcraft then placed a white cap on his head, placed the rope and a hood over Kewish's head, adjusted the rope and opened the trap door. Rev. Ferrier spoke continuously, ending with 'Lord Jesus receive, we beseech Thee, the soul of John Kewish', just as the trap door opened and the execution took place.

Reporters described a terrible silence which then followed. The whole affair had taken six minutes from leaving the cell and death was instantaneous.

The same article also contained the following description of Kewish:

> Our readers may be curious to know what sort of a man the murderer was. No one could help the thought, who looked upon his face, that they were looking at a naturally bad man. His face was devoid of any elevated or intellectual expression. It was the face of a murderer. Lustful, cruel, cunning. There was the projection at the hinge of the lower jaw, the fierce white eye, the narrow, low, receding forehead, the animal propensities behind fully developed, while there was the sneaking down-look which betokened the bloodthirsty creep of the tigerish nature. A bad face and head which God forbid we should have many more in the Isle Of Man.

The body was left hanging for a full hour before being lowered into a black painted coffin by two prisoners. An inquest was then summoned by High Bailiff J. M. Jeffcott, before the body was buried in a grave dug by the two prisoners, in a yard of the prison known as the 'stone yard', after quicklime had been place around the body. The black flag, which had been at half mast, was then lowered and taken down.

At 12.15 p.m. on 1 August another telegram was sent by the High Bailiff of Castletown to the Lieutenant Governor who was still in Macclesfield. It read 'Execution over. Death instantaneous. Your Excellency's orders strictly adhered to. I am thankful all over and done well.'

After the execution, a reporter from the *Mona's Herald* was given a copy of a confession made by Kewish to the Reverend Ferrier, and this was printed in the newspaper:

> It was through darkness I did it, because I did not know any better; I had no schooling, so I did not know my duty or what I was doing. [. . .] I never would have done it if I had schooling. I feel this from what I have learnt since I had been here. I used now and then to go

to chapel but I did not give much heed to these English preachers. I did not understand them. A day or two I prayed to God, if I was doing anything wrong to put it before me and when the evening came I could not help it. The gun was loaded a day or two before. Something came on at me that night. I took the gun. It was in my room. It was loaded with slugs. I shot him as he was sitting before the fire. I shot once only. I was about four yards off him.

If I had my life to live over again it should be a better one. I have learnt more since I came here than I did all my days. I hid the gun and I went out to see my brothers. I never looked to see if he was dead. I knew well enough from what I saw that he was well nigh finished.

I hope others will take warning from me not to live as I did, but to get schooling and attend their chapel. [. . .] I am very sorry for what I have done, but I will get leave now. I did not know what I was doing at the time. The neighbours were telling me that if they were in my clothes they would deal with him. [. . .]

I hid the gun in the thatch of an out-house and went to my brothers. It was not done with a fork. [. . .]

I wish to thank all who have had to do with me since I have been here. I may have got as much kindness from Mother, but not from Father, as I have done from all here. I pray God to forgive me all my sins. I trust in Jesus that he will save me. I wish poor father would be safe.

In making this statement I have no hope of getting off, but I hope to find the Lord. I am willing enough if I could get off, but I must find the Lord still. I know I must be executed. This is Monday. I have, haven't I, only two more whole days to live.

The mark *x* of John Kewish

6

WILLIAM H. MALINGS: FIRST WORLD WAR MURDER (1916)

During the First World War many Manx men fought and died bravely under the British flag and over 8,000 were to answer a call to arms. By the end of the conflict over 1,100 Manx men would be dead, with a similar number injured or taken prisoner. The Isle of Man newspapers of the day carried weekly reports of the latest casualties involving those from the Island or Manx men living elsewhere.

On 27 May 1916 – the year in which the case that is the subject of this chapter occurred – a headline read: 'Heavy Manx casualties – five hundred since War started. Another bad week – seven killed, four wounded.' The article pointed out that at the last census the male population had been 23,937 and already the Manx casualties totalled 500, of which 187 had been fatalities. On 15 July the *Isle of Man Times* reported 'A Record Casualty List for Manx Land!' and continued:

> Never, since the Manx roll of honour was opened in this journal, have we been compelled to make such a formidable number of additions to it, as has been our painful duty this week. It is beyond doubt that nine young men of Manx blood or Manx residence have died since the great 'push' began and nineteen have been wounded. An unofficial report, which seems to be a reliable one, gives the names of two others killed and one wounded. Two others are missing. This brings the total number of Manx casualties sustained in the Battle of the Somme to thirty three.

The following week, 22 July, the headline read, 'Still Paying the Price – Twenty-five more Manx Casualties'. On 29 July there were 'Twenty More

MANX MURDERS

Manx Casualties', and the week after, 5 August, 'Twelve Dead Soldiers' were reported.

Shortly after the war had started the British government had quickly realised that the Isle of Man would be a very suitable place for an internment camp and therefore such a camp was set up in Douglas. It was in this camp that on the afternoon of 19 November 1914, a riot took place in a dining-room and plates, knives and forks were thrown by a number of internees at the guards. After trying to quell the disturbance with bayonets, shots were fired and four prisoners were killed. A fifth died a few days later and eighteen others were injured. The jury's verdict at the inquest into the deaths of the five men was:

> The jury unanimously finds that the five deaths at the alien prisoners' camp were caused by justifiable measures forced upon the military authorities by the riotous behaviour of a large section of the prisoners interned there.

It was clear that there was a need for a second camp and Knockaloe Farm, near Peel, was chosen as a suitable site. This was to be a much larger camp and was to house around 23,000 prisoners and 3,000 staff. The camp covered 22 acres and the perimeter was 3 miles in length. By May 1916 the camp had been open for 18 months and it was to become the scene of a bizarre case in which one British officer shot and killed another without any motive ever being discovered.

Colour Sergeant William Henry Malings, aged 47, was married with several children and had been at Knockaloe as part of the camp guard for about 12 months. He came from Warrington and before the war had been a hairdresser. He was in the 306th Battalion Royal Defence Corps, South Lancashire Regiment. Sergeant John Williams, aged 46, was also in Knockaloe and as far as anyone could tell had always been on good terms with Malings. He also came from Warrington.

On the morning of Monday, 15 May 1916, several camp photographs were taken. One was of the whole company, one of the football team, one of the NCOs and another one of a boxing match. Sergeant Williams and Colour Sergeant Malings were both in the latter photograph. Later on that day, at around noon, several of the sergeants were in the mess for the midday meal. Initially there were four: Malings, Williams, Lance Sergeant James Slingsby Duncan Clare and Sergeant Major Stringfellow. The four men had a beer, ate their midday meal and then sat and talked about general matters. It was later to be reported that there had been no arguments or bad feeling between any of them. Another sergeant, named Frederick William Stoll later went to the mess. The first of the group to leave was Sergeant Williams, who went to the toilet at approximately 2.50 p.m. Malings left after this and told the men he would be back shortly. Sergeant Major Stringfellow left a few minutes later to go to Camp 4 leaving Lance Sergeant Clare and Stoll in the mess, continuing in conversation.

Malings had been suffering from back problems and walked with the aid of a stick. Private Brown saw him as he left the mess and Corporal Unsworth had walked with him towards the sleeping compartment, which was approached by a flight of steps. Shortly after he left Malings, Unsworth had heard a shot fired and, after rushing to the sleeping compartment, he had entered to find Malings lying on the floor close to the door. He could see immediately that the man was critically wounded, with blood coming from his neck. When he entered the hut Williams was standing at the other end and Unsworth asked him if he had sent for a doctor to which Williams replied, 'No.' Clare and Stoll, who had been talking in the mess, soon heard the news that Colour Sergeant Malings had shot himself and immediately rushed to his sleeping quarters. Stoll was later to say that when he entered the room Malings was lying on the floor bleeding from his nose, mouth and ears and appeared to be quite dead. Williams, by this time, was standing at the foot of his bed, smoking his pipe. Stoll had noticed a rifle on Clare's bed and another rifle on Williams' bed and saw that there were also two live cartridges on Williams' bed.

Williams had then pointed to the rifle and said to Stoll, 'Can you use one of those?'

Stoll replied, 'I don't know.'

Several other men appeared in the room shortly afterwards and many of them were later to describe Williams' whole manner as 'peculiar'. Stoll then asked Williams, 'What gun did that?' and Williams pointed to a gun on his bed. On the floor was the shell of the cartridge which had been fired.

Lieutenant Oswald Allen arrived shortly and he was also to report later that there was something unusual in Williams' manner. Sergeant Major E. Kibblewhite entered the room at about 3.15 p.m. and said, 'What's happened?'

Sergeant Williams replied, 'You had better find out.'

Williams, after pacing up and down the room, sat down on a box at the foot of his bed to smoke until Lieutenant Allen told him to put his pipe out when speaking to an officer, which he did immediately. It quickly became clear that the only other person in the room apart from Malings when the shot was fired was Williams. The police were called.

Joseph Madigan was a Scotland Yard officer and special assistant to the commandant at Knockaloe Camp. He went to the sleeping quarters of Camp 2 about 3.30 p.m. on that Monday. When he arrived there were several other people in the room and he noticed that Malings was lying on his back with his walking stick lying by his right side, his hand still resting on it. He quickly decided that Williams should be searched and, when he informed him of this, Williams said, 'Very well, Mr Madigan,' and handed over the clip containing five cartridges which he had taken from his tunic pocket. He appeared to Madigan to be 'like someone who had received a shock'. There were also the two live cartridges on the bed and the spent cartridge on the floor at the foot of it, adjoining his bed. Madigan searched Williams and found two more live cartridges in his trouser pocket and this, Madigan said, accounted for all of the ten cartridges which every sergeant had been given.

Madigan also found a letter on official notepaper in Williams' tunic pocket. The letter – which does not seem to make sense in parts – read: 'Dear Rose, please excuse me; I died in a good cause, men to men. Good [sic] bless you. Mrs Williams, 14, Shipyard, Warrington'. On the other side of the paper was written: 'Twenty years service with men mob a [indecipherable word]. Sending expert of armes [sic] [three indecipherable words, first two could be 'sincerely yours']. I enclose six and fourpence 6/4. To Mrs Williams, 14, Shipyard, off Bridge Street, Warrington'. The letter was in an official envelope and addressed to Mrs Williams at the address given. The police arrived shortly and Williams was charged and cautioned. When asked if he wished to make a statement, he replied, 'No, not at present.'

The inquest into the death of Colour Sergeant Malings started the following day before High Bailiff J. S. Gell at Patrick School House. Williams attended in the custody of two police constables. The High Bailiff explained that he only intended to take formal identification that afternoon to allow for the burial and would then adjourn the inquiry. He advised Williams that as he was the only other person present in the room at the time of the shooting, he should be legally represented.

Captain Henry Cosby-Stokes, 306th Protection Company, Royal Defence Corps, identified the body as being that of Colour Sergeant Malings. He told the court that Malings had a wife and children and that his wife was on her way to the Island that day. He added that Malings had an excellent character and had recently been on light duties because of his back trouble.

The inquest was adjourned to the following Monday afternoon, 22 May, and was resumed in the courthouse in Peel. The jury was taken to the hut where the tragedy occurred and Lieutenant Allen pointed out the position where the body had been found. Earlier that same day Sergeant John Williams had been brought before the court and charged with the murder of Malings. During the brief proceedings he had appeared to be quite unconcerned; he had no questions and was remanded in custody.

Williams was now represented by the advocate, Mr H. Percy Kelly. Mr Madigan gave evidence concerning the position of the body and the finding of Williams' ammunition. He described how he found that a pane of glass had a hole in it, apparently made by a bullet passing through it. He also said, as others would recall, that Williams' demeanour was not what he would have expected. The Coroner suggested the term 'temporary non-intelligence' and Madigan agreed that this was a suitable description.

The matter of the keys for the sergeants' sleeping quarters was explained by Private Jackson, who said, 'I act as storekeeper for this company in Camp 2 and there are some stores kept in the sergeants' sleeping room. There are two keys. I keep one and the Colour Sergeant [Malings] the other one.' On the previous Monday, when leaving the camp at around 2.10 p.m., Jackson described how he had handed the other key to Williams and explained that he always gave the key to a sergeant when he left the camp.

Other witnesses gave evidence, before Dr Robert T. McGeah told of his findings. He recalled being summoned to see the body of Malings in the sleeping quarters at about 3.30 p.m. There was, he said, a circular wound in the top of the chest and blood had come from his mouth and nostrils. He had quickly realised the man had been shot. At the mortuary he carried out a further examination. The exit wound was in the back, opposite the body of the fourth dorsal vertebra, about 2 in. from the spine. There was no mark of scorching, which would, he said, have been present if Malings had shot himself. Death would have been instantaneous. On 10 May, in the presence of Dr Syme, Dr McGeah had carried out a post-mortem examination on the body. The entry wound had been in the upper chest in the mid-line. The top of the sternum was found to be shattered and bone had been carried by the projectile into the chest. The trachea was cut at its bifurcation and the left common carotid and left subclavian arteries were severed. The fourth left rib and fourth dorsal vertebra were shattered and there was damage to the left lung.

The Coroner then addressed the jury telling them that he felt they would be 'quite satisfied' in finding a verdict of wilful murder. They then retired for only six minutes before Mr J. H. Kelly, the foreman, said: 'The jury is unanimous in finding a verdict of wilful murder against John Williams.' The next stage of the proceedings before a magistrate was due to take place later that week, on the Friday at Peel Courthouse.

On that day Williams appeared in front of Deemster Moore and Mr J. G. Corrin, JP. The defendant appeared to be bored by the proceedings and frequently glanced at the clock, showing no interest in the evidence. Moore appeared for the prosecution and H. P. Kelly for the defence. Several witnesses gave evidence, some of which was a repeat of their earlier evidence at the inquest. Sergeant Clare reiterated that there was nothing unusual about Williams' appearance or behaviour when he left the sergeants' mess-room shortly before the shooting took place and several witnesses said that Malings and Williams always appeared to be good friends.

McGeah gave his evidence, saying that the wound could not possibly have been self-inflicted, and he then described the injuries to Colour Sergeant Malings' body. Joseph Madigan also gave evidence and said that experiments made in the room where the shooting had taken place showed that the shot which killed Malings had been fired by someone seated either at the foot of Williams' bed or the adjoining bed, which was Sergeant Stoll's. He said that the expression on Williams' face after the shooting was 'like that of a person not possessing full intelligence'.

Police Sergeant Faragher of Kirk Michael then addressed the court. He stated that whilst he was in charge of Williams and another prisoner in a waiting room at Peel Courthouse on 16 May, he overheard a conversation between the two prisoners. He heard the other man say to Williams: 'You must be a strong man to shoot the soldier which you are being tried for this morning.' Williams had apparently replied, 'I didn't give him half enough, I don't believe in doing things halfway.' He said that Williams had appeared 'very excited' and that 'his eyes were rolling and the nerve of the jaw twitching'.

At the end of the hearing the decision of the Bench was that Williams should be committed for trial and he was remanded in custody.

Williams was next brought before Deemster Moore and an indicting jury of six, with the object of determining whether there was sufficient evidence to warrant the accused being sent for trial. Moore, in his opening address, told the jury they were to say whether or not there was a case to answer and went on to explain that they did not have to reach a decision as to the man's guilt or innocence at this stage. Mr Kelly then said he did not propose to raise any defence on that day. After several witnesses gave their evidence, Deemster Moore told the jury that he did not consider that they would have any doubt as to their sending the prisoner for trial on the charge. He then reviewed the evidence and commented on the letter which the prisoner had written. He said that this appeared to show that Williams had contemplated his own death. The jury consulted among themselves before they announced that they were unanimous and felt that there was sufficient evidence to send the prisoner for trial.

On Tuesday, 8 August, the trial of Sergeant John Williams for the murder of Colour Sergeant William Henry Malings began at Douglas Courthouse.

Again, Mr H. P. Kelly appeared for the prisoner while the Attorney General of the Isle of Man, Mr G. A. Ring, prosecuted for the Crown. The three men on the Bench were Lord Raglan, the Lieutenant Governor of the Isle of Man, the Clerk of the Rolls, and Deemster Moore. Williams pleaded not guilty to the charge and a 12-man jury was sworn in before the Attorney General outlined the case for the prosecution. Both men, he told the jury, were sergeants stationed at Knockaloe camp and the tragedy had occurred in the sleeping quarters of the camp. It appeared there was no obvious ill-will between the two men and it seemed that there was nothing to account for the tragic events which occurred later. He described how witnesses had recalled Williams leaving the mess-room about 3.00 p.m. and shortly after that Malings had also left, saying he would be back shortly. He then went on to say that a shot had been heard and various people had rushed to the sleeping quarters, to find Malings lying close to the entrance. When Williams had been asked if there had been anyone else apart from him in the room when Malings had been shot, he answered, 'No.'

Later, it was explained, Williams made certain statements to Sergeant Harrison. He had said, 'The cur has been the cause of all my trouble since I have been in the Company and I have made a clean job of it. He is only one of my victims.' Corporal Phillips, who had relieved Sergeant Harrison, heard Williams say, 'I am rid of that bastard. I am satisfied.' Evidence was given of Williams' strange behaviour shortly after the murder: he had sat and read the paper for a while, smoked in the presence of an officer, and generally appeared to be unconcerned by the events he had just witnessed. The Attorney General said that Dr Caird had spoken to Williams several times and a doctor from the asylum had also examined him. Neither could find anything to suggest insanity. He then briefly told the jury about the letter found on Williams and the first witness then took the stand.

Colonel Unsworth stated that he had been about 60 yards away from the sergeants' quarters in Camp 2 when he heard the shot. He immediately went to the quarters and up the flight of stairs into the room. He had been in sight of the place all the time after hearing the shot and noticed no one leave the hut. He then described the scene when he opened the door and entered the hut. He said that from the time he had left Malings to the time he heard the shot, only three or four minutes would have elapsed. It seemed clear that the shot had occurred almost immediately after Malings had entered.

Sergeant Stoll also gave evidence, telling the story he had told earlier. He was yet another witness who remarked on the 'very peculiar look' on Williams' face.

Sergeant Clare said he was in the mess-room after the midday meal when Private Jackson came into the room and gave the key of the quarters to Sergeant Williams. He explained that Private Jackson was the storekeeper and the room in the sleeping quarters where the shooting took place was also used as a storeroom. Private Jackson always handed the key to one of the sergeants when he left the camp. On this occasion he gave it to Williams simply because he was nearest to the door.

Colour Sergeant George Henry Harrison said he had examined the carbine on Sergeant Williams' bed and found that it had recently been fired. He asked who had taken the cartridge case out of the carbine and the prisoner replied, 'I did.' Immediately following this Lieutenant Allen pointed to a cartridge case lying on the ground. Several witnesses repeated the comments mentioned earlier, which appeared to indicate that Williams was pleased Malings was dead.

Dr R. T. McGeah described the gunshot wounds which caused the death of Malings and repeated the findings he had previously given at the inquest.

Mr Kelly, for the defence, said there was no reasonable doubt as to how Malings had met his death. He would not suggest that Williams had not in some way caused the death of Malings, but to prove murder, he said, the prosecution would not only have to show that Williams had fired the shot but that it was his intention to kill him by being in full possession of his faculties. Kelly then told the court, 'The Crown had suggested no motive, but sane men did not [sic] commit murder on the impulse of a moment without any motive.' He said that Williams may have become temporarily insane, and told the jury they would have to decide what the condition of Williams' mind had been when the shot was fired. The letter described earlier to his wife suggested 'a state of mental aberration'. He reminded them that up until 9.00 a.m. on that Monday, Williams had been on duty for 24 continuous hours and had stayed awake after this. If they found he was not in his usual state of mind, he would still not be freed – he would be kept in a place of confinement.

Summing up, Deemster Moore said that this was a case in which there was no question of manslaughter. They had to find that Williams committed murder or that he committed the crime during a state of mental incapacity. If they thought he was in the full possession of his faculties, they would find him guilty. If not, they would find that he had killed the man while temporarily insane.

The jury retired at 4.45 p.m. and returned after 18 minutes. The foreman announced the verdict: 'The jury find the prisoner guilty of murder, but we also find that at the time the crime was committed, the prisoner was of unsound mind.'

The deemster said, 'The jury have taken a most merciful view of the charge against you and the sentence of the court is that you be confined during His Majesty's pleasure.'

Williams then asked, 'Can I make a request?', but Deemster Moore told him that the case was over. Before leaving the court Williams turned and waved to his wife and called, 'Goodbye.'

7

ELLEN JANE LOUGHLIN (1910)

Just after 1.00 a.m. on 3 December 1909 a steamer, the *Ellan Vannin*, left Ramsey harbour bound for Liverpool. The ship had been built in 1860 and since 1883 had sailed between the Isle of Man, Scotland, Whitehaven and Liverpool, carrying mail, passengers and cargo. The ship could carry up to 299 passengers, although on this trip there were only 14, in addition to the 21 crew on board. There was a strong wind blowing as it left the Island but it did not seem severe enough to prevent the sailing. Within an hour or so, and with the ship by now well on the way to its destination, the storm had rapidly worsened, and by now in the middle of the Irish sea, the ship was battered by hurricane-force winds.

Later in the day telegrams were received on the Isle of Man; the ship had not reached its destination. As fears began to grow, further reports came in, one of which described life buoys being seen floating in the Mersey Channel. These life buoys bore the name of the missing vessel. A mail basket was also picked up in the Channel and was found to contain letters sent from the Isle of Man.

By the following afternoon it was clear that a terrible tragedy had occurred. The stricken ship was found by boats from the Mersey Docks Board, lying in 30 ft of water, roughly a mile from the Liverpool side of the Mersey Bar. All 35 people on board died in weather which was later described as the worst ever in that area. The bodies of 18 of the 35 passengers and crew were washed up following the disaster. The other bodies were never found. The crew of 21 left between them 18 widows and 70 fatherless children. A disaster fund was subsequently set up to offer financial assistance to the many dependants of those lost in the tragedy. A Board of Trade inquiry into the events of December 1909 was held in March 1910. There was some discussion of the possibility that the ship had sunk after colliding with another vessel.

However, this was discounted and it was felt it had simply sunk after being swamped by huge waves.

Later in the year of the *Ellan Vannin* inquiry, there was another tragedy. This time it occurred on land, in Ramsey, and involved two people. It was to be a shocking crime which devastated two families and was without any definite motive. Questions which would never be answered remained after the crime.

John Pearson was 54 years old. He left his home in Yorkshire in April 1908 to take up the tenancy of the Crown Hotel in Parliament Street, Ramsey, having earlier been in the army, for a while serving in India. He was known to have a violent temper and at times appeared to drink quite heavily. Local police were called several times to the premises and on one occasion Pearson's abusive language resulted in a court appearance where he was fined. He had a game licence and did some shooting, and he also took a keen interest in sporting events, being associated with the local football club.

Ellen Jane Loughlin was 18 years old and born in Whitehaven, although she had spent most of her life in Ramsey. She moved there with her mother and brothers and sisters following her father's death about ten years previously. Miss Loughlin worked in the Crown Hotel as a domestic servant for around 18 months and before this had worked in other hotels in the town. She was described as a quiet and well-mannered girl. She told her family that the work was quite hard and she had intended to leave the hotel soon and look for other employment. It was later to be revealed that Pearson had accused the girl of having given birth to a child whose body had been recently found in Ramsey harbour. Certainly it seems that there was some bad feeling between the two.

About 11.00 a.m. on Sunday morning, 14 August 1910, Pearson's wife, Mary Jane, said goodbye to him before leaving for church with a friend. She was later to say that she noticed nothing unusual in his manner that morning. About 11.20 a.m. Pearson walked to a nearby barber's shop on the quay for a shave. However, when he arrived there were seven or eight customers waiting and he arranged for the barber to visit the hotel to do the shave at about 1.00 p.m. Pearson then walked back to the hotel and the only other people there when he arrived were Miss Loughlin and another servant, Ethel Mary Walker, who had worked in the hotel for about five weeks.

Shortly after he returned to the hotel at about 11.30 a.m., neighbours and people standing nearby heard two shots fired in rapid succession. On hearing these, Ethel Walker looked out from the back kitchen window and saw Miss Loughlin lying on the ground. She then heard Pearson going upstairs. Ethel ran out of the pub, looking for help, and heard another shot. She met

Inspector Quilliam and he, accompanied by police constables Callister and Gawne, rushed to the hotel where they found Miss Loughlin dead in the back yard. She had been shot in the back of the neck and in the arm with a double-barrelled shotgun. Inspector Quilliam followed a trail of blood upstairs. He encountered Pearson rushing from a room to the left of the landing to the room on the right and took hold of his arm. Quilliam saw that Pearson had horrific injuries to the left side of his face – in fact half of it had disappeared, blown away by the gunshot. He was taken to hospital but died at 2.00 p.m. on that same day.

Two separate inquests were held into the deaths. The inquest into Pearson's death took place at Ramsey Cottage Hospital at 4.00 p.m. the day following the death, in front of the High Bailiff of Ramsey, Mr J. M. Cruickshank and a jury. The Coroner told the jury at the start that they would be unlikely to have any difficulty in deciding how the man came by his death. That, he reminded them, was all they would be required to do.

Mary Jane Pearson gave her evidence to the inquiry. She described how the couple came to the Island and gave details of her husband's past. She denied having any idea as to why, if it was the case, he might have shot Miss Loughlin and had not detected any evidence of ill-feeling between the two. Although she explained that Pearson was quick tempered, she had never heard him threaten anyone or say that he might commit suicide. She also denied that his recent drinking was excessive and said that he was not under the influence of alcohol when she had left him on the previous day to go to church. She did tell the jury that Miss Loughlin had told of her intention of leaving several times, the last being on the Wednesday before the shooting. She had in fact left that day but had returned later. The witness told the jury that she was unaware of any particular reason why Ellen wanted to leave her employment.

Mrs Pearson's friend, Mary Ellen Brain, with whom she had gone to church at the time of the deaths, said that she had detected a certain amount of friction between Mr Pearson and Miss Loughlin and said that he 'had got vexed' with her several times and sometimes found fault with her work. Miss Loughlin would answer him back when he criticised her. She told the inquiry that she had seen a gun several times in the house, both in the attic and in Mr Pearson's bedroom. She found it in his bedroom a day or two before the incident and put it in the attic.

Ethel Mary Walker also stated that Miss Loughlin would annoy Pearson sometimes by answering him back and not doing what she had been asked to do. She denied hearing him accuse the girl of involvement in the death of the baby found in the harbour, although she had heard about this incident, perhaps from Miss Loughlin herself or a customer in the pub. She had heard no quarrel between Pearson and Miss Loughlin prior to the first shots being fired. She described seeing the girl's body and hearing someone going upstairs and then how she had run out of the pub to seek help.

The barber, George Whewell, gave evidence. He said that Pearson came for a shave every day. The back door of the Crown Hotel was only about 30 yards from his shop. He said that Pearson had come in to his shop about 11.25 a.m. the day before. There were about seven or eight people waiting in the shop at the time and Pearson had said that as he was busy he would come back. He had returned about ten minutes later and the barber had told him that he would come to the Crown Hotel and give him his shave around 1.00 p.m. That was the last time he had seen Pearson.

Dr W. S. Cowan then gave his evidence. He had been called to the Crown shortly before midday on the Sunday. He described the horrific injuries to Pearson's face, compatible with a shotgun blast, and said that he felt the end of the barrel would have been placed under his chin, with the gun vertical and the shot travelling upwards. He described how, during his removal to hospital, Pearson had become violent and on several occasions said that he preferred to walk. Several police officers had to restrain him. Once at the hospital he had been anaesthetised and the wound was attended to but, as Dr Cowan had expected, Pearson died from blood loss at around 2.00 p.m. The doctor said that he had seen a gun covered with blood in the room where he had found Pearson. When the doctor asked him why he had shot the girl, Pearson had said 'Shot who? Have I killed her?' When told that the girl was dead, according to the doctor Pearson appeared very surprised and upset. The doctor also said that in his opinion Pearson did not appear to be under the influence of alcohol.

Inspector J. T. Quilliam then addressed the jury. He described finding the girl's body in the yard. She had been lying face down. He had then gone upstairs, found Pearson, and later discovered the double-barrelled shotgun. Two empty cartridges were lying next to it and there was one empty cartridge in the right-hand barrel of the gun. He claimed that Ethel Walker had told him she had twice heard Pearson accuse Ellen Loughlin of being the mother of the baby found in Ramsey harbour, although she had denied saying this earlier in the inquest.

The Coroner told the jury that Inspector Quilliam was the last witness they would hear. He felt they would have no doubt that the man committed suicide. The question of the man's state of mind was discussed by the Coroner and the jury gave a unanimous verdict of 'suicide while of unsound mind'.

The inquest into the death of Ellen Jane Loughlin was held in the courthouse in Ramsey at 6.00 p.m. on the same day. Rose Kelly, Miss Loughlin's sister, gave evidence to the inquest. She described how Pearson had begged her sister to return to work on the Wednesday before her death, after she had said she wanted to leave. She said that Pearson had told her sister that if she came back to work, he would stop drinking. She was not sure why he had said this. Rose Kelly was not aware of any ill-feeling between Pearson and Miss Loughlin.

Dr Cowan again gave evidence. He had seen the dead body of Miss Loughlin. He described a wound on the back of her neck which had severed the spinal column and said that death would have been instantaneous. There was also a wound on her right upper arm, which had also been caused by a gunshot. The gun had been fired at close quarters and the shot causing the wound to the neck had been fired from behind. The doctor felt that this wound, which had resulted in destruction of the spinal cord in the neck, had caused her death. The jury found that Miss Loughlin had died from gunshot wounds inflicted by John Pearson.

The jury then expressed their thanks to Inspector Quilliam for the way he had conducted the inquiry. The Coroner agreed with this view and said that he had been very courageous to go upstairs where he expected to meet a man with a loaded gun. The Coroner told the jury that he intended to inform the appropriate authorities of their feelings about Inspector Quilliam.

The funeral of John Pearson took place the following day on the Tuesday. Miss Loughlin's body was laid to rest the day after.

8

PERCY WILLIAM BROOKE (1930)

Lhergyrhenny Cottage still stands to this day, although, being invisible from roads which pass nearby, it will not have been seen by many Manx people. It is reached by walking along a rough track leading from the road between The Bungalow at the foot of Snaefell, which passes down to Tholt-y-Will and then on to Sulby. The track runs parallel to the north-eastern shore of Sulby Reservoir and ends at the cottage after about half a mile. The isolated cottage is a sad reminder of a murder which shocked the whole Island in 1930. The two people involved in this case were Percy William Brooke, who owned the property – although it was not lived in at the time of the murder – and Thomas Edward Kissack.

Percy William Brooke, who in 1930 was 62 years old, was a son of the late Mr John Brooke of Druidale, Lezayre, a well-known farmer who had once been a member of the House of Keys for Ayre. As a child, Percy had lived at Druidale and for a while he had worked in Parliament Street in Ramsey where he was a motor engineer and cycle dealer. He was extremely well known and respected in the north of the Island and had also worked as a sheep farmer in Sulby Glen and Andreas. He was a director of the Ramsey Waterworks Company. He had been described as a very friendly man, popular with all who knew him and one of the newspapers of the time reported that it would be difficult to believe he had an enemy in the world. For the previous year or two he had lived in Churchtown, Lezayre in retirement. He had an interest in bee keeping and had recently been the secretary of the newly formed Manx Bee Keepers Association. His wife was a school nurse in Ramsey and he had a son who was a student at King William's College in Castletown.

Thomas Kissack was the son of the late Mr William Henry Kissack who had lived in a cottage at Balladromma, Lonan. Thomas was described as 'mentally disordered for many years'. He had served in the army for a while and had been a fireman on ships. Kissack had been involved in an accident as a young man, and this may have contributed to some of his subsequent mental problems. He had fallen down the rocks on the coast near Groudle, just outside Douglas, and sustained head injuries. During this incident, he had lain trapped in the rocks all night and was eventually rescued the following day.

After serving in the army he returned to the Isle of Man and made several court appearances, being eventually committed to the psychiatric hospital. Later he had lived in the south of England and again had been arrested and imprisoned. He had a particular liking for guns, was unmarried and had a brother who worked in Douglas. Born in 1883, he was of average build and height with black hair. His previous crimes had included burglary, vagrancy and stealing a gun in 1914. His crimes seem to have started after his accident.

On Monday, 13 October 1930, Percy Brooke decided he would spend some time shooting on land near his cottage, Lhergyrhenny. The cottage was unoccupied but Mr Brooke kept guns and ammunition stored there. He set off from his home in Churchtown, Lezayre, on a bicycle on the Monday morning and arrived at the cottage about noon. When he got to Lhergyrhenny he found that he could not get in and there appeared to be a problem with the lock. He heard noises inside the cottage and found that a pane of glass in one of the windows was broken. Realising there was someone inside, he set off to look for help. In a nearby field William Kinrade was busy ferreting for rabbits and Mr Brooke asked him if he would accompany him back to the cottage to investigate. Kinrade agreed and they returned together to the cottage where Brooke managed to get in through the broken window and opened the door from the inside to let in Kinrade. Brooke found that there was a wire stuck in the lock preventing him from putting in the key from the outside. The two men looked round the house and Percy Brooke quickly realised that someone had taken his guns. He shouted upstairs, 'Who's there?' but there was no response. There were two flights of stairs leading to the room above and Percy Brooke started on his way up them. After climbing five steps to the first landing, a shot was fired from the landing. Kinrade was still at the bottom of the stairs when this happened and Brooke fell back downstairs and lay next to him. Kinrade believed that Brooke was dead and, fearing for his own safety, he quickly left the cottage and ran for help. After about a mile he found a group of men working on the Tholt-y-Will Road, including Mr William Christian, who tenanted the mountain farm owned by Percy Brooke. One of the men, Ernest Fargher, took Kinrade to Ramsey police station in his lorry, while the others made towards the cottage. When they reached it, the men positioned themselves around it but did not enter and awaited the arrival of the police.

Sergeant G. W. Corkhill was in charge of the station in Ramsey, and after summoning Dr Kitchen, and in the company of Constable Lancaster and Kinrade, travelled by car the seven miles to the cottage. There they found the men surrounding the cottage, who told them that no one had left while they had been there. After the police had fired off several shots, two through the kitchen window and three through the upper windows from about 20 yards, they entered with the doctor and found Percy Brooke lying dead at the bottom of the stairs. His body was then taken to the mortuary at Ramsey and two armed police constables were left to guard the house overnight.

It was felt by the doctor that Mr Brooke would have died instantaneously when he was shot in the back. It seemed that Brooke had turned round or bent down when he had seen the man on the landing above, about to fire at him. The doctor found a large hole in the man's back.

It was subsequently found that another man, Arthur Comish, who was employed by William Christian and lived at Mill View, Starch Mills in Sulby Glen, had met Mr Brooke earlier that day. Brooke had called at Comish's house around 10.00 a.m. and asked him to accompany him to Lhergyrhenny as he had heard that a man was seen acting strangely in the area the previous day. Comish had told Brooke that he was unable to go and Brooke had then set off on his bicycle. It appeared that no one had seen Mr Brooke between this time until he asked Kinrade to accompany him to the cottage. William Christian had been the foreman of the group of men working on the roads at the time of the murder.

The man who had been acting strangely the day before became the main suspect for the murder. It was soon found that he had called at the home of Mr John Cowley, The Creggan, near Tholt-y-Will, who gave him some bread. It was also found that Mr Brooke had kept about six guns, a pistol and a revolver in the house. All the weapons except one were found in the cottage by the police and all were loaded. One gun and several rounds of ammunition were missing.

A huge manhunt got underway, supervised by Colonel Madoc, the Chief Constable. This involved both police and volunteers and was to last for over 24 hours but the search was hampered by poor weather conditions with severe fog limiting visibility to a few yards. Every available member of the Manx police force was called in and armed with guns, as knowing that the man was armed made the search extremely dangerous; the hunt rapidly spread over a very wide area. Kissack had become the main suspect after he had escaped from Ballamona Hospital near Douglas, where he had been detained. He was known to have an extremely good knowledge of the mountains and was used to living outdoors. The police searched for him in pairs.

At midday on the Tuesday, Kissack was seen by an employee of the Highway Board, who contacted two of the searchers. He told them he had seen a man wearing a pair of waders and carrying a gun, hiding in the culvert of a bridge. However, by the time the men arrived at the spot where he had been seen, Kissack was found to have escaped. The police later found some bread in the culvert.

Later on the Tuesday, at about 3.00 p.m., Sergeant P. H. Watterson and other men approached a group of old ruined houses near Druidale. As Sergeant Watterson entered one of them he came across Kissack standing by the old fireplace, a dead rabbit lying at his feet. Kissack had not seen the police officer and was taken by surprise. The police sergeant drew his gun and shouted, 'Hands up, Kissack'. Kissack dropped his gun, put up his hands and with help from the other men he was then handcuffed. Both barrels of the gun he had been carrying were found to be loaded and he was also found to be carrying 23 cartridges when caught. He was taken to Douglas police station, arriving about 4.45 p.m.

On the Saturday before the crime, Kissack had escaped from the mental hospital where he had been an inmate for several years. He had broken out before but had never been violent on the previous occasions.

An inquest on the murdered man was opened at Ramsey Courthouse on the Tuesday afternoon, before Mr W. Lay, the High Bailiff of Douglas. The court was packed for the hearing but only identification evidence was given. Percy William Brooke was identified by his brother-in-law, Robert Lees. He had last seen the dead man on the Monday morning as he had passed Lees' house at 9.30 a.m. riding his bicycle on his way to Lhergyrhenny.

The church at Lezayre was crowded for the funeral of Percy Brooke on the Wednesday afternoon, and on that same day Thomas Edward Kissack appeared before High Bailiff Cowley for the formal preliminary hearing. Kissack was charged with Percy Brooke's murder and Police Sergeant Watterson gave evidence. He explained how he had arrested Kissack and had later charged him with the murder. He told the court that Kissack had replied, 'I will tell you what I done. I just levelled the gun to frighten him. If I had had any intention of killing, I would have killed the two of them.' The prisoner was then remanded until the Thursday.

The preliminary hearing continued on Thursday, 16 October at Ramsey Courthouse. The court was opened by High Bailiff Cowley. Mr William Frederick Christian gave evidence. He said he had known Mr Brooke very well and was a tenant of his. He also knew the house at Lhergyrhenny very well and had lived there for years. He identified the waders worn by the accused as belonging to Mr Brooke. The gun which Kissack had in his possession had also belonged to the murdered man. The last time Christian had seen the gun it was hanging over the mantelpiece in the cottage, where it was always kept. Christian said that he did not know of any dispute between Brooke and Kissack but did describe an interesting incident. He said that two or three years earlier, when his father was a tenant of Brooke's, Kissack went to Lhergyrhenny with a gun. He went on, 'He met my father at the stable door and asked for food. My father said, "No, Kissack, you're not to get in the house – you shall get food outside."' He added that his father had warned Kissack that the police were after him on Snaefell and Kissack had then bolted. Christian also said of Kissack: 'I thought he was a harmless man.'

William Kinrade, aged 72 years, was a rabbit catcher by occupation. He told of the events on that Monday when he had accompanied Mr Brooke to the house. He explained that he was in a field on the west side of Lhergyrhenny when Mr Brooke came up to him and said that there was someone in his house and he had been unable to get the key in the lock. The two men went to the cottage and he described how Brooke had climbed through the broken window and let him into the house. He said they looked in the kitchen and Brooke said, 'The house is ransacked.' Then Brooke looked up to the joists of the ceiling and said, 'My gun's gone.' Kinrade went on to describe how Brooke had then shouted upstairs, 'Whoever is up there speak and show yourself', but there was no answer so Brooke started to climb the stairs. Kinrade explained that when he was about three-quarters of the way up the first set of stairs, he was shot. He went on, 'The deceased fell right across on the stairs before my feet. I stepped back off the stairs and went into the pantry and stood about three feet from the body. There was no sign of life and I concluded that he was dead so I stepped out of the door and made for the highway to get help. I had seen no one but the deceased in the house.' He added in response to a question by a juror, 'I heard no one upstairs at all. The deceased told me that when he was passing he saw someone upstairs like a woman. When I left the house the deceased's head was on the top stair. When the deceased was on the stairs, I heard the click of the hammer of a gun.'

Dr Kitchen of Ramsey said that he had seen the body lying at the foot of the stairs, partly on the left side with the head lying in the room on the right side. He had been dead between two and three hours and there was a large pool of blood in front of the body and around it. The body was then taken to the mortuary, and in the company of Dr Skene, Dr Kitchen had found that there was a ragged hole through the coat, waistcoat and shirt, at the back, just over the right shoulder. On removing the clothes, a round hole with ragged edges about half an inch in diameter, just on the inner side of the right shoulder blade, was found. The cause of death was haemorrhage. The direction of the wound was from above, downwards, forwards and to the right. The doctor believed that the gunshot wound had been inflicted from above on a man who was stooping down.

The layout of the house was described by one of the police officers, then Sergeant Watterson gave his evidence about the arrest of Kissack. After the preliminary case had been completed Kissack was asked if he had anything to say. He replied, 'No, sir', and was then remanded into custody. He was taken to the cells and later to the Isle of Man Prison where he remained until the start of his trial.

The last murder trial on the Isle of Man had taken place on 8 August 1916. On this occasion, Sergeant John Williams, a member of the Royal Defence Corps at Knockaloe POW Internment Camp, had been charged with the murder of Sergeant W. H. Malings. Williams had shot Malings in a room at the camp and he was found guilty but insane and was ordered to be detained at His Majesty's pleasure. The last time a Manx person was charged with murder had been in 1890 when William Kelly stood trial for his wife's murder in Douglas. On that occasion the defendant was found guilty of manslaughter and given ten years' penal servitude.

Kissack's case was heard before Deemster Reginald Douglas Farrant at Douglas Courthouse. The prosecution for the Crown was led by Mr Ramsey Bignall Moore and Junior Counsel was his son George Moore. Leading Counsel for the defence was Mr John Henry Lockhart Cowin, and Junior Counsel was Mr Howard G. Lay. The trial started at 11.00 a.m. on Friday, 28 November 1930 before a packed courthouse. When the charge was put to Kissack by Deemster Farrant that he had murdered Percy Brooke, Kissack replied, 'Not guilty. It was an accident.' A 12-man jury was sworn in, and the Attorney General outlined the case for the jury. He told the court that Kissack was charged with the most serious crime apart from treason: that he had murdered Percy Brooke on 13 October 1930. He told the jury that the defendant had a long record of both crime and confinement in lunatic asylums, both on the Island and in England, and had been for some time an inmate in the Isle of Man lunatic asylum. He had been seen in the kitchen of the asylum on Saturday, 11 October about 9.00 a.m. but shortly after this he was found to be missing. A search had commenced but by Monday there was no trace of him.

The Attorney General then described the events leading up to the death of Mr Brooke at Lhergyrhenny. He explained how, using a wooden model of the cottage, Percy Brooke had entered the house and then opened the door to allow William Kinrade to enter. He told the court that Mr Brooke quickly realised a gun was missing. Having ascertained that there was no one downstairs, Brooke had then called upstairs several times for whoever was there to come down. The Attorney General told the court how Mr Brooke had ascended the first flight of stairs and been shot on the landing. He told the jury, 'I don't think you will find yourselves troubled in any way with the identity of the man who shot Mr Brooke.' Kissack was found in possession of several articles, including the lethal weapon which was missing from the house when Mr Brooke went into it. After the arrest Kissack was taken to Douglas Police Station and was formally charged by Sergeant Watterson with having murdered Mr Percy William Brooke and after being cautioned in legal form, he made this remark: 'I just levelled the gun to frighten him, because if I had any intention of killing, I would have killed the two of them.' It was clear therefore, said the Attorney General, that Kissack had killed Brooke. He also told them that they would have to consider whether the killing was intentional or whether there was any possibility of it being accidental. They would also need to consider the man's state of mind. The jury did not, he explained, have to decide whether Kissack had meant to kill or wound Mr Brooke, as either of these would amount to murder. He did say it was clear that Kissack was not a normal sane man, but a certified lunatic. This however did not automatically mean that he was not guilty of murder as there were 'degrees of lunacy' he said. The jury had to decide if the defendant knew at the time of the killing, the difference between right and wrong. The Attorney General told the jury there were four possible verdicts they could find:

- not guilty
- guilty of murder
- guilty of manslaughter
- guilty but insane

The deemster said he was not sure if the jury could in fact find him guilty but insane. It was decided however that this point would be argued later.

Prison Surgeon Robert Marshall gave his evidence. He had seen Kissack on seven or eight occasions since his arrest six weeks earlier. He described him as 'of very low mentality, feeble minded, and he could not engage in a serious conversation without sniggering and laughing'. Kissack did not seem to understand the seriousness of his predicament and showed no evidence of regret for himself, Mr Brooke or Mr Brooke's family, for what he had done. He said that in his opinion 'the man [was] utterly irresponsible for his actions'.

The trial resumed on the second day, Saturday. George William Corlett, an expert on guns was called by the defence. Corlett had tested and examined the gun used in the killing, which was a double-barrelled 12-bore shotgun. He had been to the cottage and said that the distance from the top landing by someone firing at a person on the first landing was only about four feet. Corlett felt that if the defendant had picked up the gun with his finger on the trigger it might have gone off.

In his final address to the jury, Mr Cowin said that Kissack was not aware of the difference between right and wrong. He told the jury that whatever happened at the end of the trial, Kissack would never be free again but would be in custody for the rest of his life. He told the jury that if they felt Kissack had fired without intending to kill Mr Brooke, he would be guilty of manslaughter and reminded them that several doctors had felt he did not have homicidal tendencies. He explained that Kissack had not himself given evidence because he could not carry on a conversation without becoming confused.

The Attorney General for the Crown said that he could not really argue with the doctor's opinion that the defendant could not distinguish between right and wrong. He told the jury that he felt they would conclude that Kissack was insane. He said that if they found that the whole tragic episode was simply an accident, he would be returned to the Isle of Man mental hospital. If they found otherwise, he would be treated as a 'criminal lunatic'. He reminded them that Mr Brooke had called out to him from the foot of the stairs and asked him to come down. He felt that the verdict could be guilty but insane. He also added at the end of his closing speech, that no blame for his escape should be levelled at the staff of the hospital where he had lived.

Deemster Farrant began his summing up at noon on Saturday, 29 November. He told the jury they had to decide if the killing was accidental or not. If it was an accident, they must find Kissack not guilty. If they did not feel it was an accident, they had to then decide if he was guilty of murder or manslaughter. All the evidence, he said, pointed to Kissack being insane – they had to consider if this would excuse his killing of Mr Brooke. The deemster added that it was not clear that the Manx jury could bring in a verdict of guilty but insane. This would have been an option in England although there was, however, a precedent in the Isle of Man (in the case of Williams in 1916 – *see* Chapter 6).

The jury retired at 12.40 p.m. and returned at 2.48 p.m. to inform the deemster they were unable to agree on a verdict. Although the foreman told him there was little chance of their coming to an agreement they again retired to give the matter further consideration. They came back to the court later to ask what step Brooke had been standing on when the shot was fired. The deemster said no one could be absolutely certain, that it was probably the third from the bottom but may have been the fourth. The jury retired again, the foreman taking the photograph of the body with him to the jury room.

They returned almost immediately. The foreman said, 'We find the prisoner guilty of murder but insane at the time he committed the offence.' The deemster then ordered the defendant to stand and told him: 'Thomas Edward Kissack, you have been found by a jury of your fellow countrymen, guilty of feloniously killing with malice aforethought, Percy William Brooke. They have also found that you were insane at the time you committed that felonious act. The sentence of the court is that you be removed to the place from whence you came, and that you be therein detained until His Majesty's Pleasure shall be further known.'

Kissack showed no emotion during the sentencing and was led away. He was subsequently sent to Broadmoor Criminal Lunatic Asylum and detained there for life.

One week after the trial, an article in the *Isle of Man Examiner* said: 'The end of the trial was the culminating moment in the appalling tragedy which began at a lone spot in the Manx mountains seven weeks earlier.' The article went on to say that one needed to feel some sort of pity for Kissack in view of his mental illness.

It continued: 'Kissack was a born poacher. From early boyhood he displayed a passion for rabbit hunting and right on through his whole adult life, rabbits and guns seemed to hold some strange fascination for him.' The article went on to say that his mental problems may have resulted from the 'mishap' on Clay Head in which he sustained head injuries and goes on to look at Kissack's criminal career, which began at the age of 19. He overstayed leave from the army by two weeks and broke into an old cottage, stealing some money, for which he was jailed for one month. This conviction led to his dismissal from the army. After his release, he was almost immediately re-arrested for another burglary at a shop. This time he was given two months in prison. Another conviction shortly after this resulted in three months in prison. His next conviction earned him four months in prison and resulted in the judge suggesting he be mentally examined, and he was found to have psychiatric problems and was sent to the mental institute. Over the next few years he had several jobs as a fireman on ships and also accumulated more convictions.

On the night of 11 November 1913 he escaped from the asylum and broke into a house in Onchan and took food and a gun. After a long search he was caught and again sent to prison. In November 1916 he was sentenced to six months' hard labour by Deemster Moore, who told him, prophetically as it turned out, 'You seem to have a mania for stealing guns and that is a very serious thing, for although you have never attempted to shoot anyone, a man with a gun, in a moment of passion or forgetfulness, might do very serious injury and you might thus find yourself in a very serious position. I take this opportunity of letting it go forth to the public that with a man like you about, it is most important that people keep their guns carefully and in an unseen position, where you may not get hold of them, and use them against some member of the public.'

In July 1918 he was convicted of 'indecency with a male person aged 10 years' at Lewes, Sussex. He received a 12-month prison sentence but was then transferred to East Sussex Mental Asylum from Sussex County Gaol and then returned to the asylum in the Isle of Man in 1922. Although he escaped for two days in 1928, he remained there until the escape which culminated in the murder of Percy Brooke.

9

JANICE McCALLUM (1978)

In the February of 1978, Summerland, the scene of the tragedy five years earlier when fifty people had lost their lives in the terrible fire, opened its doors again to the public. It was claimed by the then general manager to be one of the most modern, well-equipped sports and recreation centres in Europe. It included, among other facilities, fourteen squash courts, one five-a-side pitch, a judo room, eight badminton courts and an indoor hockey pitch. On 22 June, Lieutenant Governor Sir John Paul unveiled a plaque in the main auditorium of the new building to commemorate its re-opening.

At the end of May, thousands of motorbike fans made their annual pilgrimage to the Island for the TT (Tourist Trophy) festival. Extra money had been made available to attract top names to the races and the fans especially looked forward to the return of their hero, Mike Hailwood, with his record number of TT wins, after an absence from the races of 11 years, during which he had concentrated on car racing. He had spent the previous week re-familiarising himself with the course. This paid off when, riding a Ducati, Hailwood thrilled the crowds by winning the Formula One race on the Saturday at the end of Practice Week, his 13th TT win and 10th World Championship. 'Mike the Bike', as he was affectionately known to his many fans, returned to the Island the following year and won the Senior Race, his 14th and final TT win, with a new lap record of 114.02 mph. He was to die in tragic circumstances along with his nine-year-old daughter in a road accident in March 1981 when their car crashed into a lorry.

In 1978, though, despite the excitement surrounding Hailwood's return to the TT, there was also sadness with the deaths of five of the riders during the fortnight's racing. Three were killed during the first sidecar race, when a previous TT winner, Mac Hobson and his passenger, Ken Birch, crashed on Bray Hill seconds after the start. The horrific accident was witnessed by a

86

large crowd of spectators at what was always a popular spot for watching the bikes. The third rider who died, Ernst Trachsel from Switzerland, crashed at the bottom of the hill after negotiating the wreckage from the first accident a few seconds later and his passenger suffered a broken leg in this accident.

In May 1978 Janice McCallum was 18 years old and worked as a shop assistant in Largs, Ayrshire, on the west coast of Scotland. Eight months earlier she had moved out of her parents' house there to live nearby with a friend, Anne Cuthbertson, who was 22 and also a shop assistant. On Sunday, 28 May, the day before practices started for the TT, the two young women set off for a two-week holiday on the Isle of Man. Arriving in Douglas later that day they soon found their accommodation at Ravenswood, Clifton Terrace and spent the next day or two looking round places of interest in Douglas, including the Manx Museum and the Waxworks on the Promenade. During this time the girls also met up with some boys they knew, one of whom they had met on the boat on their way to the Island. When their money began to run out, they moved into cheaper accommodation at 1 Castle Mona Avenue, on Wednesday, 31 May, and that same day they both went to see about a job in a hotel. Although Janice took the job, Anne decided she did not really want it and decided that she would rather return home. That evening the pair relaxed watching television in the guest house before going out for a meal. After their meal they called in at the Central Hotel's Broadway Bar, in the middle of Douglas Promenade, close to their lodgings in Castle Mona Avenue. That evening Janice was wearing a white T-shirt which she had bought shortly after arriving in Douglas; the T-shirt had her name printed on it and the slogan 'I like it when I can get it'.

After a glass of coke, Janice told Anne she was going to ask her landlady if it would be all right if she took the landlady's puppy, Biggles, for a walk. Having collected the dog from the guest house, she then returned to the bar and spoke to her friend again, leaving at about 10.00 p.m., saying she would be back 'in a minute'. As Anne watched her cross the road outside the hotel and set off along the promenade with the dog, she was not to know that it would be the last time she would see Janice alive. She stayed in the bar with John Bow, a young man who was also staying at the same guest house, until around 10.45 p.m. She then went outside to wait, but with still no sign of Janice, she returned to Mrs Kelly's boarding house. Anne and John later went to look for Janice, but even as they set off to search, the dead body of her friend had already been found.

At 10.15 p.m. that evening, Michael John Howard, managing director of Howard Amusements Ltd, and his wife, arrived at the garages in Market

Street close to the rear of the Strand Cinema where he kept his car each night. Mr Howard noted that, unusually, the folding garage doors were open. His wife opened the door further so that he was able to reverse the car in, and as she did so she discovered a girl's body lying behind the door. The girl had been brutally battered about the head, which was heavily smeared with blood. Her nose and jaw were later found to have been fractured. The girl's trousers were ripped and pulled down to her ankles and her knickers had been torn in two and the T-shirt pulled up to her chest. She also had injuries to her neck, suggesting that she had been strangled by her attacker. Minutes later the puppy was found running free, still with its lead on, and it was handed into the police the following morning. Mr Howard's wife contacted the police immediately and the first police officer arrived after a few minutes. A full-scale murder hunt was then launched. A team from the North West Forensic Science Laboratory in Chorley, Lancashire, was contacted and set off immediately for the Isle of Man to help with the inquiry. Twenty officers from Lancashire were also flown in and the inquiry was led by Lancashire's Head of CID, Chief Superintendent Wilf Brooks. He had last visited the Island in 1973 to help with enquiries into another death, which became known as the 'Golden Egg Murder' (*see* Chapter 1). An incident room was set up in nearby St George's Hall, Hill Street, Douglas. Shoe prints were found in dust a few feet away from the body and it was felt by the police surgeon who attended the scene, shortly after the body was discovered, that death had occurred very recently, probably in the last two hours.

Over the next few days all departures from the Island's airport at Ronaldsway and the Sea Terminal were closely watched by the police. Passengers' luggage was searched for bloody clothing and police mingled with the crowds of TT fans, who were by now flocking to the Island in anticipation of the races, which were to start with the Formula One on the Saturday after the murder. Posters giving details of the crime and requesting information were distributed around Douglas, and women were warned to take extra care when out on their own, particularly in quiet parts of the Island. The public were asked to look out for and report to police any blood-stained clothing. Appeals were made in both English and German and people were asked to report any incidents of women being followed or accosted by men. Clothing, blood samples, and fingerprints found at the scene were sent to Chorley's Forensic Science Laboratory.

At 9.00 p.m. on Friday, 2 June, 48 hours after the murder, a local girl who had volunteered for the task took part in a police reconstruction of the murdered girl's last known movements. Wearing similar clothes to those Janice had worn on the fateful night she traced the route Janice had taken on her final walk from the Broadway Bar in the middle of the Promenade to Castle Street then into Market Street, close to the spot where Janice met her death. She also took the dog, Biggles, with her on her walk. Several people soon came forward to say that they had seen a girl matching Janice's description walking in and around Strand Street. Some reported her as being in the company of a man, aged between 20 and 25 years and approximately 6 ft tall with dark-brown collar-length hair. Several witnesses also described the girl's white T-shirt with the slogan on it and the small dog on a lead.

It was early on the morning of Sunday, 4 June, four days after the murder, that Police Sergeant John Teare was on mobile patrol in Douglas when he received a request to attend a house in nearby Onchan. When he arrived at the house he was shown the body of a man, lying in a double bed. His wife had awoken to find her husband, dead, beside her. A police surgeon was called and attended shortly afterwards, confirming that the man was dead. Various items of clothing were removed from the house and later sent to Chorley for forensic tests. A pair of training shoes found under the stairs in the hall under a pile of clothing, were also taken. It appeared to police that these shoes might have been hidden under the clothes.

An inquest was opened on Friday, 2 June by Deputy Coroner Weldon Williams into the circumstances surrounding the death of Janice McCallum, in front of a seven-man jury. Her mother gave evidence about Janice's trip to the Island and told the inquiry that she had last spoken to her daughter by telephone during the evening of Tuesday, 30 May.

Dr Roger Harry Ritson, deputy police surgeon and general practitioner, stated that he had examined the girl's body at 10.45 p.m. on the night of the murder. He estimated the girl had been dead for approximately two hours and described her injuries. He said there was a 2 cm split in the left corner of her mouth and a large 6x1 cm area of clotted blood over the right eyebrow and a large area of clotted blood over the left side of the girl's face. Her trousers were pulled down and ripped at the seams. The right shoe was still on her foot but the left was off. Her T-shirt was pulled up, exposing her left breast, and her knickers were torn in two and lay across her upper chest.

The Home Office pathologist, Dr Brian Beeson, attached to the North West Forensic Science Laboratory, Chorley, explained his findings at a post-mortem examination which he carried out at 2.00 p.m. on Thursday, 1 June. There were numerous grazes and bruises and she had suffered a broken nose and fractures to other facial bones. The pathologist said that in his opinion the injuries would have resulted from at least four blows. He also reported that marks on her neck were caused by pressure, possibly a 'manual stranglehold' and that these marks pointed to strangulation. Dr Beeson said that the cause of death was asphyxia caused by both the inhalation of blood due to blows on the head and pressure on the neck.

John Bow, who was also a resident at Mrs Kelly's boarding house, said that on the evening in question he had met the two girls in the Central Hotel and recalled that Janice had a small puppy with her. He told the inquiry that she had left around 10.00 p.m. with the dog and that was the last time he saw her. Several other witnesses described seeing her walking in the direction of Strand Street with the dog.

Mrs Joyce Prescott worked at the Picture House cinema in Strand Street. She told the inquiry how, at around 10.30 pm on the evening in question, she left the building by its rear entrance and walked down Market Street. She went on to say that she came across a little dog running free with its lead attached. She took it by the lead and looked around for its owner, but when she could not see anyone she let the dog go. The director of a local taxi firm described how he found the dog a few minutes later and handed it over to police earlier the following morning.

Mrs Christine Curphey of Willaston told the inquiry that she had seen Janice that evening. She was in the Wimpy Bar in Strand Street with her boyfriend and left at 10.10 p.m. She remembered the time as she was planning to catch the last bus home, which left at 10.25 p.m. She walked towards Granville Street and it was then that she saw Janice coming in the opposite direction with the small mongrel puppy. At that time, she said, there was no one with Janice.

Another witness to give evidence was Miss Vivian Woods. After leaving the Strand Cinema she had briefly visited the Dogs' Home public house before walking back along Strand Street. She said that she saw a couple turning up the lane by the Strand cinema. She recalled that the girl nearly tripped over her dog's lead and said, 'The man just put his arm round her to steady her. They seemed to know one another, they were walking up the lane holding hands.' She added that the girl was about 5 ft 3 in. tall with brownish hair and was wearing a white top and blue jeans. The man was taller by about five or six inches and was wearing a white shirt and dark trousers. He appeared to be in his early 20s, of medium build with just longer than collar-length hair. The couple had been walking towards her but she only noticed them when the girl tripped and so only received a rear view of the couple.

The inquest into Janice's death also heard evidence concerning the finding of the Onchan man's body. The jury at the inquest were also told about the post-mortem findings and the removal of clothing and other items from the man's house. A Home Office forensic scientist, Mr Philip Charles Rydeard, gave evidence. He described how he had examined and photographed the footmarks found in the garage and compared them with the training shoes removed from the man's house. He had found four footmarks and felt that it was highly unlikely that these had been made by another pair of shoes. However, he did say that there was a remote possibility of this being the case.

Robert John Kelso, from Widnes, told the jury that he was in the Regent Hotel on 31 May at around 5.30 p.m. with Michael Cowin when they were joined by the Onchan man at about 6.30 p.m. Kelso explained that he and the Onchan man had known one another for four or five years. Some women came into the bar and the man left with one of them but later returned between 8.00 and 8.30 p.m. on his own. He recalled that 'he seemed to be a bit more drunk' at that time and he bought the man a drink, as he said he had no money. He went on: 'He talked to me for a while then a girl came in – she was wearing a white T-shirt with a slogan on it and she had a small dog with her on a lead.' The man then told Kelso in crude terms that he intended to have sexual intercourse with the girl, before going to sit with her, then returning to the bar. After finishing his beer, the man and the girl left together. Kelso estimated the time they left the pub to be 'well before 9.00 p.m.' He said that the man had appeared to be 'obsessed by sex that night' and he had been 'talking about sex all the time'.

Michael Cowin also gave evidence, telling the jury that the man had also indicated to him that he hoped to have sex with the girl. He added that when the man left with her he seemed 'quite drunk'.

The woman mentioned by Kelso as having left the Regent Hotel at around 6.30 p.m. with the Onchan man was Valerie Agnew. She said she had seen the three men there and had left with the man, whom she had known for about three months and they had gone to the nearby Dogs' Home. When they left this pub she had gone to the Athol and the man had returned to the Regent. Later that same evening she saw the man again outside one of the cinemas in Strand Street and they had briefly spoken.

John Houghton told the jury that he saw the man, whom he knew, twice that evening. Mr Houghton and his girlfriend were in Strand Street between 9.45 p.m. and 9.55 p.m. on the first occasion. The couple had later decided to look at the new multi-storey car park in Chester Street and they walked to the top of it. From there he again saw the man at about 10.20 p.m. immediately below them, walking from the direction of the back of Strand Street towards Church Road Marina. Mr Houghton added that the man was walking in 'a brisk fashion' and had been wearing a white T-shirt and light blue jeans.

Detective Chief Inspector Moore told the jury that he had measured the distance from the garage where the body had been found, to the man's home in Onchan. He found this to be 2.4 miles if the route taken was along the promenade then up Summer Hill. Another route, along to the end of the promenade to Port Jack then up Royal Avenue was slightly longer at 2.7 miles.

The Onchan man's wife told the inquiry that he had arrived home that evening around 10.00 p.m. He lived approximately two miles from the scene of the murder, and she claimed that he had brought her a cup of coffee as she lay in bed just as the Border Television news at 10.00 p.m. was starting. She said that there was nothing unusual in his manner that evening and he had undressed and got into bed. Her husband had told her he had had a few drinks, but not many, and had walked home through the town and along the promenade, but she said he was not at all drunk when he came home and added that, over a period of 2–3 weeks before his death, he had been concerned about his unemployment and their financial problems. At his wife's request, the man had visited his GP a few weeks earlier, who described him as tense and irritable. However, when the GP had seen him a week later, he said that the man seemed 'better'. The man was subsequently found to have died from a massive overdose of a drug called Tuinal, which was a sedative-barbiturate. There was no suicide note.

On Tuesday, 13 June, almost two weeks since the girl's murder, the *Isle of Man Weekly Times* reported that the murder squad had left the Island and the intensive police enquiries into the hunt for the killer had ended. The murder headquarters had been closed down and the posters appealing for information on the death were removed from doors, walls and billboards.

At the end of the week-long inquest and three hours' deliberation, the seven-man jury named the unemployed Onchan man as the man who had murdered 18-year-old Janice McCallum. The deputy Coroner took just over an hour to sum up the evidence to the jury. He told them: 'If you are satisfied that you can name the assailant then you are bound to do so, and you will do so without regard to the fact that the person is dead and is not here to speak on his own behalf.' It took the jury three hours and ten minutes to make up its mind. By a vote of six to one they found that Janice had been maliciously killed 'with malice aforethought' and that the man in question had been responsible for her death.

The case was closed. No one else was sought by the Manx police in connection with the crime.

MANX MURDERS

NOTE

In order to minimise any distress to the family of the man named by the jury as the killer of Janice McCallum, he has not been named in this account.

10

HERBERT SMITH COWELL (1900)

The classic definition of murder was that given centuries ago by Coke:

> Murder under English Law is when a man of sound memory and of
> the age of discretion, unlawfully killeth within any county of the
> realm any reasonable creature in *rerum natura* under the King's peace,
> with malice aforethought, either expressed by the party or implied by
> law so, as the party wounded, or hurt etc. die of the wound or hurt
> etc. within a year and a day after the same.

As stated, that was the classic definition of murder but over the centuries it
has been modified by statute and decisions of the court. Nowadays the usual
definition of murder (which also applies to the Isle of Man) is as follows:
subject to three exceptions, the crime of murder is committed where a person
of sound mind and discretion unlawfully kills any reasonable creature in
being and under the Queen's peace with intent to kill or cause grievous bodily
harm (note: the common law requirement that death must follow within a
year and a day has been abolished).

In order to prove murder, therefore, it must be necessary to show that
the defendant was 'of sound mind and discretion'. This simply means the
defendant must not be insane or under ten years of age. The act causing
death must have been done 'unlawfully', i.e. without legal justification or
excuse. Such legal justification or excuse might arise in the case of self
defence or bona fide surgical treatment. The onus is on the prosecution to
prove that the killing was unlawful. It is also necessary to show that the
defendant *killed* his or her victim. Any act which is a substantial cause of
death renders the doer responsible for that death if the other elements of
murder are proved.

The reference to 'any reasonable creature' relates to the appearance rather than the mental capacity of the victim. As regards 'in being', to kill a child in its mother's womb is neither murder nor manslaughter. For there to be an offence of murder, it must be shown that the entire child has actually been born into the world in a living state.

The use of the words 'under the King's (or Queen's) peace' was to except from murder killing in the course of war and possibly rebellion.

The last ingredient – and generally the most important – to be proved by the prosecution is that the killing was done 'with intent to kill or cause grievous bodily harm'. (In this context grievous bodily harm means injury that is really serious but not necessarily dangerous to life.) Section 18 of the Criminal Code 1872 refers to 'with malice aforethought'. This concept has a long history but since more recent decisions it is no longer necessary to explore this concept in order to expound the modern law. It can now be stated that it consists in:

1. an intention to kill any person;
2. an intention to cause grievous bodily harm to any person.

For the sake of completeness I might add that an offence which would otherwise be murder is reduced to manslaughter if the accused:

3. was provoked;
4. suffered from diminished responsibility; or
5. was acting in pursuant of a suicide pact.

Leaving aside the above three special exceptions, generally the elements of manslaughter are the same as those of murder *except* there is no need to show an intent to kill or cause grievous bodily harm.

I have indicated that the definition of murder has been modified or amended over the course of time. For example, in the vast majority of cases in this book, the 'objective test' of liability for murder was then the law. That test of intent was 'not what the defendant himself contemplated but what the ordinary reasonable man or woman would in all the circumstances of the case have contemplated as the natural and probable result'. The test is now a subjective one, namely what did the defendant himself or herself intend as the consequences of his or her actions. Furthermore, it was only in the latter half of last century that the concepts of provocation and diminished responsibility were introduced whereby offences which would otherwise be murder may be reduced to manslaughter. It is extremely likely (if the present definition, 'defences' or exceptions applied) that some of the 'older' convictions for murder would not have been forthcoming, and that verdicts of manslaughter would have been returned instead.

Over the years there have been many cases on the Isle of Man where manslaughter was the final outcome of a trial. In some of these the accused person had been initially charged with murder but at the end of the trial was found guilty of the lesser charge of manslaughter. In other cases the charge was manslaughter from the start. For example a person may have been initially charged with murder but before the main trial the charge had been reduced to the lesser one. We will next consider a case where the initial charge of murder was levelled at two men but this charge was later reduced to one of manslaughter.

William Corlett was a married man aged 25 years, who worked as a butcher in Douglas. On the evening of Monday, 7 May 1900, he was in the Bijou Billiard Club in Regent Street, Douglas. The 70 members of this club paid a subscription of 5s a year and the club was open from 11.00 a.m. until about 2.00 a.m. the following morning. Around 11.00 p.m., Herbert Cowell, aged 30 years, was playing billiards with a man called John Davies and William Corlett had offered to mark for them during the game. At some point Cowell accused Corlett of marking the game wrongly in favour of his opponent and a dispute then took place. In the ensuing scuffle, Corlett struck Cowell, causing a wound to his cheek. Davies and James Roberts, the manager of the club, parted the two fighting men and one was put out of the front door while the other was ejected from the rear of the building. The pair left the club at approximately 1.00 a.m. on the Tuesday morning and it was later to be claimed by Roberts that Cowell was perfectly sober although Corlett appeared to have had a few drinks.

Later on that Tuesday, 8 May, around 9.20 a.m., Cowell was in the bar of the Villiers Hotel on Douglas Promenade. A barman there, Thomas Hales, had spoken to him while he was having a beer and he pointed out to Hales the injury to his left cheek. When Hales had asked him how he got the injury, Cowell replied that he had been involved in a row the previous night with William Corlett and added that he was going straight up to the shop to 'finish him'. He had said, 'There never was a Corlett in Douglas that could beat a Cowell.' Hales was to say that although Cowell was sober, he was very excited and 'looked full of fight'. Cowell had later left The Villiers in the direction of Bucks Road on his trap, which had been left at the door of the pub.

Cowell had then gone to the butcher's shop on Bucks Road where William

A policeman guards the entrance to the Golden Egg Restaurant on the morning the body of Nigel Neal was discovered in August 1973 (Chapter 1).
Courtesy of Manx National Heritage

The murder weapon used by James Richard Lunney in the Golden Egg Restaurant, Douglas. Lunney's bloody fingerprint is indicated by the arrow.
With kind permission of the Chief Constable, Isle of Man Constabulary

LEFT: The lane between Clarke Street and Tynwald Street. Mrs Quayle's garden was behind the wall on the right, where the telegraph pole stands (Chapter 2).

BELOW: Map in local newspaper showing location of garden where the body of Frances Quayle was found in 1914 – position of body marked with X (Chapter 2).
Courtesy of Manx National Heritage

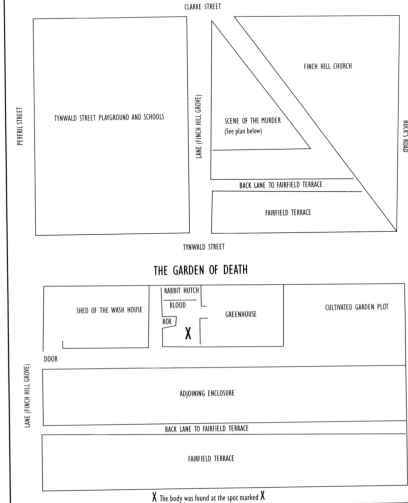

LOCALITY OF THE TRAGEDY

CLARKE STREET

FINCH HILL CHURCH

PEVERIL STREET

TYNWALD STREET PLAYGROUND AND SCHOOLS

LANE (FINCH HILL GROVE)

SCENE OF THE MURDER
(See plan below)

BUCK'S ROAD

BACK LANE TO FAIRFIELD TERRACE

FAIRFIELD TERRACE

TYNWALD STREET

THE GARDEN OF DEATH

SHED OF THE WASH HOUSE

RABBIT HUTCH

BLOOD

BOX

X

GREENHOUSE

CULTIVATED GARDEN PLOT

DOOR

LANE (FINCH HILL GROVE)

ADJOINING ENCLOSURE

BACK LANE TO FAIRFIELD TERRACE

FAIRFIELD TERRACE

X The body was found at the spot marked X

Mooragh Camp, Ramsey during the Second World War. In 1943 the Finnish POW was fatally stabbed on the pavement midway between the two fences in the centre of the photograph (Chapter 3).
Courtesy of Manx National Heritage

Castle Rushen, Castletown. John Kewish was executed here in 1872 – the last execution on the Isle of Man (Chapter 5).

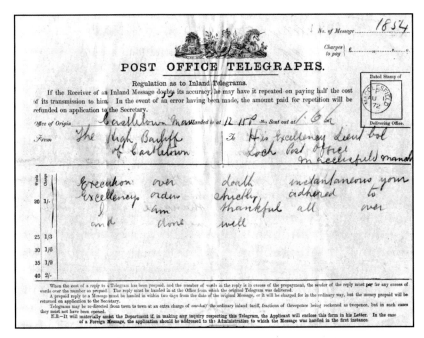

Telegram sent by the High Bailiff of Castletown to the Lieutenant Governor, informing him that the execution of John Kewish had gone according to plan (Chapter 5).
Courtesy of Manx National Heritage

MANX MURDERS

Lhergyrhenny Cottage near Druidale.
Scene of the murder of Percy Brooke in 1930 (Chapter 8).

The inside of Lhergyrhenny
Cottage. Percy Brooke
was shot as he climbed the
stairs shown on the right.

The Central Hotel at the bottom of Broadway, on Douglas Promenade. In 1978
Janice McCallum was murdered shortly after she had left this hotel to walk her
landlady's dog (Chapter 9).
Elizabeth Galsworthy's fatal journey began here in 1899 (Chapter 13).
Edith Cooper was working here as a barmaid when she met George Cooper. He
was to become her husband and killer in 1892 (Chapter 14).

The garage in Market
Street, Douglas. Janice
McCallum's body was
discovered behind the
doors on the left in
1978 (Chapter 9).

Part of the Old Douglas Road near Ramsey. The body of Betsy Crowe was found on the left side of this path in 1888. She had been brutally battered to death (Chapter 11).

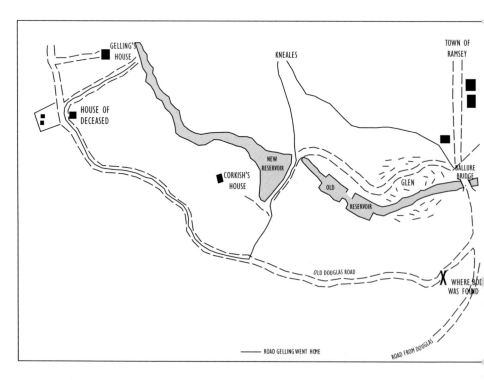

Map in local newspaper showing murder scene (position of body marked with X). Old Douglas and the path taken by Gelling are shown (Chapter 11).

Courtesy of Manx National Heritage

Bottom of Summer Hill (formerly Burnt Mill Hill). Scene of the altercation between Patrick Gallagher and Edwin Wilmot in 1864, which led to Wilmot's death (Chapter 17).

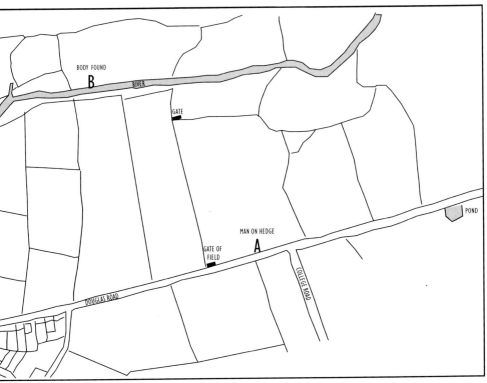

Map used at the inquest into the death of John Kermode in 1866 showing location of body (B) and the position of man on 'hedge' (A). Castletown is at bottom left (Chapter 19).
Courtesy of Manx National Heritage

John Kermode's body was found in the river at this spot on the outskirts of Castletown in 1866. The killer was never caught (Chapter 19).

The site of the Mill Dam in Onchan where the body of Melvina Kewley was found in 1859. She had been murdered by her father (Chapter 20).

Corlett and his father, Thomas, also a butcher, worked. William Corlett had left the shop earlier, at about 9.30 a.m., on his bicycle to get some orders. His father, Thomas, was later to say that Cowell came up to the opposite side of the road in his trap and stopped across the road from the shop where he had waited for around 20 minutes, watching the shop all the time. Thomas Corlett knew that Cowell had been a friend of his son and had gone across the road to talk to him and asked him what he was doing there. Cowell, he said, had replied, 'I am looking for that son of yours. I want to give him a damn good hiding.' According to Thomas Corlett, Cowell had then driven off angrily up the road. About five minutes later William Corlett arrived back at the shop on his bicycle and Thomas had asked him what had happened between himself and Cowell. Very shortly after this, Cowell returned, coming down the road and he stopped the trap near the butcher's shop. William, who had been putting his bicycle away in the yard at the back of the shop, had then returned and he and Cowell had met in the middle of the road. Thomas said that Cowell had hit his son first but his son, after taking off his coat and throwing it to his father, had then retaliated, and struck Cowell who fell to the ground. Cowell had got back up again and Thomas shouted, 'Give him another.' William had then punched Cowell again and he had again fallen, this time striking the back of his head on the kerb.

After receiving this second blow, it became clear that he was badly injured. Thomas tried to lift him up but he could not stand. Blood was seen to flow from his mouth and the two Corletts lifted him into the trap, then took him to the nearby hospital. He was unconscious on arrival and later that day he deteriorated, and shortly after 10.00 p.m. that evening he died. Earlier, William Corlett, after taking Cowell to the hospital, had gone to the police station to give his account of the incident. He had said that the blows were struck in self-defence and it had been a fair fight. After initially being released, he was arrested later on that Tuesday.

The following morning William Corlett was brought before the High Bailiff and charged with unlawfully killing Herbert Cowell, of 48 Finch Road, Douglas. He was remanded until the Saturday and the High Bailiff said that in the meantime he would order a post-mortem examination of Cowell's body.

The inquest into the death of Herbert Cowell began on the following day before Mr Samuel Harris, Coroner of Inquests, and a jury of 13 men. Cowell had been 30 years old, married and a horse-drawn carriage proprietor in Douglas. Mary Jane Cowell, his widow, gave her evidence. She told the inquest that she had identified the body in the mortuary as being that of her husband. John Joseph Callow said that on the Tuesday morning he was in

Bucks Road and had seen William Corlett taking off his blue jacket. He was standing at the corner of Mona Street where it joined Bucks Road. Corlett, he said, had rolled up his shirt sleeves and struck Herbert Cowell on the right side of his face. Cowell had fallen down and he had heard Thomas Corlett say 'Give him another.' William Corlett hit Cowell again in approximately the same place with his fist, and Cowell fell on to his back so that his head was lying on the path and his body in the road. After receiving this second blow, Cowell did not get up again and the Corletts lifted him into the trap and drove him away.

Several other witnesses gave a similar story. Alfred Fitton told the inquest that he had seen Cowell and Corlett on the opposite side of Bucks Road on that Tuesday. Thomas Corlett was also there. He had seen William throw off his coat, roll up his sleeves and hit Cowell on the right side of the face. He also heard Thomas Corlett shout 'Hit him again', or 'Give him another', or words to that effect. William had then hit him again in about the same place and Cowell fell to the ground once more. Fitton had said to William Corlett, 'Hold hard! This is not fair.' William Corlett said that Cowell went into the shop and challenged him to the fight. Cowell lay still on the ground after the second fall, before father and son picked him up and put him into the trap.

Dr John Alfred Deardon told the inquiry that he had made a post-mortem examination of Cowell's body, along with Dr Goldsmith, the house surgeon. Also present at the post-mortem were Dr Pantin on behalf of William Corlett, and Dr Mackenzie on behalf of the police. He found the man to be about 5 ft 7 in. in height, well developed and well nourished. There was a bruise on the right side of the chin, the edge of the right side of the lower lip was cut and there was a cut on the inside of the lip in the same position. There was also a slight bruise on the left cheek and a large bruise and puffy swelling on the left side of the back of the head. There were abrasions to the right arm and skin of the knuckles on the second and third fingers of the right hand, although these did not appear to be recent. He found a large blood clot around the brain and a large skull fracture. In his opinion death had resulted from pressure on the brain from the blood clot which had accumulated due to the skull fracture and he also felt that the fall on to concrete would have been sufficient to account for the injuries described.

At the end of the inquest, the Coroner criticised the conduct of Thomas Corlett. He felt that he had virtually 'patted his son on the back'. He said that without the encouragement given to William by his father, things may have turned out differently. The foreman of the jury said: 'After due

consideration the jury find that the deceased met his death by misadventure.'
William Corlett was then remanded until Saturday.

Around 8.00 a.m. on the Friday morning, Thomas Corlett was arrested and
remanded into custody on the charge of being concerned in the unlawful
killing of Herbert Cowell.

On Saturday, 12 May, Thomas and William Corlett were brought before
magistrates in Douglas and charged with murder. The evidence was similar to
that of the earlier inquest. The magistrates were G. Drinkwater, D. Maitland,
and W. A. Hutchinson. There was much discussion between the lawyers about
whether the charge should be murder or manslaughter. Mr William Creer, for
William Corlett, was about to apply to the court for the prisoners to be
released on bail, when the Chairman of the Bench said that there was a
question as to whether the defendants should be committed for murder or a
lesser charge. Mr Creer said that the evidence of Hales, who had described
Cowell's threats before he went to the butcher's shop, was important. At the
inquest the jury had given a verdict of misadventure, although the Coroner
had disagreed with them. One of the magistrates, Mr Drinkwater, said there
was not a particle of evidence to show the greater offence (of murder). Mr
Hughes-Game, for the prosecution, pointed out that as Cowell had not
defended himself it could not be considered to have been a fight and was
therefore murder. At the end of the hearing the magistrates retired for two
minutes before returning to announce that they would commit the prisoners
for trial on the charge of manslaughter.

At the end of July the prisoners were back in court again. The Attorney
General, Mr G. A. Ring, prosecuted for the Crown; Mr Creer defended
William Corlett and Thomas Corlett was defended by Mr Lay. The court was
held before a six-man jury, who had to decide if there was sufficient evidence
to warrant a case for General Gaol Delivery. The Attorney General outlined
the facts in his opening statement.

After evidence had been heard, Deemster Kneen told the jury that the
evidence appeared to be very clear. He said that the elder Corlett had, instead
of restraining his son, apparently encouraged him in the attack on Cowell.
Deemster Kneen said in his opinion there was enough evidence to justify the
prisoners being tried at the court of General Gaol Delivery on the charge of
manslaughter. The jury agreed with this and the prisoners were released on
bail to await their trial.

The trial took place at the end of November 1900 in the Tynwald
Chamber, Government Buildings, Douglas, before a jury of 11. The Attorney
General outlined the case, reminding them that the two men were charged

not with murder, but the reduced charge of manslaughter. Killing in self-defence, he explained, was only excusable when a man had done all he could to escape. He went on, 'but if a man stood and fought, he was doing an illegal act and if death took place in the course of that illegal act, it amounted to manslaughter.' Witnesses who had given evidence at earlier hearings were called to describe the events of the morning of 8 May 1900.

Thomas Corlett then gave his story. He said that at around 9.30 a.m. that morning Cowell had stopped outside his shop on the opposite side of the road and signalled him to come out, which Corlett had ignored. After ten minutes Cowell had called to Corlett who had gone over and asked him what he wanted. Cowell said he was looking for William Corlett and intended to give him a 'damn good thrashing'. Thomas Corlett had advised him that he might come off worst and after a few words Cowell had driven off up Bucks Road.

Cowell returned after 15 minutes, shortly after William Corlett himself had got back to his father's shop. Thomas Corlett told the jury that the two men had met outside the shop at the top of Mona Street and Cowell had pushed his son, who had taken off his coats and thrown them to his father. William Corlett had struck Cowell and knocked him down. When he got up again, it appeared that he was crouching, about to attack William again and Thomas Corlett admitted encouraging his son to 'give him another'.

Catherine Corlett, Thomas's wife, explained that she was in the shop that morning with her husband and daughters. She recalled how Cowell had called to her husband and spoken to him opposite their shop. Later when Cowell had returned, he had parked his trap across the top of Mona Street before the two men had fought.

William Corlett said he had tried to avoid a fight with Cowell but that Cowell had called him a coward and had struck him, hitting him in the chest and knocking him back. He went on to describe how he had retaliated, knocking Cowell down twice and how he (Cowell) had not got up after the second punch.

Mr Creer, defending William Corlett, told the jury they would have to decide whether William was defending himself or 'trying his abilities as a boxer'. William Corlett had asked Mr Creer to convey his regret over the death of Cowell but it was clear, he said, that Cowell had been the aggressor and Corlett had only defended himself. 'If he had not done so,' Mr Creer went on, 'it might have ended up with Corlett's skull being broken instead of Cowell's.'

On behalf of Thomas Corlett, Mr Cooil, defending, also expressed his client's regret at the accident which had caused Cowell's death. He submitted that Cowell had brought it on himself. He said there was no doubt as to who had struck the first blow. It was not the blow that killed Cowell, he said, but the kerb, adding that if the fight had been in a field the fatal occurrence would not have happened. The Attorney General, however, said it was not right to suggest it was a case of self-defence. He said that despite Thomas Corlett's denials, several witnesses had described how he had lifted Cowell up after he had been first knocked down before telling his son to 'give him another'.

Deemster Moore told the jury the difference between murder and manslaughter. He said that if in a fair fight a man caused his opponent's death, it was manslaughter. The deemster told the jury that although Thomas Corlett did not strike the blow, he was, according to law, equally guilty if it was shown that he aided and abetted his son.

The jury retired and returned after 20 minutes to say that they had found both prisoners guilty but recommended mercy. The judges, the Lieutenant Governor, the Clerk of the Rolls, Deemster Kneen and Deemster Moore, then retired to consider the sentences and returned after five minutes. Deemster Moore addressed William Corlett. He told him that the jury had found him guilty of manslaughter and sentenced him to imprisonment for six months with hard labour. He sentenced Thomas Corlett to imprisonment and hard labour for three months.

11

ELIZABETH 'BETSY' CROWE (1888)

Elizabeth Crowe was a 45-year-old spinster who lived alone in a small cottage called Dreemlang, on the Old Douglas Road above Ballure Bridge, on the outskirts of Ramsey. Remains of the cottage can still be seen today at the end of the Old Douglas Road where it meets the road to the Gooseneck. Although called a 'road', it was in fact little more than a rough narrow track. Known to most people as 'Betsy', she had two cows and managed to make a living by going into Ramsey twice a day to sell milk.

At around 5.00 p.m. on Thursday, 20 December 1888, she had walked into Ramsey as usual. One of her regular customers was Jane Duffy who lived in Bark Lane. At about 7.55 p.m. Betsy called at her house, where she stayed for a few minutes. Jane Duffy paid her some money she owed and received half a pint of milk. Betsy had put the money into a piece of old stocking and then gone on her way. Later that evening she had called at the house of another friend, William Caine, whom she had known for about 18 months. She visited him almost every night and often had her supper in his house. On the night of the 20th she had taken a meal at Mr Caine's house and left about 10.45 p.m. Mr Caine was later to relate that Betsy usually left earlier than this, between 8.00 and 9.00 p.m.

Also out that evening was a sailor called Robert Edward Corlett who lived in Maughold – about a mile from Ramsey. He had been drinking that evening in the Queen's Hotel with a friend, Thomas Radcliffe. Having left the hotel around 11.00 p.m. they then waited for a while for two friends who had been drinking with them. When their friends failed to appear Corlett and Radcliffe set off for home without them. On the way out of Ramsey they came across Betsy Crowe and walked with her before she turned off at the Old Douglas Road. Her cottage lay about a mile up this road at its far end. The pair were later to recall that they probably spent seven or eight minutes walking with her before she turned off the road. The two men then waited a few more minutes for their friends who soon appeared and the four then set off for home.

William Goldsmith was a labourer employed by Ramsey Town Commissioners, who worked at the quarry by the side of the hill at Ballure, on the outskirts of Ramsey. On the morning of 21 December he was on his way to work shortly after 7.00 a.m. and was making his way up the Old Douglas Road when he was shocked to find a body lying at the side of it. As it was dark he could not tell if it was a man or a woman but he could see that there was blood on the face and wondered initially whether the person was merely drunk. He set off immediately to inform the police in Ramsey. James Corkill also worked for the Town Commissioners and he too was on his way to work that morning when he met William Goldsmith. Goldsmith told him he was on his way for help but Corkill said that he would go for assistance. Around 7.30 a.m. he found Police Constable William Caley and told him that there was a body lying on the Old Douglas Road. On the way back the pair met William Goldsmith who informed PC Caley that the body was that of Elizabeth Crowe.

PC Caley then informed Inspector Cannell and Dr John Gell who both arrived at the scene around 8.00 a.m. They saw that she lay on her back with her hands close to her chest. There were numerous wounds to the head and the face was covered in blood. There was marked swelling around both eyes. It seemed clear that the lady had been murdered and the body was taken to the Queen's Hotel at 10.00 a.m. An inquest was held at 2.00 p.m. in the hotel to investigate the circumstances surrounding the death of Betsy Crowe. The Coroner was Mr Samuel Harris of Douglas. Goldsmith, Corkill, PC Caley and Dr Gell gave evidence.

Dr Gell said that there were about 14 separate wounds on the head and superficial scrapes around the knees, which he felt were caused as a result of Betsy Crowe being dragged along the road. He added that the injuries could not have been self-inflicted and went on to explain that the body appeared to have 'been arranged' and added 'it is very improbable that it could have got into that position by falling'.

PC William Caley described how he had seen two large wounds above the woman's eyebrows. Her dress appeared to have been 'carefully tucked in just about the knees'. He saw that her bonnet was lying about 15 yards further up the road where there was blood on some stones. He produced a stone with blood and hair on it and this was thought to be the murder weapon.

The Coroner said that no expense would be spared in finding the murderer, if this had indeed been a murder. The inquest was then adjourned until the following Thursday.

One of Betsy Crowe's close neighbours was John Henry Gelling, aged about 25 years, who lived with his mother and sister approximately 200 yards from Betsy's cottage. It appeared to be common knowledge among some of Betsy's friends that there was ill-feeling between Betsy Crowe and the Gellings. As a result, John Gelling was arrested on the day following the discovery of the body. He was questioned over the weekend and on the Monday morning following the murder, he was brought before the High Bailiff of Ramsey. As word had spread about Gelling's arrest, there was much interest in the proceedings and a large crowd had gathered at the Courthouse in Ramsey. Gelling's mother and sister sat behind him when he was brought into court and the pair frequently wept while the case was being heard.

Mr C. B. Nelson prosecuted on behalf of the Crown and Mr F. M. LaMothe appeared for Gelling. Mr Nelson explained that Gelling had been arrested on suspicion of the murder of Miss Crowe. Inspector John Cannell gave his evidence and explained how on the morning of 21 December he was informed at about 8.00 a.m. by William Goldsmith that a body of a woman had been found on the Old Douglas Road. Inspector Cannell had gone there at once and found the body lying on the left-hand side of the road. It was about 100 yards from the main road and he recognised it as being that of Elizabeth Crowe. He said that Gelling's house was about 200 yards farther up the road from where Miss Crowe had lived. The route to Gelling's house from the town would have been via the Old Douglas Road, he said, adding that Gelling would have had to pass Betsy Crowe's cottage to get home. He described briefly the head injuries he had seen and felt these would have been the cause of death. The Inspector told the court that Gelling had been arrested on the Saturday morning, following information they had received and enquiries they had made.

Mr Nelson told the High Bailiff he did not wish to call for further evidence and wanted to defer this until the inquest had been completed. Mr LaMothe, on behalf of the prisoner, objected to the arrest, saying that there was really nothing to connect Gelling with the crime. The High Bailiff told Mr LaMothe that, as it was clear the police had very strong suspicions about Gelling, he would, at their request, remand him into custody for a week. Gelling was then taken from the dock and formally remanded until the following Monday.

The inquest was resumed at the Courthouse in Ramsey on Thursday, 27 December. John Henry Gelling was brought to the court from Castle Rushen Gaol. Mr G. A. Ring and Mr LaMothe watched the proceedings on his behalf, while Mr C. B. Nelson looked after the interests of the police. Again large crowds had gathered for the hearing and the 13-man jury returned to hear further evidence.

Dr John Gell explained that he had made a post-mortem examination of the body. There were, he said, some bruises over the right knuckles and wrist as if the woman had used her arm to protect herself. On removing the scalp, he had found a quantity of blood between the scalp and the skull. When he removed the skull he had found blood on the surface of the brain and also a fracture at the base of the skull. Two other fractures were discovered involving the left cheekbone and temple. The wounds on the base of the skull were, he said, quite sufficient to cause death and this was, in his opinion, the cause of Betsy's death. There were a lot of blood marks on the bank nearby and on the road, extending over 30 yards higher up the road from where the body had been found. He felt the body may have been placed there after death. He said she must have bled a lot, but some of the blood had been washed away by the stream.

Police Constable Caley was then called. In response to questions from Mr Nelson, he said that he was aware of a court case over a year ago when Elizabeth Crowe had accused John and Catherine Gelling of assault and battery and using abusive and provoking language. That case had subsequently been dismissed.

Jane Duffy and William Caine gave their evidence and Robert Edward Corlett repeated his earlier evidence, explaining how he and his friend had met up with Betsy Crowe on their way home from the Queen's Hotel after closing time.

William Skillicorn then took the stand. He said he remembered that on the night of Thursday, 20 December, John Henry Gelling had been at his house. He said he could not remember what time he had arrived, but was sure that he had left about midnight. He did, however, feel that it was after 11.00 p.m. when he arrived. Another man, James Cormode, was also in Skillicorn's house that evening as were Skillicorn's daughter and wife. PC Caley said he had gone to Skillicorn's house on the Saturday and Skillicorn had said that Gelling left about 11.55 p.m. and that Cormode had left about ten minutes before Gelling. Isabella Skillicorn, William Skillicorn's wife, and Ellen Skillicorn, his daughter, both said that Gelling had left their house around 11.55 p.m. The inquest was then adjourned to the following day.

The inquest was resumed on Friday, 28 December and Gelling was again brought to Ramsey from Castle Rushen by train, and at all stations along the track many people had gathered in order to try to catch a glimpse of him.

John Corlett addressed the court and said that on the night of Thursday 20 December he had been in the house of Mrs Gelling, having arrived about 10.20 p.m. He had passed Betsy Crowe's house in order to get there. Mrs Gelling and the young girl had been alone in the house, as Gelling was out. Gelling, he said, had arrived home at about 12.45 a.m. although Corlett was not certain of the time. He had, however, heard Gelling's mother complain about him coming back so late. Gelling had his supper and sat in front of the fire for half an hour or so. John Corlett, John Gelling and Gelling's mother had then sat until about 5.30 a.m., when Corlett left to go home, returning the way he had arrived. He had not walked right down the Old Douglas Road and therefore had not walked past the spot where the body was found.

John Kennish told the inquiry that he lived in a cottage on the Douglas Road, a short distance from the old road. He had not seen anything of Elizabeth Crowe that night and had heard nothing suspicious. He did say he had seen the Gellings going up and down the old road, and so far as he was aware, that was the only road they used, although he could not swear that he had never seen them going any other way to their house.

John Dickson said that he lived about 300 yards from both Betsy Crowe's house and from the Gelling family. He knew all of them and had seen Mrs Gelling and John Henry Gelling at Betsy's house several months earlier. At that time, he claimed, he had heard sounds as if they were arguing and said they were speaking in loud, angry tones.

Eleanor Crowe told the inquiry she was the widow of Neil Crowe, Betsy's brother. She also had heard an argument between the Gellings and Betsy but she did not hear what was being said. Betsy had told her that she was in fear of 'them brutes down there' and that they had 'thumped and lashed' her. Betsy had also told her that 'they would take her life'.

John Skillicorn was another witness called to give evidence. He said that he had formerly been a tenant on Betsy Crowe's land and had heard her say that she was in fear of her life from her neighbours. He said threats had been used. The inquiry was then adjourned to the following Monday and Gelling was again returned to Castle Rushen.

On Monday, 31 December the inquest continued in Ramsey Courthouse and Gelling was again brought from Castletown by train, in the care of Mr F. E. Keene, governor of Castle Rushen.

John Henry Gelling took the stand and was told by the Coroner, 'You were brought here to this inquiry and it is my duty to tell you that you are not bound to answer any question in whatever form it may be put, that will tend to incriminate yourself'. Mr Ring on behalf of the witness, told Mr Harris, the Coroner of Inquests, that Gelling was willing to answer any question. Gelling told the court that he had lived in the house near Betsy Crowe's for about six years, and was then asked to explain his movements on the night of Thursday, 20 December.

Gelling thought he had left his home at about 9.00 p.m. His first stop was at the house of the auctioneer, Mr Chrystal, with whom he had business. Gelling explained that when he went to Chrystal's he did not go down the Old Douglas Road. Instead he went via another route into Ramsey and had gone past John Dickson's house and then down past Kewey Kneale's house (*see* map of area). He said he had gone this way in order to stop off at Kneale's house to drop off a cart rope which his mother had asked him to give to Kneale. He left Kneale's about 9.30 p.m. He then went into town to Parliament Street as he wanted to see a man called John Corlett, to ask him about his plans for Christmas, but as there was no light on he had not gone in. He also said that around this time he had bumped into a man called Peckham, the son of the fishmonger. He had walked with him for a while and then Gelling went to Mr Chrystal's house on the Lezayre Road. He only spoke to Mr Chrystal for about ten minutes, he said, and then had carried on to the quay, in the company of Peckham. There they met up with Peckham's brother and the three men walked to Peckham's home, where Gelling had left them.

Gelling said he then went around the corner of the marketplace to Parliament Street where he crossed over to look for John Corlett and walked as far as East Street. He said he had gone into Cubbin's sweetshop and recalled being served there by a young girl. He was in the shop about two minutes before he left and walked down Parliament Street. He then went up Church Street and then to Kirk Maughold Street, before reaching the Skillicorn house. Gelling said when he arrived at the house, John Cormode, the greengrocer, was there with Mr and Mrs Skillicorn. Mr Skillicorn was sitting in the kitchen when Gelling arrived and a minute or two after he came in, he said he remembered Skillicorn's daughter arriving. Gelling was unsure how long he stayed there, but he remembered Cormode leaving about ten to fifteen minutes before him. He then said he left the house at about 11.55 p.m. and was not certain if the young girl was still in the house when he left. After leaving he went up Kirk Michael Street in front of the Queen's Hotel and up Ballure Road to the bridge. Just before the bridge, he had turned right and gone up by Kewey Kneale's house again, by the quarry. He explained that he had not gone up the Old Douglas Road, which was just past Ballure Bridge on the right, but had gone through a field to reach the Old Douglas Road and on to his mother's house. He said he had not seen anyone on the entire road from

Ramsey, estimating that he reached home about 12.45 a.m. He approximated the distance from Skillicorn's house to his own home as being about a mile and a half to two miles. He explained that it was quicker to walk into Ramsey than it was to return because the latter journey was all uphill.

Gelling explained he had not gone up the Old Douglas Road because it was 'dirty and mucky'. He said he never went up it at night unless he was in company. When asked what difference company would make, he said the road he had used was 'not so lonesome'. A juror asked Gelling if it would not have been quicker to have gone straight on past Kneale's house. Gelling admitted it would have been, but said that, as it was a fine, moonlit night, he had gone across by the reservoir and through the field. After passing Kneale's house therefore, the next house he would have reached was Betsy Crowe's, before his own house 200 yards later. Further on, after passing Kneale's house, however, he had turned left and joined the Old Douglas Road about halfway between the main Douglas to Ramsey road and the point where the Old Douglas Road went right after passing Betsy Crowe's cottage (*see* map showing the area around the murder scene).

Gelling explained that he reached home at about 12.45 a.m. saying he had looked at the clock when he arrived. He remembered his mother grumbling about the late hour and remembered that Corlett was in the house when he got home, along with his mother and sister. After having his supper, he said he had sat by the fire, but his mother had later asked him to go out and check on the horses though he was outside for only a minute or so. He thought his sister had gone to bed when he got back in and he then sat by the fire until approximately 5.00 or 6.00 a.m. talking to Corlett. He told the court that they often sat talking until the early hours. Gelling said after Corlett left he had gone to bed at about 6.00 a.m.

Gelling was then asked about a blue coat, which he had sponged on the Thursday, the day of the murder. He explained that some toffee had melted and stained the pocket of the coat. When asked to explain a dish containing some blue water, which the police had found on the Saturday morning, Gelling said the water was not blue because his coat had been washed in it but that the colour was caused by a blue tablet (called 'Dolly Blue'), which his mother had put in to make the white clothes look whiter after washing. He said he had washed the coat upstairs and denied that there was any reason why he was concealing what he was doing to the coat.

Gelling said he got up between 8.00 and 9.00 a.m. on the Friday morning, had fed the cattle and then had breakfast. A man called John Joughin had called at the house about 1.00 p.m. and informed Gelling about the woman found dead on the old road. Joughin had later said that Gelling had replied with words to the effect that Betsy Crowe had 'deserved it, as she had been going round telling lies about people'. Gelling said he did not remember saying this to Joughin. He explained that John Dickson had told him that Betsy Crowe had informed him that Gelling had stolen a spade belonging to her. He said Dickson had told him this about seven or eight months prior to the murder. Gelling told the court he had seen some men passing by his house earlier, near Betsy Crowe's house and thought they were policemen. When asked if he had not been curious on seeing the men he said that he had not taken that much notice. Gelling also admitted that a year or two previously, Betsy Crowe had falsely accused him and William Skillicorn of stealing some of her hay. He said that he had not mentioned the men around her cottage that morning. After Joughin had gone he attended to the cattle, pulled some turnips and generally pottered about until the evening.

Gelling was questioned again about why he had sponged the coat on that particular day, as he had noticed the toffee stain on the previous Sunday. He replied that he had been 'too busy'. Mr Nelson told Gelling that the coat was wet from the shoulders down to the tail and it was not just the area round the pocket which was damp. Gelling said he was not aware that the whole of the coat was wet. He was also questioned about his relationship with Betsy Crowe and he acknowledged that they were not speaking to each other, because of earlier trouble. He was not aware that she had told people she was in fear of her life from his family. There was some discussion about some sheets Betsy Crowe loaned to the Gellings at the time of his father's funeral. It was said that his family had refused to give back the sheets and this had caused further bad feeling but Gelling denied this and said that she had never asked that the sheets be returned.

He was then asked if he had seen Betsy Crowe during the night of Thursday, 20 December and he explained that he had not seen her after dinner-time that day, nor had he seen her in town when he was on his travels there. He explained how he had walked uphill out of Ramsey on his way home that evening and estimated it was a distance of 50 yards or so between the reservoir road and the start of the Old Douglas Road. Gelling was asked if it would have been possible to have seen the body from the reservoir road and he said, 'Oh, no.' Several of the jurors confirmed this and said it would only have been possible to see the body if passing close by it on the Old Douglas Road. Gelling confirmed he had seen no one else after he left the main Douglas to Ramsey road on his way up the reservoir road, passing between the reservoirs to reach the Old Douglas Road and then his home. It was reported by the press that throughout his examination Gelling had been remarkably cool and answered all the questions which appeared in any way damaging to him.

Gelling's mother was the next witness to enter the box. She said her name was Catherine Gelling and remembered that on the Thursday night, 20 December, her son had left about 9.00 p.m. to go into town. She said he had asked her to go with him but she told him that she was too busy. She said she had asked her son to take a cart rope down to Kewey Kneale and asked him to see Mr Chrystal while he was in Ramsey. She told the court that John Corlett had called at her house around 10.15 p.m. that evening, and her son returned home about 12.45 a.m. She denied ever saying to the police that he had come home at midnight and remembered that she had asked him which road he had taken and why he was so late. Mr Nelson asked her several times if she had ever said that he came home around midnight but she continued to deny this. His mother said that Gelling had told her he had been at Mr Skillicorn's house that evening and had then come up the Ballure Road and round by the reservoir. She told the court she did not think it extraordinary that he should come that way as he never came up the Old Douglas Road. She thought he took that route because it was 'cleaner'.

She described how, after her son had entered the house, he had a cup of tea and she had told him to put some coal on the fire. She had then asked him to check on the horses, which he did, and this took about two minutes. After returning to the house mother and son sat next to the fire until about 5.30 a.m. Mr Corlett was there during all of this time and the three talked about various topics including the Christmas show in Ramsey. Corlett had left about 5.30 a.m. and both she and her son went to bed.

She had got up at about 8.00 a.m. and said she thought she had done some washing. She said the coat, which the police had claimed was damp, was not the coat her son had been wearing on the Thursday evening, adding that the coat he was wearing in court as she was speaking was the one he had worn that night. The first she had heard about Betsy Crowe's death was just after Joughin had left. Her son had told her that there were men at Betsy's house and thought they were policemen and had also informed her that Betsy's body had been found in the Old Douglas Road.

At this stage, the inquest was adjourned until the Wednesday and Gelling was again remanded into custody.

The inquiry resumed on the Wednesday, and Mrs Gelling continued to give her evidence. A juror asked her, 'On the night of the 20th were you out on the Old Douglas Road after 10.00 p.m.?'

She answered, 'No.'

She was then asked, 'Was Corlett out from the time he came to your house to the time he went in the morning?'

She replied, 'No, sir,' before adding that he had never left the house that evening.

James Cormode next entered the witness box. He said that on the night of 20 December he had gone to William Skillicorn's house at about 10.30 p.m. Only Mr Skillicorn had been in the house when he arrived, but his wife had come in later and then his daughter had arrived. While he was at Skillicorn's house a young man he did not know came in, whom he said looked like John Gelling. Cormode had left Skillicorn's house at about 11.30 p.m. and Mr and Mrs Skillicorn and the young man were in the house at this time – the daughter had left earlier.

Inspector Cannell was called next. He explained how, with constables Caley and Moore, he had gone to the Gelling house at about 8.15 a.m. on Saturday, 22 December. Gelling had been upstairs in bed when they arrived, but his mother had told them that he arrived home on the Thursday night 'after 12 o'clock'. He told the court that John Gelling had said to him that he arrived home 'near about one o'clock' and he had been in Ramsey that evening, leaving William Skillicorn's house about midnight. He described finding the wet coat and when he was examining this, Gelling had shouted to him, 'Mr Cannell, there is a stain in the pocket which was caused by toffee.' Inspector Cannell said that when they searched Betsy Crowe's house they had found very little, indeed it was barely furnished. They found no money at all, either on her body or in the house.

Assistant Superintendent Fayle was then called. He said he had gone with Inspector Cannell to the Gelling house on the Saturday between 8.00 and 9.00 a.m. He had asked Mrs Gelling what time her son had come home on the Thursday evening, and she had told him, 'between 11 and 12 o'clock.' When he had later asked John Gelling the same question, he had replied 'quarter to one.' He said that Gelling had been taken to the police station and had been charged on the Sunday, with being involved in Betsy Crowe's death.

Dr Clucas was then called. He said he had been asked by the police to examine the clothing of John Gelling, to see if there were any traces of blood, but stated that he had not found any.

William Goldsmith again described how he had found Betsy's body, before the Coroner began his summing up. He described the death of Betsy Crowe as 'One of the most mysterious events that has ever taken place in the Isle of Man'. He told the jury that 'if a person of sound mind, memory, and understanding, unlawfully kills any reasonable creature with malice aforethought, either expressed or implied – that is murder'. He then described the meaning of 'circumstantial evidence'. On the night of the 20th, he said, it appeared that Elizabeth Crowe had left home as usual about 5.00 p.m. to go into town to supply her customers with milk. Around 8.00 p.m. she had gone to Mrs Duffy's house and later went to the Alexandra Hotel, owned by Mr Caine. After having her supper at Caine's house she left about 10.45 p.m. and later met the two men from the Queen's Hotel, walking with them until she reached the Old Douglas Road. She had then set off up this road on her own. He reminded the jury of the trip they had made to the murder scene, approximately 200 yards from the main Douglas to Ramsey road on the Old Douglas Road. He reminded them of a stone that had been found there with blood and human hairs on it – this appeared to have been the murder weapon.

He then told the jury that Gelling had come to Ramsey about 9.00 p.m. and explained there was a dispute over certain times, but it appeared he had left Skillicorn's house between 11.40 p.m. and midnight, and it was clear that he must have been fairly close behind Betsy Crowe on his journey home. He had told the jury he had taken a different route home from that of Miss Crowe, but for a time they must have been quite close to each other. He went on to describe the events at the Gelling house, after John Gelling had arrived home in the early hours of Friday morning. The Coroner remarked disdainfully that it was strange to sit up until 5.30 in the morning talking, and said, 'It may be a custom of the country, but the sooner it is done away with the better.' He then briefly mentioned the ill-feeling which appeared to exist between the Gellings and Betsy Crowe. He reminded the jury of Joughin's visit to the Gellings' house later in the morning, after the body was discovered. The Coroner told the court he thought that the Gelling house should have been searched much earlier, saying it should have been done on the Friday morning. He said that every house in the area should have been searched thoroughly that morning. If there had been any evidence at Gelling's house, he had had ample time to dispose of it.

The jury then retired at 3.40 p.m. The Coroner called them back into court at 4.00 p.m. and told them that their verdict need not be unanimous. They were told they could find a person culpable in respect of a murder – they did not have to bring in a verdict of wilful murder. The jury again retired and at 5.03 p.m. they returned with their verdict.

The Coroner then read the verdict aloud: 'We find that the deceased, Elizabeth Crowe, was wilfully murdered on the night of 20 December or the morning of the 21st, on the Old Douglas Road, in the parish of Maughold and we further find, from the evidence adduced, that strong suspicion is attached to John Henry Gelling, of The Rhoan, Intack, of the said parish. We quite concur with the remarks of the Coroner as to the unfortunate delay occasioned before investigations were made by the police, in this case.' The Coroner said he was satisfied with their verdict and said there was sufficient to justify him in committing John Henry Gelling. Gelling was removed from the court before being returned to Castletown. His mother wept on hearing the verdict.

On Monday, 7 January, Gelling was again taken back to Ramsey. Interest in the case was as great as ever and a large crowd of people were at Douglas railway station, hoping to catch a glimpse of Gelling as he changed trains on his way from Castletown to Ramsey. This time Gelling was brought before the High Bailiff of Ramsey, Mr J. C. LaMothe, the presiding magistrate. Mr C. B. Nelson prosecuted the case and Mr F. M. LaMothe defended Gelling.

Over the next two and a half days or so the evidence previously heard was repeated to the jury. When Gelling himself took the stand he said, 'I have nothing to add to what I said before the Coroner.' On Wednesday, 9 January, all the evidence had been heard. Mr Nelson told the High Bailiff he felt the prisoner should be committed for trial and gave his reasons for this. Mr LaMothe for Gelling said, 'I strongly contend that there is not the shadow of a case upon which Your Worship should be induced to commit him for trial.' He then asked the High Bailiff to release the prisoner and allow him to leave the court a free man. The High Bailiff told him, however, that in his opinion, although the evidence was circumstantial, there was enough for him to commit Gelling to trial. The High Bailiff then summarised his reasons for finding that Gelling should be submitted for trial, on a charge of the murder of Betsy Crowe.

On Monday, 18 February 1889, John Henry Gelling was brought before His Honour, Deemster Gill, at Ramsey. This time there was less public interest, as it was generally felt that Gelling was about to be released. His mother and sister were at the back of the court for the proceedings. After the jury was sworn in, the Attorney General stood and said, 'I do not propose to put any evidence before the jury.'

Mr LaMothe replied, 'Then, sir, on behalf of the prisoner, I ask that a formal verdict be entered on his behalf of not guilty.' The deemster then addressed the jury, telling them that as the Attorney General did not propose to put any evidence before them, all they had to do was to say that there was no evidence on which to indict the prisoner. The jury then did this and Gelling was ordered to stand. He was warned that if he was not innocent of the crime and any evidence in the future was forthcoming against him, he could be re-tried. He then discharged Gelling.

Although a large crowd had gathered at the back of the court building, Gelling and his mother waited for a while before leaving by the front entrance and walking down Parliament Street. Gelling had been aware that he would be released, as a result of the Attorney General's failure to offer any evidence against him. He spoke highly of the way he had been treated in Castle Rushen.

Many years later in 1923, Mr Thomas Christian made a sworn statement before Mr T. H. Midwood JP. Mr Christian, a Methodist local preacher, said: 'At the time of the murder of Betsy Crowe a man who was ill at the time told me that he had murdered Betsy Crowe. He said he was hard-up for money and followed her up the Old Douglas Road with the object of getting her bag of money, which he saw her taking out of her dress whilst in a house where she was delivering milk. He told me he tried to get the money from her but she resisted and began to shout. He then caught up a stone and struck her on the head and she fell down. He said he got frightened and ran down Ballure Glen to the shore and came home along the shore. I informed the police, but they made light of it. The man who made the confession to me died shortly after. I am strongly of the opinion that the man who made this confession did so genuinely. He was in a very distressed condition of mind, but was, in my judgement, sane and sensible and knew what he was talking about. He repeated the statement to me several times.'

This statement was sent to the Lieutenant Governor and in the Tynwald Court in Douglas in 1923, he was asked if he had considered the affidavit and if he felt it would be appropriate to appoint a commission to enquire into the facts of the case. The Governor replied: 'I have considered the affidavit of Thomas Christian but in as much as the murder of Elizabeth Crowe took place 35 years ago, and no evidence could be found at the time upon which to indict John Henry Gelling, I do not see that any useful purpose would be served by appointing, at this late date, the suggested commission of enquiry.'

The name of the man who made the alleged confession was never published, and today, 114 years later, the mystery still remains.

NOTES

1. In his book *The Isle of Man Constabulary* (1984), George Turnbull gives brief details of the case and its subsequent investigation. He describes how the then Chief Constable of the Isle of Man, Colonel William Freeth, requested the services of a detective from London. Pretending to be a tourist, this detective stayed at a hotel in Ramsey and

began unobtrusively to make his own enquiries into the circumstances surrounding the case. He too was apparently unable to come up with any real new evidence.

2. Having visited the track which was formerly known as the 'Old Douglas Road' and walked up it from the main Ramsey to Douglas coast road, I have to agree with John Gelling's description of it. He explained that on the night of the murder he had not used that track as it was 'dirty and mucky' and 'lonesome'. Even today a stream runs over most of the stones and rocks forming the track and it is extremely muddy and wet throughout most of its length as well as being very steep in parts. The route he said he took was reached just before the Old Douglas Road travelling from Ramsey and he would have joined the Old Douglas Road well past the point where Betsy's body was found.

12

THE KILLEY FAMILY TRAGEDY (1868)

Now and then we see, hear or read the sad news of a parent who has killed, or attempted to kill, all of his or her family before committing suicide. There may have been marital or financial problems which have driven the person to commit such an awful act, but in other cases there may be no apparent reason. Such an event is not a new phenomenon and the case you are about to read occurred in an isolated cottage in 1868.

James Killey was 33 years old and worked at the Foxdale Mines as a miner's labourer. In addition to this job he also farmed approximately nine acres of land. He had been married for seven years and his wife's name was Esther. They lived in a tiny, isolated thatched cottage at Doarlish Ard, which was an area about half a mile to the west of Foxdale. They moved there six months after their marriage and the couple had five children, all girls. The oldest was Selina Agnes, aged seven years, then there was Emily, Anna Louisa, Elizabeth Esther (known as 'Esther') and the youngest, Madeline, aged three months. His wife was later to say that James was a good father to his children, worked hard and was paid relatively well and indeed had recently employed his brother-in-law, Archibald Shimmin, as a labourer. James rarely drank alcohol and seemed to spend his money carefully; the family lived relatively comfortably. All seemed to be well in his life until March 1868.

During that month James Killey had one day gone to a public house in nearby Glen Maye after receiving his pay. His wife was later to say, 'He returned home on that day about nine o'clock at night. He did not appear to be altogether sober. He stated that when at Glen Maye he had been speaking of people whom he ought not to have spoken about, but he hardly knew what he had been talking about.' She then went on: 'From enquiries I have since made, I have ascertained that he had not been speaking of the persons or of the things he told me of.'

From that day James Killey changed. According to his wife he had always been a cheerful man, but now he appeared to be depressed and would not answer when spoken to. His wife had asked him on several occasions what was the matter but she never received a proper answer from him. Although he continued to work, over the next few weeks his behaviour continued to be strange and it is clear that his wife was very worried about him.

On Wednesday, 1 April 1868 he came home from work and told his wife: 'There is no use stopping here as there is nothing to be got.' He also said he would 'prepare for America'. He informed her that they were about to be turned out of the farm and the captain of the mines where he worked had received a letter, saying that James was not to work there any more. His wife's subsequent enquiries again showed that none of this was true. Two days later, when James returned from work, he told his wife, who was cutting potatoes, 'You are not to cut much as the potatoes are not going to get leave to grow, as when they come up the blossoms will be pulled.' He was also reported as having said, 'My cows may be burnt in the cow house, my sheep will be killed on the mountains and the house burned over our heads.' He went to work the following morning despite his wife's advice that he should stay at home and rest.

On the Thursday evening, James was very restless and his wife felt he was brooding over the strange things he had said the previous day. She asked him if he felt any better but he said he did not. His wife later reported that he did not sleep at all that night.

On Friday, 3 April he rose early at 7.00 a.m. and later that morning took three of his children to see the corpse of a little nephew who was to be buried in the afternoon. The body was lying in the house of James Killey's mother at Ballanass, about half a mile from the Killey home. James had taken the day off work as he intended to go to the funeral and he showed his children the little child's body before returning home shortly afterwards. His wife spoke to him but he did not appear to hear her or take any notice of what she was saying. At around 11.30 a.m. he told her it was time to attend the funeral, though it was not actually due to take place until 2.00 p.m. As she was later to relate at the inquest: 'I was obliged to push him and shout to him to get a reply from him, but when he did speak he gave an intelligible answer.' She went on to describe another strange event during that day, saying, 'I sent my two eldest children to the village. He [James] was out at the time and, meeting them [the children], would not let them go and brought them back again. It was a very unusual thing for him to do and I asked him his reason for doing so – was he sick or what? He replied that he was not very well but he did not feel very bad.'

His wife was quite concerned about his behaviour and when he wandered off into the fields she sent her brother, Archibald Shimmin, to keep an eye on him. When James later returned to the house, Shimmin went off to work in the field. Inside the cottage his wife asked him what was wrong but he said that he wished he was dead and added that he would 'have to see them all gone first'. He then went outside to the well, which stood in the corner of the garden about six yards from the front door of the cottage. It was about 20 ft deep and the water at the bottom was about 8 ft deep and pulled up in a bucket on a rope. James toyed idly with the bucket for a time while his children played nearby. He returned to the house and apparently destroyed some valuable papers, which caused his wife to become even more worried about him. Her concern increased when he went to where he kept his tools and also the place where he kept his razor. As she was to say later, 'I then got frightened as I had never seen him do such a thing and I sent Emily for my brother to tell him to come down.'

James had once more gone out into the yard where his children were playing. She subsequently recalled that she had just taken the youngest child out of the cradle when she heard a scream from one of her other girls, 'Dadda! Dadda!' and she had then rushed out of the cottage. Earlier there had been three children playing in the yard but now she saw that two were missing. James had the third one and was about to throw her into the well. His wife ran towards him but he let the child fall into the well and then turned on her and told her that they 'were all going together'. He then grabbed the baby from his wife and the pair fought over the child. After a struggle he managed to get the baby from his wife's arms and then threw the child down the well. Esther pulled herself away from him and ran off down the road. Emily, who had been sent to look for her uncle, had just arrived back in the yard as her mother ran out screaming. Her father also picked her up and threw her into the well before jumping in himself.

Archibald Shimmin arrived shortly after with another man called Philip Corkill. He was later to describe how he looked into the well, but could not see anything. He had then gone down in the bucket and had grabbed a child and pulled her up, but had dropped her as he got to the top and had to go down again. This child, he said, was Emily, who had been the last to go into the well, and she was unhurt. He had then brought up Anna Louisa, who was dead and then little Esther who was unhurt. He had gone down again and brought up the baby, Madeline, who was also dead. The bodies of the eldest child, Selina Agnes, and of James Killey, had sunk to the bottom of the well and they were brought up later after being dragged out with a boat hook.

The four bodies – James, Anna Louisa, Madeline and Selina Agnes – were taken to the house and laid side by side on a bed.

The inquest took place in the Cottage at Doarlish Ard the following day at 2.00 p.m., before the High Bailiff of Douglas, Samuel Harris, and an 11-man jury was sworn in.

A report in the *Manx Sun* included the following description of the scene outside the cottage:

> An air of solemn, sombre and oppressive silence hangs over the spot; not a policeman or other officer of the law is to be seen. No gaping crowds have yet penetrated thither to satisfy that craving for the horrible which is inherent in human nature. At the door of the cottage stands a little girl some five years old who gazes about her with a timid, half-frightened air, as well she may, poor child, having been one of those rescued from such imminent peril of death.

The report describes the scene inside the cottage:

> [There] sits a woman, whose frame is convulsed with the agony of grief, while at a little distance from her are two fine little girls, one about five, the other about two years of age. We turn into a room on the left and there, stretched on the humble bed covered with white counterpane, which is rivalled in colour by the faces of the dead, are four bodies – a father and his three daughters. The father is a man of some three and thirty years, a handsome man [. . .] Beside him is his infant daughter Madeline; next is the eldest daughter Selina, nearly seven years of age [. . .] last Louisa, about four years of age. Hard indeed would be a heart unmoved by so touching a spectacle.

The Coroner said he would hold an inquest first on the three children and then on the father. The first inquest was into the deaths of Selina Agnes, aged nearly seven years, Anna Louisa, aged about four years, and Madeline, aged about three months.

Esther Killey, the wife of the dead man, was the first witness to be called. She explained how they had come to live in Doarlish Ard and described her husband as always having been a cheerful man until the last four or five weeks of his life. She spoke of his trip to Glen Maye and his steady deterioration following this. She later explained the awful events of the previous day and how she had become extremely worried about his behaviour, sending her daughter, Emily, to look for her brother. A report in the *Mona's Herald* gives an indication of the harrowing details revealed at the inquest. At one point, while giving her evidence:

> Mrs Killey was so overcome with emotion that she could not proceed for a length of time. Indeed, everyone present was visibly and deeply affected and you could see the eyes of the strong, stalwart men suffused with tears, none being more visibly affected than the worthy Coroner himself.

Archibald Shimmin then described how he had been summoned by his sister, and had then gone down the well several times to bring out all the girls, including those who were dead. He said he had gone down twice to try and retrieve the bodies of James and his eldest daughter but had been unsuccessful.

A friend of James Killey, John Skiller, gave his evidence. He said he had worked with James for about five years and did not notice anything wrong with him until the preceding two or three days. He thought James seemed rather depressed and was not speaking very much, and said he had also told Skiller he had lost his appetite.

Philip Corkill had been talking to Archibald Shimmin at the moment when Esther came running up to them, screaming that the children were in the well. He confirmed Shimmin's evidence was correct and added an interesting detail. He described how, as the bodies were being brought out of the well, a 'strange man' who was passing at the time, rolled one of the girls on a 'tub' (the witness was almost certainly referring to a barrel) at the same time putting his finger in her mouth. The report in the *Mona's Herald* describes how he then 'rolled the child backwards and forwards and thus restored her'. Corkill told the jury that he did not know the man and had not seen him 'before or since'. It would appear from Corkill's description that the stranger saved the life of one of the two surviving girls.

Dr Percy Ring then gave details of his examination of the bodies. All three of the girls had died from drowning, he said. The doctor also mentioned that he had been told James had been bitten by a dog about four years earlier, but he did not feel this was relevant to the events of the previous day.

James Killey's mother then gave evidence. She stated that she had noticed her son was 'low in spirits' when he had been to her house over the previous few weeks. She said that he would sometimes sit with his head in his hands and added that there was 'no man in the parish more fond of his children as my son was' and described how he would often have one or two of them on his knee.

The Coroner then summarised details of the case for the jury. He praised the actions of Archibald Shimmin for saving the lives of two of the girls. It was clear he said that 'the unfortunate man had committed the act when he was in a state of temporary insanity'. The jury at once returned a verdict to the effect that the three children had come to their deaths by drowning, in consequence of being thrown into a well at Doarlish Ard, in the parish of Patrick, by their father, James Killey. They also found that at the time he committed the said act, James Killey was in a state of temporary insanity.

The inquest on the body of James Killey was then held. The only witness examined this time was Dr Ring. His opinion was that he had also drowned. The Coroner said, 'What possible motive could the deceased have for deliberately destroying himself and his children, if it were not that he was insane and not accountable for his actions? Here was a man in the prime of life, in a comfortable home, surrounded by his children of whom he was extremely fond, throws those children one after the other into the well and then springs in himself. Could they put any other explanation upon his conduct, except that when he so acted he was not in a rational state of mind?'

The jury returned their verdict. They found that, 'The said James Killey did come by his death by drowning, after first throwing his five children into a well, at Doarlish Ard in the parish of Patrick on Friday, 3 April 1868; that the said James Killey at the time he committed the said act was in a state of temporary insanity.' The spokesman for the jury said that they wished to express their approval of the conduct of Shimmin. They said he had bravely gone down the well on several occasions, risking his own life, to save the lives of two of the girls. They also expressed their deep sympathy to James Killey's widow.

The funeral took place the following day, the Sunday afternoon, a description of which appeared in the *Mona's Herald* on Wednesday, 8 April:

> Early in the day, a rumour gained currency that the interment would take place at two o'clock; and at that hour, the weather being fine, the roads in all directions for miles around were thronged with people to witness the mournful scene. The bodies, however, did not arrive at the church until four o'clock, and in the meantime people were left to occupy themselves as best they could. Judging from the expressions of opinion we overheard, the unfortunate deceased James Killey had but few sympathisers and it is doubtful whether, if his case had been left to

the decision of the crowd, he would have been allowed Christian burial. They were also anything but pleased at the finding of the jury [. . .] The bodies were conveyed in a cart and never before was there so melancholy a load in this Island. The first taken out was that of the father, which was borne into the church by his neighbour and fellow-workmen. Then followed that of the eldest girl, which was carried by four youths, the two younger children being carried by little girls [. . .] The bodies were all interred in a double grave, the father being first placed in it and the children by his side. At the time the service at the grave was going on, it is estimated that there could not have been fewer than from two thousand to three thousand persons present and there was scarcely a dry eye to be seen. Indeed callous must have been the heart which could have witnessed such a mournful spectacle and still remain unmoved.

It seems clear that the terrible tragedy of the Killey family had touched the hearts of many people on the Isle of Man.

13

ELIZABETH GALSWORTHY (1899)

In September of 1899 Elizabeth Galsworthy was 48 years old. Her husband, John, had died ten months earlier. His business had been in leather manufacturing and he had bought several properties. His widow was therefore relatively wealthy as a result of interest from his investments of around £300 to £400 a year and she also had about £2,000 in the bank. Elizabeth had never had children and since her husband's death had lived alone in Leeds. She had not enjoyed good health for many years and was known to have a liver complaint for which she was receiving medical treatment.

She lived at 12 Armenia Place, Sheepscar, Leeds, and was a prominent member of the Leeds Central Ward Liberal Association. She was described as a very energetic worker at election times. Having often taken holidays in the Isle of Man, when her doctor recommended she should visit Harrogate as part of the treatment for her medical problems she instead had decided to return to the Island.

On Saturday, 26 August she set off with some friends from Leeds, William Thorpe Pearson, his wife and two children, on a holiday to the Isle of Man. The group arrived at their lodgings at 10 Broadway, Douglas, owned by a Mrs Knowles. After ten days the Pearsons left to return home, but Mrs Galsworthy stayed on, and by 23 September she had been on the Island for four weeks.

Mrs Galsworthy had known William Franklin for around seven years, since the time that he had been a neighbour of hers in Leeds. He was by now the landlord of the Old Strand Inn, Strand Street, Douglas, and during her stay on the Island she called at his house every night for a cup of tea and sometimes had an evening meal there.

William Pearson had clearly been concerned about Elizabeth Galsworthy's health, as he had asked Franklin to keep an eye on her after he had left to return home. Franklin last saw Mrs Galsworthy on the evening of Friday, 22 September. She had complained that evening of feeling rather poorly and Franklin's wife had asked her if she would like a cab home, but she replied that she could manage. She had taken away a small bottle of gin when she left that night.

Since his return to England, Mr Pearson had collected rent for Mrs Galsworthy and had sent her three lots of money: £5 on each occasion. It was later to be revealed that Mrs Galsworthy almost certainly had a drink problem. She had an enlarged liver and the landlady at her lodgings had noted that she seemed to drink quite a lot on two or three occasions whilst she was staying with her. It was also to become clear that almost every day Mrs Galsworthy went drinking in a public house at the bottom of Broadway – the Central Hotel, about 250 yards from her lodgings.

On 18 September Mrs Galsworthy had gone to Ramsey as one of a party of seven. Ellen Duggan, a servant at the guest house on Broadway, also went on the trip and the driver of the wagonette in which they had travelled was a man called Ellis Corlett. Mrs Galsworthy had also gone for a drive on the Thursday, when she had travelled to Peel and Glen Maye. The last time Ellen Duggan had seen her was on the Saturday morning, when she had gone to Mrs Galsworthy's bedroom to see if she wanted anything. She had asked for some milk, which Ellen had given her. Mrs Galsworthy told her that she was planning to go out for a drive later that day, but, if she changed her mind and decided not to go, she added, that she might see Ellen on the promenade later.

It is clear that Mrs Galsworthy then went to the bottom of Broadway and into the Central Hotel, where she ordered a glass of whisky and milk. She had stood at the bar until she finished her drink and then left the public house. At around 1.15 p.m. she returned, ordering the same drink which she took into a sitting room where there were some men drinking. Two of these men were Ellis Corlett and Alfred Kelly. Corlett was a cab driver employed by William Clague, a cab proprietor who had several stables in Douglas while Kelly acted as a foreman in the stable yards. Behind the bar that day was John Burton, a barman who was later to recall that Mrs Galsworthy had ordered three drinks from the bar – a small gin and milk, a small whisky and a glass of beer. As they had their drinks he overheard them discussing going for a drive. Shortly after this the trio – Kelly, Corlett and Mrs Galsworthy – had left and set off on a long drive in a horse-drawn carriage (a phaeton), during which they had stopped off at several public houses. As we shall see, the spree was to end in tragedy.

By 9.00 p.m. the three were at the Bowling Green public house in central Douglas, close to the stables in Derby Square and the boarding house at 10 Broadway. It was to become clear that the three were very much under the influence of alcohol by this time, and it was at this point that Alfred Kelly left to return home. William Christian, another cab driver who worked for Mr Clague, was in the Bowling Green public house that evening. After Kelly had left, he took over the driving of the cab and in the company of Corlett and Mrs Galsworthy, he set off towards the Quarter Bridge and then Mount Murray. The group had several more drinks on the way and Christian unsuccessfully tried to convince the pair that they should go home. Christian then decided to go home himself. He left the cab and walked home, leaving Corlett to take over the driving of the cab.

Shortly after leaving the Quarter Bridge, Corlett then turned the horse around and travelled back to Derby Square. He was later to say it had been too late to look for lodgings for the lady. He added, 'I put her into the hay store and I put the cab in another yard'. Another cab driver, Joseph Martin, shared a room with Corlett. He was later to describe how Corlett had come into the bedroom between 1.00 a.m. and 2.00 a.m. on the Sunday. Martin said he had looked at his watch when it was 12.50 a.m. and it was shortly after this that Corlett came in. Corlett had not said much to him and Martin said that he appeared to be sober at this time.

William Clague owned seven livery stables in the neighbourhood of Derby Square, including one, which he called Stable 2, in Brisbane Street. Ellis Corlett was a driver of one of Clague's cabs – a double horse wagonette. Corlett's horse and cab were kept at Stable 2 yard. On the Saturday, Corlett had swapped cabs with another driver, called Kissack. Clague had been told on the Saturday that Corlett's cab and horses had been put in Stable 2, and was also informed by some other drivers that Corlett had taken Kissack's cab in order to take out a lady, whom he had taken out earlier in the week. He was also told that Kelly had accompanied them on the trip that day. Clague had waited up until 1.00 a.m. for Corlett to return with the cab, as his was the only one still out. Clague checked at stables 1, 2 and 5 to see if Corlett had returned to any of those but found there was still no sign of the missing cab. Clague then went back to his home in Brisbane Street and had gone to bed. The back door of his house opened into the yards of stables 1 and 2.

The following morning, just before 9.00 a.m., Corlett went to Clague's house. Clague's wife answered the door to him. Clague was still in bed but he heard Corlett say to his wife 'There is a woman dead.'

Clague shouted to him, 'Where is the woman dead?'

Corlett replied, 'In Number 2 yard.'

Clague told Corlett to go and inform the police immediately and he then got up, dressed as quickly as he could, and went to Stable 2. There he found the body of a woman lying in the hay store, and shortly after this Police Sergeant McLaughlin and two constables arrived at the stables. Corlett had arrived just before the police, but had then left the stables, saying he had to take someone to Ramsey later that morning and needed to get ready for the trip.

Dr MacKenzie was contacted by the police and arrived shortly after them. The lady's body was lying in the hay store, about four yards from the doorway. Her hat, umbrella and satchel were lying close to her head and the satchel contained an empty half-pint bottle, and another empty half-pint bottle was lying close to her head. At Dr MacKenzie's request, Sergeant McLaughlin removed some of the lady's clothes, and as he did so, he discovered her underclothing was saturated with blood. When the body was moved a large pool of blood was found underneath it. Some blood was also found at the entrance to the hay store, and when the police examined the phaeton which Corlett had used on the previous day, they found that the cushions were dirty and also had blood stains on them. The phaeton was found in Number 5 yard, which was about 200 yards from Stable 2, where the body had been found.

It was clear that Mrs Galsworthy had not died from natural causes and Corlett and Kelly were questioned about their movements on the previous day. The two men were subsequently arrested and the inquest into the circumstances surrounding the death of Elizabeth Galsworthy was opened the following day, Monday 25 September.

At 1.45 p.m. on 25 September at Douglas Courthouse, the hearing began in front of Mr Samuel Harris, High Bailiff and Coroner for the Douglas district. A large crowd were at the Courthouse that day and 13 members of the jury were sworn in. The two men who had been arrested, Ellis Corlett and Alfred Kelly, sat in the dock during the inquest. They were represented by Mr C. W. Hughes-Games.

Mr James Cowle, an architect and builder, submitted a plan of the premises in which the body of Mrs Galsworthy had been found. On this plan was a red mark indicating where the pool of blood had been found.

He was followed into the witness box by William Franklin, landlord of the Old Strand Inn, and a long-time friend of the deceased. He described how he had known Mrs Galsworthy in Leeds as a neighbour, and how she had come to the Isle of Man with friends on holiday in the past, and on the last occasion, four weeks ago, had arrived with Pearson and his family. He had seen her on a regular basis at his home, the last time being on the previous Friday. He told the jury that he was aware that Mrs Galsworthy's health had not been good, although he did not feel she had a serious drink problem. He had identified her body in the mortuary.

Ellen Duggan was then called to give her evidence and explained that she was a servant of Mrs Knowles, working at her guest house, and had only recently met Mrs Galsworthy, who was staying there during her holiday. She stated that on the previous Monday Mrs Galsworthy had gone on a trip to Ramsey with several other people, herself included. On Thursday of the previous week, she added, Mrs Galsworthy had gone on another trip, this time to Peel and Glen Maye although on this occasion they did not share the same cab. Mrs Galsworthy had been quite sober on both these trips, said Miss Duggan. She went on to describe how she had taken her some breakfast on the Saturday morning, and had then been asked to go to the saddler's to pick up her satchel. She told the court that Mrs Galsworthy had been in possession of between £5 and £6 in gold, in a little leather bag in a pocket sewn inside the top of her corset. She explained that Mrs Galsworthy had changed a £5 note on Friday morning at her lodgings and added that she had kept two half-pint bottles, one containing gin, the other rum, in her room, and she also kept about a dozen bottles of beer. She did say, though, that she had never seen Mrs Galsworthy drunk while she was staying at the guest house.

Dr T. A. MacKenzie was next to give evidence. He had been asked by the police to go to the stables in Derby Square on the Sunday morning and had made an external examination of the body, which was lying in the hay store. The woman's body had been lying on its back when found. When it was moved so that it could be taken to the mortuary, a large amount of blood was found underneath it. The woman's underclothes were also saturated with blood, he said, and there was also blood on her right hand. Dr MacKenzie then explained that her death would have been a gradual one, caused by blood loss from an injury to the vagina and this bleeding would have been both internal and external. He said the wound was behind and to the left side of the uterus and the perforation was large enough to admit the tips of two fingers.

He also agreed with Mr Hughes-Games that because of her chronic alcoholism, her tissues may have been more friable than normal tissues, and therefore may have been more prone to injury. Although he felt it was unlikely, Dr MacKenzie said it was possible that the injury was caused by sexual intercourse. He also told the court that he found a vaginal discharge and considered that she had probably been suffering from gonorrhoea.

The inquest was adjourned and re-opened the following day, Tuesday, at

10.00 a.m. The two accused men returned to the court which was again packed with spectators.

Mr William Thorpe Pearson was the first witness of the day. He explained how he had known Mrs Galsworthy for many years, and he described himself as an 'agent' for the deceased lady, collecting her rent and also carrying on her husband's business after his death. He then went on to describe how he had come to the Isle of Man with Mrs Galsworthy, but had left after ten days, while she had stayed on. He told the court that as soon as the Coroner could release the body he intended to return it to Leeds and make appropriate arrangements for the funeral.

Mrs Betty Knowles then gave her evidence to the court. She described how the Pearsons and Mrs Galsworthy had come to stay at her boarding house on Broadway on 26 August. She did say that Mrs Galsworthy had a drink now and then, but she had never had occasion to speak to her about being the worse for drink. She had stayed up until about 1.00 a.m. on the Sunday morning, but when Mrs Galsworthy did not arrive home had presumed that she had stayed the night with friends. She said that she had no knowledge of her daily trips to the Central Hotel and added that she seemed to be a 'very nice lady' and was very quiet in the house.

James Quinn was the next witness. He was a barman at the Central Hotel on Broadway, and told the jury that Mrs Galsworthy had come into the bar around midday on the Saturday, when he had served her with a glass of whisky and milk. She had left shortly after this but returned later and then began speaking to several men. Angus Clague, a cab driver, was one but he did not know the names of the others. He added that she came into the bar every day around lunch time and usually had about two drinks and sometimes got into conversation with men who were also in the bar.

John Burton, the head barman of the same hotel, was next called as a witness and he explained that he had relieved the previous barman shortly before 3.00 p.m. on the Saturday. He said that at that time Mrs Galsworthy had been talking to several people in the bar, two of them being Corlett and Kelly, and added that he had overheard them planning a drive before the three of them left the public house.

The next witness, John Kissack, was another cab driver in the employment of Mr William Clague. He explained that Corlett had come to him on the Saturday when he was waiting with his one horse phaeton, hoping to hire it for a trip. Corlett had asked him if he could borrow his carriage to take a lady for a drive. The pair had swapped cabs and he had then taken Corlett's two-horse wagonette back to Stable 2. He had last seen

Corlett heading off towards the Central Bar on the promenade to pick up his fare.

The next few witnesses were various bar staff from public houses in and around Douglas. It was clear from their evidence that the three had gone on a journey, stopping off for drinks every now and then along the way. Their first stop was at Crebbin's Hotel in the Crescent on Douglas promenade. Alice West, a barmaid there, described Corlett and Kelly coming in around 5.00 p.m. on the Saturday. After having three drinks, Kelly had come back in and asked for a brandy, which she gave him and they left shortly after this. Annie Maloney, the barmaid at the Groudle Hotel, some two miles up the coast, gave evidence next, telling the jury that Corlett, the driver, had come into the hotel and she had served him two small whiskies and a glass of beer. He had taken the drinks out on a tray. Another witness who worked in Groudle Glen told the court that he had seen a man and a woman in the back of the cab and the woman had appeared to be 'the worse for drink'. Mr John Gresty was the licensee of the Liverpool Arms Hotel on the Laxey Road and he said that the group had arrived at his hotel about 6.00 p.m. and although he did not see the woman at that time, the two men had come into the hotel. He said they seemed quite sober at the time. They had one drink each before leaving, and about half an hour later, the group arrived at the Prince of Wales Hotel in Onchan. The wife of the man in charge had refused to serve them alcohol as they appeared to be drunk. It was clear that Corlett was unhappy about this, but Frederick Collins, the owner of the public house, again refused to serve him and the pair had a soft drink each before leaving.

By about 8.30 p.m. on the Saturday evening, the group had arrived at the Quarter Bridge Inn on the outskirts of Douglas. John Frederick Rylance told the inquest that Kelly had come in and asked for two small whiskies and a glass of beer. Again the barman refused to serve him because he felt he was drunk. He also added that later on that evening, around 9.45 p.m. the same phaeton had come to the hotel again. This time the driver was a man named Christian. He had come into the bar and ordered two small whiskies and a bottle of beer. He had drunk the beer in the public house and taken out the two small whiskies. Christian had later returned and ordered a half pint of whisky and a half pint of gin in two bottles. He had then driven off in the cab and he had heard a voice from inside telling him to drive to Mount Murray. Prior to this second stop at the Quarter Bridge, however, the group had gone to yet another public house in the centre of Douglas, the Bowling Green, close to Derby Square. Several witnesses gave evidence to say that they had seen the group in or outside the Bowling Green public house that evening.

William Christian, another cab driver working for Mr Clague, had gone to the Bowling Green about 9.00 p.m. where he had met Kelly and had given him some money he owed and explained to the court that he had advised Kelly he should go home. Kelly had then left and returned home. Christian had known that Kissack, the owner of the cab, was looking for it and he had wanted to take the cab back to the stables. However, Corlett told him that Mrs Galsworthy wanted to travel on further, so Christian himself took over the driving of the cab. The group then travelled about 300 yards to the nearby Woodbourne Hotel. Christian had gone inside and ordered three drinks, but Corlett and Mrs Galsworthy had stayed in the cab. They had then requested that Christian take them to the Quarter Bridge again. When he arrived there, he described getting more drinks, including a bottle of gin and a bottle of whisky. After he had given them the drinks, the others said they wanted to go to Mount Murray. Christian said he did not want to go with them so after travelling a short distance, got down from the box and set off to walk home while Corlett carried on driving. He told the court he had not really taken much notice of the condition of the lady. In answer to a question by a juror he said he was unaware of Corlett's whereabouts between 10.15 p.m. that evening and 1.00 a.m. on the Sunday. He arrived home himself around 11.15 p.m. after stopping off at the Woodbourne again for another drink.

On the third day of the inquest William Clague gave evidence to the court. He explained that he owned the seven stables in the neighbourhood of Derby Square in Douglas. He described how he had been out on that Saturday afternoon and on his return, found that Corlett's horses and cab were in the stables, but that Corlett had borrowed Kissack's phaeton to take out a lady and gentleman. He waited at Stable 1 until 1.00 a.m. on Sunday for the phaeton to come in and had called at the other stables, but when it had not returned, had gone to bed. The following morning his wife had answered the door to Corlett, who informed her that he had discovered a body in Stable 2 (the cab being in Stable 5). He went on to describe how he discovered that on the bottom of the cab and on the doors there were little clots of blood. There were also blood stains on the seat cushions in the cab.

Joseph Martin was the next witness. He was yet another cab driver and lodged with Corlett's father, occupying the same room as Corlett. He described Corlett coming in on the Sunday morning between 1.00 a.m. and 2.00 a.m. but added that he had not said anything, and Martin could not say whether Corlett was sober or drunk when he arrived home. He said Corlett had got up on the Sunday morning between 7.00 a.m. and 7.30 a.m. and then left.

Sergeant McLaughlin was called next. He confirmed that he had been told of a body in a stable in Derby Square and described its condition. Dr MacKenzie had examined the body and asked for it to be removed to the mortuary prior to sending for Corlett, who made a statement about the previous day's trip. In this statement, said Sergeant McLaughlin, Corlett described meeting the lady in the Broadway Hotel on Saturday at lunch-time. She had asked him to take her for a drive and in the company of Kelly they had set off on the trip. By the time they got back to Derby Square, Corlett said, it was too late to look for lodgings for the lady, so he left her in the hay store before putting the cab in another yard.

Kelly had arrived around this time and the pair were taken to the police station for further questioning. Sergeant McLaughlin had asked Corlett if he had harmed the lady in any way or if he had had any sexual contact with her. This was denied by Corlett. The police officer later returned to the hay store and examined the cab which Corlett had driven the day before. In the bottom of the cab he had found a penny and two black buttons corresponding to buttons missing from the lady's blouse. He agreed with the previous description of the cushions being blood stained. He then said he had found blood stains on Corlett's trousers and shirt but none on Kelly's clothes.

Kelly was then questioned. The Coroner reminded him that he did not have to answer any questions that may incriminate him and Kelly explained how they had met the lady and she had requested they take her for a ride in the cab for 3d. The court was then cleared of all ladies before the following evidence was given. Mr Hughes-Games asked Kelly what he was doing in the cab and enquired, 'Did you take any liberties with the lady?' Kelly denied any improper behaviour and said that he had done nothing to cause any injury to the lady. He also said he had not seen Corlett do anything to her, and added that during the time he was with the other two, Mrs Galsworthy had remained in the cab throughout the trip.

Dr Dearden gave medical evidence for the defence, explaining that he had been present at the post-mortem on the deceased. He agreed with the earlier evidence of Dr MacKenzie, who felt that the lady had drunk more than was good for her and thought that the injury which caused the lady's death could have been caused by normal sexual intercourse. He told the jury that he had heard of similar cases in America.

Dr M. Mathieson said that he had conducted an independent examination of the deceased and had come to the same conclusions as the previous witness. He explained that the cause of death was clearly haemorrhage from a wound in the vagina and in his opinion the death was due to natural causes. He also stated that death would have occurred three or four hours before the body had been found.

Dr Dearden was recalled and said that he felt it was not possible to say for sure what time the woman had died.

Ellis Corlett then entered the witness box, saying that he had listened to all of the evidence and agreed with it. He told the court that at no time did Mrs Galsworthy ask to go home, but had insisted on him driving her to Mount Murray. He admitted he had lied to Sergeant McLaughlin when he said that he had not had any sexual contact with the lady. However, he said that what took place was with Mrs Galsworthy's consent. He said the incident had occurred before they reached the Quarter Bridge. He then explained how they had eventually returned to Derby Square and Mrs Galsworthy had said it was too late to return to her lodgings. He claimed that she had asked him if he had any place to take her, and he had said the only place he had was the hay store. He said he helped her out of the cab and admitted that she was 'the worse for drink' by that time. He said there was no sign of any bleeding when he left her and she had not complained of being hurt in any way. He estimated that they had arrived at the stable between midnight and 1.00 a.m. and after leaving the lady in the hay store, he had gone to bed. Corlett then explained how he had gone to the stable the following morning where he had found the body. He then went to tell his master, William Clague, about the discovery.

In his summing up, the High Bailiff explained the events as 'a most extraordinary case'. He reminded the jury of the drive, the many stoppages on the way and the numerous drinks which the group had consumed. He complimented the police on their work. It was fortunate for Kelly, he said, that he had left the group at the Bowling Green public house, where Christian had taken over the driving of the cab. Christian had also left the pair shortly after leaving the Bowling Green, leaving Corlett and Mrs Galsworthy alone in the cab. He said it was a 'very unkind act' for Corlett to have left her alone in the stable after driving her around all day. The High Bailiff said that there appeared to be some money missing from Mrs Galsworthy and also a purse she owned had not been found. It was not clear what had happened to this. He described Corlett as a 'monster' for behaving in the way in which he had and then, being a married man, returning to his wife after the incident.

The jury retired at 5.45 p.m. and returned at 6.30 p.m. with their verdict. The foreman said, 'We are agreed that Elizabeth Galsworthy was found dead at Clague's livery stables, known as Stable 2, Derby Square, on Sunday morning 24 September 1899, and that her death was caused by haemorrhage from a wound in the vagina; and that Ellis Corlett was blameable for her death through his inhuman treatment of her. We are of the opinion that the conduct of Kelly is deserving of censure.'

Kelly was then ordered to stand. The High Bailiff told him:

> You have, along with your companion Corlett, been guilty of an exceedingly improper act. You took advantage of the opportunity afforded you of having a drive with this unfortunate woman [. . .] You say she coaxed you – a woman at her age, 48, is scarcely what you would expect a married man like you to be coaxed to take such a liberty as you did on this unfortunate woman, and in doing so, you must have encouraged your companion, whom the jury have found to be blameable to a certain extent for the offence committed. [. . .] I do hope sincerely that the recommendation of this Court and the censure I am bound to give you will have the effect of making your tears remembered, and that you will go home now and give a vow to your wife and children to give up drink and be a steady and sober man and bring up your family as they ought to be brought up. Otherwise, if you are brought before me again for drink you will be branded as an 'habitual drunkard'. You are now discharged and most fortunate you are. You are indebted to the jury for your discharge, and not to me.

The article goes on to describe how

> Kelly had a rude awakening from the idea that he was free to return to his wife and family. He was then taken downstairs only to find himself placed under arrest and on a charge of murder, along with Corlett. Up to this, they had been merely detained men, and were not before the Coroner for committal or discharge. The Coroner and jury's duty were merely to find the cause of death.

Both Kelly and Corlett were removed from the court by the police to be charged before the Magistrates.

On Thursday, 28 September, Ellis Corlett and Alfred Kelly were charged at the Courthouse, Douglas, before his Worship, Mr J. M. Cruickshank, High Bailiff of Ramsey, with unlawfully and feloniously killing Elizabeth Galsworthy. The witnesses called were the same ones who attended the previous inquest, and the hearing ended on the following day around 2.00 p.m. Neither man had anything to say. Mr Hughes-Games, addressing the court on behalf of the prisoners, said that although the conduct of both men was indefensible from a moral point of view, there was nothing in the evidence to substantiate any criminal charge against them. Mr Cruickshank said he agreed that in regard to Kelly there was no real case to answer, and Kelly was then discharged. Corlett however, was committed for trial on a charge of murder.

Ellis Corlett was again brought before the court on Saturday, 21 October. The Attorney General, Mr Johnson, prosecuted the case and Mr Hughes-Games again defended. The Attorney General outlined the case. He admitted that it was not a crime for Corlett to have left Mrs Galsworthy in the state he did, as long as he had not realised the severity of her injury. He did add however, that the behaviour of the pair 'raised the strongest feelings of disgust and loathing towards the prisoner'. The jury agreed that there was really no case against Corlett. Dr MacKenzie was called to the witness box and said that in his opinion, it might have been possible that the injury was caused by 'violent sexual connection'. The Attorney General said that he did not intend to call further evidence, and the Clerk of the Rolls, presiding, then said to the jury: 'It is my duty to put to you – do you or do you not consider that a sufficient case is made out to send this man for trial?'; 'No, sir' was the reply. The Clerk of the Rolls then asked Ellis Corlett to stand before telling him:

> A fortunate combination of circumstances has told in your favour, and enabled the jury to find that you should not be sent for trial. I may say this: that while you escape being committed on the charge of murder, you stand convicted in the eyes of all your fellow men of the most abominable conduct – conduct that is an absolute disgrace to yourself, and calculated to bring discredit upon every person in any way connected with you. I hope this will be a lesson to you for your life and the best thing will be for you to withdraw from this place to someplace where you are not known. You are now discharged.

14

EDITH ANNIE COOPER (1892)

Edith Annie Cooper came from Shirley, Birmingham. Her parents were well respected in the area and she had two brothers and one sister. After leaving school she took up a position as a barmaid at the Central Restaurant in Birmingham. She later worked as a barmaid at the Kensington Hotel in High Street, Birmingham and after this position went to the Isle of Man in 1888 or 1889 to work in the Central Hotel on Douglas Promenade. She was described as very attractive with a dark complexion and dark hair. It was while working at the Central Hotel as a barmaid that she met her future husband, George Barker James Cooper (coincidentally, Edith's maiden name was also Cooper).

George Cooper was described by many as a flamboyant character. He was slightly below average height, of slight build, with black hair, beard and moustache. He wore gold rings, pince-nez spectacles, expensive clothes and often a sombrero hat, and was sometimes described as 'Spanish looking'. His mother was Manx and had earlier lived in Athol Street in Douglas, while his father was a partner in a wealthy Manchester firm, I. & J. G. Cooper. Both he and his father were well known in the north of the Island and his father had owned property in the Tholt-y-Will area.

Despite his fortunate upbringing George Barker James Cooper was to have his share of problems later in life. He was involved in several scandals, which must have caused acute embarrassment to his parents. He developed a reputation as something of a womaniser and on one occasion eloped with a married woman, with whom he travelled to America. After living with her there for some time he returned and was later given a beating by the woman's husband. His first marriage ended in acrimony, his wife obtaining a divorce on the grounds of his cruelty and infidelity. During one argument with his first wife he had fired a revolver and was subsequently arrested and charged with her attempted murder. He later faced a court on this charge but was acquitted. A frequent visitor to the Island, he became well known there, often staying with his father.

A relationship developed between George Cooper and Edith and they soon became engaged. After working in the Central Hotel in Douglas for six months or so, she had returned to Shirley in early 1891 and began making arrangements for the forthcoming wedding. The pair were married in November 1891 in Shirley Church but the marriage was to be short-lived, ending in tragedy and a trial that was to become one of the most sensational ever on the Isle of Man.

Following their marriage the pair made several journeys to the home of Edith's parents. They also made several trips to the Isle of Man and always stayed at the Regent Hotel on Loch Promenade, Douglas. On 2 September 1892, when George Cooper was 39 and Edith 25 years old, they travelled to Douglas from Fleetwood by boat. On the trip they shared a private cabin and Edith was seasick on the journey over to the Island. After arriving in Douglas they went to the Regent Hotel, having stayed there on six previous occasions and Edith was shown to their room, number 16 on the second floor, while Cooper remained downstairs until about 9.00 p.m. He went to bed at about this time but then came back downstairs about 3.30 a.m. to ask for some champagne for his wife. He was told the bar had closed and he instead took her a soda water.

Cooper came down again about 8.00 a.m. for breakfast and left the hotel at around 9.00 a.m. in order to attend to some business. He then met Mr Bradshaw, a portrait painter and photographer, and the pair visited a local bank before returning to the hotel. Mr Bradshaw waited downstairs in the smoke room while Cooper went up to his room. When he did not return Mr Bradshaw left the hotel. Cooper meanwhile had ordered a small bottle of champagne and a maid had taken this to the bedroom he occupied with his wife. Shortly after this, another maid, who was working in a nearby bedroom, overheard an argument between George and Edith and not long after this heard a woman's scream and a thud, as if a body had fallen to the floor.

The maid summoned help from the hotel manager who, in the company of the head porter, went to the bedroom and demanded entry. When George Cooper opened the door they were shocked to find the apparently dead body of Edith lying on the floor naked, with her husband standing over her. On closer inspection the manager saw that there was a wound in the left side of the woman's chest which was bleeding. The head porter then went for the police and shortly afterwards several police officers arrived with a doctor who had been summoned to the hotel, and who confirmed the death.

George Cooper was arrested and taken away for questioning. Although he had earlier appeared to be unconcerned about the events in the bedroom, he suddenly exclaimed, 'Oh my God! Oh my God! Let me go back and kiss her before I am taken away.' The Coroner was then informed and a jury was hastily assembled. The inquest was opened that same afternoon in the Regent Hotel in front of Mr Samuel Harris, the Coroner for Douglas. The body was viewed by the jury and they saw what appeared to be a deep stab wound about one and a half inches in length above the left breast. There were also marks on the right arm and some bruising on the right leg.

The first witness called was William Welden, the manager of the Regent Hotel. He explained that he had known the deceased, as she had stayed there several times as a visitor over the previous year or so. On each occasion she had been accompanied by her husband, George Cooper, who was also present in custody at the inquest. The pair had arrived at the hotel the previous evening, Welden said, and he explained how the chambermaid had come to him earlier that day after she had heard squabbling in room number 16. Initially, Weldon did not take much notice, thinking it was merely a minor disagreement, but shortly after that the maid had returned to say she had heard a scream and someone fall to the floor. He had then gone upstairs and found the door locked, but added that when he had knocked on the door Cooper had opened it immediately. He had not noticed any blood on Cooper's hands. Mr Welden had then seen the lady lying on the bedroom floor and Cooper initially said, 'She is in a dead faint.' The hotel manager estimated that when he first saw the body it was about 20 minutes since the maid had told him of the scream and the sound of a body falling in the room. He noticed blood on the pillow and on the bedclothes and when the head porter had turned the body over slightly, he saw the wound to the chest. The head porter had then gone for the police and the first policeman on the scene, Police Constable John Henry Whitfield, had arrived some three minutes later and asked the manager to send for further police officers.

Mr Welden stated that he had seen Cooper earlier that morning about 8.00 a.m. when he was sitting quietly on a seat at the entrance to the hotel and at that time he appeared to be sober. On their previous visits to the hotel Mr Welden said the couple had always appeared to be on good terms.

John Champion Bradshaw next gave his evidence for the inquest, stating that he had known both Mr and Mrs Cooper for some time and had identified the body of Edith Annie Cooper earlier that day. He explained that he had gone to the bank that morning with Mr Cooper in order to receive payment for two portraits he had made of Edith. The pair had then gone to the Regent

Hotel, arriving there at around 10.30 a.m. Mr Cooper had asked him if he would like a glass of champagne and he had gone inside with him and waited in the smoke-room. However, Mr Cooper did not return and shortly afterwards Bradshaw left the hotel. He told the inquiry that he had noticed the smell of drink on Mr Cooper and did not feel that he was 'completely sober' when he left him. Mr Cooper had told him, he said, that his wife had 'got drunk' on the boat coming from Fleetwood and was still feeling ill that morning. After Bradshaw's evidence the inquest was adjourned and the body was removed from the hotel and taken to the hospital mortuary where a post-mortem was carried out. During the inquest Cooper sat on a sofa and apparently appeared unconcerned by his predicament.

The inquest was resumed the following Monday at 10.30 a.m. in Douglas Courthouse. Telegrams had been received from the fathers of both Edith and George Cooper, requesting an adjournment so that they could attend and the jury agreed to adjourn until the following day.

Large crowds gathered on the Tuesday morning. Mr Kneen was Cooper's advocate at the inquest and the first witness called was Mr James Cowle, an architect, who produced a sketch showing the situation of the room in which the death had occurred. He was followed by Miss Polly O'Brien, who worked as a chambermaid at the Regent Hotel. She had met the couple when they arrived on the Friday evening and had shown Mrs Cooper to room 16. Miss O'Brien said that the woman had looked ill and assumed this was because she had had a rough sea crossing. She did not feel that the hotel guest was drunk. The maid took Edith Cooper a small brandy and later George Cooper had asked her to go and ask his wife if she wanted another drink. When she returned to the room Edith Cooper was lying on the bed fully dressed and said she did not require anything else and the maid saw nothing more of the couple that evening. She said that she had seen Mr Cooper very briefly the following morning, and later she saw him again when she took a small bottle of champagne to room 16. Mrs Cooper had drunk a glass of champagne and Mr Cooper had told her that his wife was ill. The maid returned to the room between 9.30 and 9.45 a.m. and found the woman still lying in bed in her nightdress. Edith Cooper told the maid that she still felt ill.

Miss O'Brien said that at around 10.30 a.m. another chambermaid had come to her and said, 'I think Mr and Mrs Cooper are quarrelling.' Shortly after this Miss O'Brien had gone past room 16 and had heard the sound of an argument. Later she had heard a slight scream and when she was in room 17 she heard the noise of someone falling on the floor in the adjoining room, number 16. She then looked through the keyhole of room 16 and saw the woman lying naked on the floor between the bed and the wash stand. Mr Cooper was leaning over her and wiping her face with a towel. One of the hotel staff knocked on the door and complained about a disturbance and it was quiet for about quarter of an hour after this. The manager had then knocked at the door of number 16 and asked if everything was all right. Mr Weldon told Miss O'Brien that if she heard any further commotion she should call him. Shortly after this the maid was in room 2, which was underneath room 16, when she heard another noise of someone falling on the floor. She immediately sent for Mr Welden who, with the head porter, then demanded admittance to the room.

David Joseph O'Malley MD, a doctor who had a practice in Bucks Road, said that he had gone to the Regent Hotel about 11.45 a.m. on the Saturday morning. He had found the body of a lady lying partly on her right side, naked, apart from a cloth covering the lower part of her body. He saw the wound on the left side of her chest and confirmed that she was dead. He measured the wound and found it to be 3 in. in length. He also found bruises on the upper part of her right arm. He described how he had been shown a pen-knife by the police with one blade open, and the blade was covered with blood. That evening he had made a post-mortem examination of the body. He found some discolouration around the eyes which he felt may have been caused by recent blows, and discovered that the chest wound extended in an oblique direction and upwards towards the left shoulder. He thought that the knife he had been shown could have caused the injury and he told the inquest he felt the wound was not self-inflicted.

Miss Matilda (Tillie) Yeaman, a barmaid at the Regent Hotel, said that she had seen the Coopers arriving on the Friday evening about 7.00 p.m., adding that Mrs Cooper appeared to be sober at that time. She later saw Mr Cooper and asked him what he had been doing to his wife, as she had looked so ill. She said that Cooper had replied that he had given her 'a good thrashing' with a horsewhip the night before.

Gilbert Cannock, head porter at the hotel, gave his evidence and explained how he had gone to room 16 with Mr Welden around 11.30 a.m. When they had entered the room he had seen Mr Cooper standing beside the bed and the body of his wife lying on the floor, with her feet under the bed and her head near the washstand. The inquest was then adjourned again for the day and resumed on the Wednesday morning at 10.00 a.m.

John Alexander Clarke, a steward on board the SS *Mona's Queen*, gave evidence. He said that he was on duty on the Friday when the Coopers travelled to the Island. He recalled that Mr Cooper had ordered a glass of brandy for the private cabin he was sharing with his wife but apart from one other brandy served to the cabin later, he was not aware of any other drinks consumed on the boat by the couple. Clarke said that when they disembarked they were both sober and he was not aware of any arguments in the cabin during the crossing.

John Henry Whitfield of the Manchester Constabulary explained that he was a police constable attached to the local force and had been working near the hotel on the Saturday morning when the head porter had asked for his assistance at around 11.45 a.m. He described seeing the body and the wound on her left breast. When he asked Cooper, 'Who has done this?', Cooper replied, 'I don't know. I have been to Dumbell's Bank in company with Mr Bradshaw and on my return I found her like this.'

Shortly after this exchange several other police officers and Dr O'Malley arrived in the room and George Cooper was then taken to the police station. Just as he was leaving the bedroom he exclaimed, 'Oh, my God! Oh, my God! Let me kiss her before I am taken away.'

The police officer then went on to describe how the lady's blood-stained nightdress had been found on the floor near the foot of the bed. He also said there had been a wash basin three parts filled with blood-stained water and he had found the blood-stained pen-knife lying next to the sink. He had also discovered various other items of clothing, which were stained with blood, under the bed.

Several witnesses then gave fairly unimportant evidence before the Coroner began his summing up to the jury. Mr Harris said that the wound was either self-inflicted or inflicted by Cooper. If it had been self-inflicted it would have been expected that Cooper would have sent for help. The fact that he did not proved to the Coroner's mind that the victim did not cause her own death. The jury left and returned after an absence of 25 minutes. The foreman said they had unanimously come to the following verdict: 'We find in conformity with the evidence laid before us, that the death of the deceased was caused by a wound on her left breast, and that the wound was inflicted by George Barker James Cooper, now in custody.' The Coroner pointed out that they had not said if it was feloniously done and there then followed some discussion about the wording of the verdict. The majority of the jury felt that Cooper should be tried for murder and the inquest ended.

On Thursday, 8 September, George Cooper was brought before Mr Samuel Harris, High Bailiff of Douglas and was charged by Superintendent Boyd of the Isle of Man Constabulary, prosecuting, that he 'wilfully and feloniously killed his wife Edith Annie Cooper'. The court was quickly adjourned until the following day and much of the evidence previously heard at the inquest was repeated.

At the end of the hearing the High Bailiff asked Cooper if he had anything to say and he replied 'I desire to reserve my defence.' The High Bailiff then committed him for trial on the charge of the 'wilful murder of Edith Annie Cooper'. It was reported that Cooper showed no emotion and he was then taken to the Isle of Man Gaol to await his trial.

The funeral of Mrs Cooper took place on the Thursday morning in Shirley, Birmingham, at the same church in which she had married her husband, her body having arrived there on the Wednesday evening.

A report in the local press on 17 September gave a description of George Cooper's life in prison while awaiting his trial. It described him as the only son of a wealthy Manchester merchant. He was not confined to his cell but instead had an apartment assigned to him and was not compelled to do any work, having as much reading material as he needed apart from newspapers. He was also allowed to exercise separately from other prisoners and his meals were supplied by the nearby Falcon Cliff Hotel. The article stated that he had a good appetite and that he ate well, often washing down his meals with a small bottle of champagne. Cooper was also allowed to smoke Havana cigars and the report ended by saying that he slept well while he was on remand.

On 27 September Cooper was brought before a special criminal court of inquiry in front of Sir W. L. Drinkwater. A six-man jury was sworn in. The jury were told that they could either send Cooper to Gaol Delivery for trial on a charge of murder or a reduced charge of manslaughter, or alternatively they could decide to discharge him. Cooper was represented by Mr T. Kneen and Mr G. A. Ring and Sir James Gell prosecuted the case with his son, James S. Gell. Again, much of the evidence was as heard in the previous hearings.

Miss Matilda Yeaman was a young barmaid at the Regent Hotel. She described a conversation with Cooper in which he said he had given his wife 'a good thrashing with a horsewhip' the night before. He told her that he had had an 'awful time' with Edith, as she had been 'boozing' all the time they had been away from the hotel.

William Henry Cooper, a brother of Edith Cooper, said he had stayed with his sister and her husband at their home near Manchester, and described how an argument had started between the couple. William had stepped in and hit George Cooper several times. A few nights later William had seen George Cooper hit his wife in the eye with his fist and he had then 'thrashed' Cooper with a riding whip. He also described another incident during his stay where

George had held a knife to his wife and again William had intervened and taken the knife off him.

Dr Joseph O'Malley again described the condition of the body in room 16, in the Regent Hotel, on the morning of 3 September and later that same day he confirmed that he had carried out a post-mortem examination at the hospital mortuary. Several other doctors were present including Dr Wood and Dr Buxton. There were recent bruises to the right upper arm and on the left breast above the wound, as well as a small abrasion on the right cheek. Dr O'Malley felt that the discolouration of the eyes may have been recent bruising.

The fatal wound was 3 in. long. It had passed between the second and third ribs on the left side and pierced the pleura and the lung itself, the pericardium (a covering of the heart) and the pulmonary artery. The depth was about 2.5 in. The wound had definitely caused the death of Edith Cooper, the doctor added, and the other doctors present at the post-mortem agreed with this opinion. Dr O'Malley confirmed that the knife he had been shown by the police could have caused the wound described.

William Davis, a police constable in the Lancashire Constabulary, gave evidence and explained that he worked in the area where the Coopers lived near Manchester and had known them for about eight months. One night, while on his beat at around midnight, he had heard screams from the Cooper house and the following day had seen Edith with black eyes. He saw her again on 1 September, the day before she travelled to the Isle of Man and remembered that her eyes were also bruised at that time. He also described her as 'a very nice person'.

Police Superintendent James Bent worked in the same force and explained how he had given George Cooper a verbal warning on Saturday, 8 May concerning his ill-treatment of his wife. He told Cooper he had received reports from police constables of hearing his wife cry 'murder!' and 'police!' late at night. He was aware that a constable had on several occasions warned Cooper about these disturbances and Bent had also cautioned him about threatening his wife with a revolver. It is clear that Cooper had been told in no uncertain terms that if he continued to behave in this way he would be arrested. He promised he would mend his ways in future.

George Cooper himself then gave evidence. He recalled his trip to the Island with his wife and their arrival at the hotel and described going up to the room after leaving Mr Bradshaw downstairs following their trip to the bank. When Cooper had gone into the room, he said, his wife was still lying on the bed and complained of feeling unwell. He asked her when she intended to get up as he hoped to go out later that day to Sulby, and then clipped his nails with the pen-knife which had been lying on the dressing table. After telling his wife that she should have something to eat as she had done nothing but drink since leaving Manchester, an argument ensued between the pair and she had slapped his face. He retaliated, not realising the knife was still in his hand, and Edith cried out 'George, you have cut me.' He saw that there was a wound on her chest, he explained, but thought initially it was only trivial. After moving her from the bed towards the washstand so that he could bathe her wound, he found she was unable to stand and fell heavily to the floor. He cut away her nightdress and bathed her wound, adding that at this point he thought she had merely fainted.

After extensive summing up by the prosecution and defence, the jury found an indictment for murder.

Cooper's trial started on Monday, 14 November 1892. The court was composed of His Excellency the Lieutenant Governor, Mr Spencer Walpole, who presided, Deemsters Drinkwater and Gell and the Clerk of the Rolls, Mr A. Dumbell. Twelve jurors were selected. Prosecuting for the Crown were Mr J. S. Gell and Mr J. M. Cruickshank. For the defence, Mr G. A. Ring and Mr T. Kneen again represented Cooper, who said, when asked to plead, 'I am not guilty.' Mr Cruickshank outlined the case for the prosecution.

Miss Louisa Mary Cooper, a sister of Edith's, was called to give evidence. She described how, on the previous New Year's Day, she had gone to the house of her sister in Higher Broughton, Manchester, where she found her sister had two black eyes and a bruise on her forehead. Over the next few days she heard numerous disturbances between the pair and said that George Cooper would ask his wife for spirits but she would refuse to give him any. On another occasion George had bitten Edith's wrist. She added that to her knowledge her sister drank very little in the way of alcohol.

William Henry Cooper, Edith's brother, repeated the evidence given at an earlier hearing describing how he had beaten George Cooper after he had seen him abuse his sister.

Many of the witnesses from the previous hearings again gave their evidence to the court. A new witness at the trial was Robert Callin, a warder at the Isle of Man Gaol. He told the court that Cooper had been in the gaol since 9 September and on Sunday, 11 September, he had written a letter. Callin remembered that it was addressed to Mr Harold Cooper but could not remember any other details. He had taken the letter to the gaoler's office. William Fayle, another gaoler, remembered that the address was 38 Richmond Street, New Brighton, Liverpool.

Mrs Miranda Jackson followed William Fayle, explaining that she owned the house in New Brighton and had let it to a lady called Mrs Cooper and her son Harold, who was about five years old, in May of that year. A few weeks later she met a man at the house whom she now identified as George Cooper, who was introduced to her as Mrs Cooper's husband. She had seen him there on several other occasions, the last time being 1 September.

The 'Mrs Cooper' living in New Brighton was identified by several witnesses as a Mrs Hunt who was being divorced by her husband, Arthur Earle Hunt. It was Hunt who had earlier given Cooper a thrashing after he eloped with his wife. Arthur Hunt gave evidence, saying that he had not lived with her for seven years and had been trying to discover her whereabouts without success. Five witnesses from Liverpool and Manchester then gave evidence that proved that George Cooper was regularly seeing Mrs Hunt and her son but she had then left the New Brighton address on 13 September and despite intensive enquiries had not been traced.

The gaoler, William Fayle, was recalled and explained that he had copied the letter sent by George Cooper on 11 September and Mr J. S. Gell read it to the court. In it Cooper described his version of the events in the Regent Hotel. In part of it he said, 'You know how I liked the little girl and would never have harmed her, having raised her from a barmaid to my own level, one dress to twenty and more.' He also wrote, 'Returning from the bank I found her as stated in the papers and tried to bring her round.' He went on to describe the ordeal of the inquest and subsequent court appearances. He also wrote, 'I never imagined I should be placed in a suspicious light', adding, 'we all know she was drinking herself insane for months'. He then went on to describe various articles he wished her to have (it seems clear that the letter was sent to Mrs Hunt), including a set of valuable engravings and items of furniture. The letter ends with 'You remember me when I last saw you [sic]. I thought you might have crossed with me, not her. Destroy this when read'.

It is apparent from the letter that George Cooper was involved in a relationship with Mrs Hunt and was anxious that she would not be identified. It seems that having been with her on 1 September, the day before his crossing to the Island, he had wished that she had gone with him instead of his wife. He denied this when questioned by the Clerk of the Rolls and Mr Ring.

Cooper was questioned by the Clerk of the Rolls about this letter. He said, 'You said that when you wrote that letter you were in such a state as not to know what you were doing.'

Cooper replied, 'Yes and I have been all along. When you come to consider that the doctor had given me sleeping draughts you can understand.' When he was asked, 'Then you don't think you ought to be held to what you said?', Cooper replied, 'Certainly not.'

Mr Ring said to him, 'Cooper, you say at the end of that letter of 11 September, "You remember when I last saw you, I thought you might have crossed with me not her"? Was there any intention of anyone else coming?'

Cooper's reply was, 'Certainly not.'

Sergeant James Bell had been present when Inspector Boyd charged Cooper at the police station. He told the jury that Cooper had said, 'It is a sure case of suicide.' Cooper had later been heard to say, 'I am an innocent man and my conscience is clear.'

When the case for the defence began Henry Buckingham, a steward on the Peveril boat, said he knew George Cooper and his wife. He described seeing the woman drink excessively on a trip from Liverpool about three weeks before her death and said that by the end of the trip she was in a very intoxicated condition. He felt that Mr Cooper was very kind to his wife. Other witnesses gave evidence that although Cooper was often the worse for drink, his wife was also often in a similar condition.

Allan Pearson, a porter at the Athol Hotel, said that Edith Cooper had lived with his mother after leaving the Central Hotel. He had seen her then and on many occasions since and described her as having a very nasty temper. She was often, he said, either drunk or partly drunk.

After a trial lasting six days, the jury retired to consider their verdict on Monday, 21 November, and after an hour and three quarters returned to find that George Cooper was guilty of manslaughter. Deemster Drinkwater said, 'Prisoner at the bar, you have been found guilty after a long trial, of the crime of manslaughter. The jury have taken a merciful view of your case and one [with] which the court is not inclined to disagree. The court, however, see that this is not the first act of violence committed by you; but that various assaults upon your wife have been committed, causing her considerable bodily injury and that these have at last culminated in her death.'

Cooper was then sentenced to ten years in prison. The moment of sentencing was described in the *Mona's Herald* on 22 November: 'Cooper blanched a deadly white when he heard the punishment announced, but on recovering, leaned over the dock and was heard to say, "In seven years I'll be out of it." Prisoner was removed to the cells immediately afterwards.'

Two days later the *Mona's Herald* reported:

> It is impossible to accept this story of a severe blow on the prisoner's own statement and there was no evidence whatsoever to support it.

[. . .] From these points of view we cannot but regard both the verdict and the sentence with profound dissatisfaction. We cannot feel that the demands of justice have been met. While the law remains as it is, an act like this must be more than a milder form of manslaughter. If manslaughter at all, it is surely the highest degree of that crime, for which a sentence of ten years' penal servitude is utterly inadequate.

It is interesting to note some of the comments in the English press, the reporters of which attended the trial. The *Liverpool Courier* said that although Cooper had lied at times, he would probably still have been found guilty of manslaughter if he had been tried in England. The paper said that he had 'a life of gross over-indulgence of every kind', and did not deserve 'an atom of sympathy'. It also reported that there would have been few regrets had he been found guilty of murder and executed. They did however add that ten years' penal servitude for him was a harsh sentence in view of his previous lifestyle.

The *Liverpool Echo* felt it was clear that the jury had been swayed by the powerful defence made on Cooper's behalf. They had heard Edith Cooper described as 'nagging, drunken and quarrelsome'. The paper said it was clear that most people felt loathing and disgust for Cooper.

The *Daily Chronicle* said it felt there was 'greater repugnance in the Isle of Man to hanging anybody' and this may have induced the jury to be rather more merciful than they should have been. The article added that the only real evidence in Cooper's favour was his assertion that his wife had provoked him. It was clear that Cooper had been in the habit of abusing and threatening his wife and there had been previous assaults on her. The paper was also concerned that Cooper would eventually return to live in society again.

It is also interesting to look at the reaction of the people in and around the courthouse after the verdict was given. The spectators in court were said to be astonished by the leniency of the verdict and when the members of the jury came out of the building they were greeted with loud hisses and an angry mob who rushed at them had to be restrained by police. The jury were then escorted to the railway station by the police and more hissing was heard when two of the judges exited the court. The general feeling was that the sentence was far too lenient.

Cooper was not removed from the court to the Isle of Man Gaol until people had dispersed and was then taken to gaol to start his sentence. He was later transferred to a prison in England to serve his time.

15

JOHN GOLD (1870)

William Edward Makepiece Williams came from Solihull in Warwickshire. In the late summer of 1869 he had moved to the Isle of Man and stayed at the Castle Mona Hotel on the promenade in Douglas. While staying at the hotel he met a young lady called Emma Caroline Goldthorpe and the pair later became engaged. In February of 1870 they were married in Deansgate, Manchester and after the wedding the pair honeymooned on the continent. Several weeks later, when the honeymoon ended, the couple returned to Manchester, to stay at the Albion Hotel.

On 14 May 1870, about three weeks after returning to Manchester, the pair travelled to the Isle of Man, accompanied by Emma's brother, William Cliff Goldthorpe. They travelled by boat and on their arrival in Douglas at around 7.30 p.m. went to Miss Hickman's lodgings in Castle Terrace, Douglas, where they were to stay. Over the next few days Williams visited some old friends he had met during his earlier stay on the Island. He had three brothers and one of them, Ridley, had earlier bought him a revolver pistol. This had two barrels and twenty chambers and William Goldthorpe was later to say that Williams appeared to have a strange fascination for the gun.

On Thursday 19 May, Williams, Emma and her brother travelled to Laxey. Goldthorpe and Emma went in a pony trap and Williams travelled on horseback. They had stopped off on the way to Laxey for a drink, where Williams had a glass of beer, and when they arrived in Laxey he had a small bottle of claret. After leaving, the three had then set off for Douglas but Williams had gone off on his own to look at a house, Cooil Roi. The other two lost Williams when he went up a private road looking for the house. This occurred at about 5.00 p.m. and Goldthorpe and his sister then went back to the lodgings. When they arrived they found that Williams had not returned and Goldthorpe set off in the trap to look for him. Not far from the Castle

Mona Hotel Goldthorpe came across Williams, riding quickly on his horse in the direction of the town centre. The two men then went for a drink at about 8.00 p.m. in a nearby pub where Williams had another glass of beer. After this the men returned to the lodgings and the man from whom Goldthorpe had borrowed the trap, Tom Smith, also went with them.

The three men went into the sitting-room at the guest house where they were staying. On the mantelpiece was a box containing the revolver. Williams took the revolver out of its case and although the gun was loaded at the time, he pointed it at Tom Smith, who quickly ran out of the room; Goldthorpe was later to describe Williams's manner as 'strange'. After putting the gun back in its case the men sat down for a meal, although Williams did not eat anything. He did have another drink and a smoke but after ten minutes or so he got up, put on his boots, which he had only taken off a few minutes earlier and again took the gun out of its case. He put on his coat and put the gun in the inside pocket. He then took it out again and pointed it at the wall separating the sitting room from his own bedroom; Emma was in that room at the time. He fired one of the chambers and the bullet went into the wall to a depth of about 3 in. Williams then opened the window and fired the other 19 chambers over the Castle Mona Road. Goldthorpe tried to get the gun off him but was unsuccessful and Williams reloaded some of the chambers in the gun, again returning it to his breast pocket before saying that he was going out. Goldthorpe begged him to leave the revolver there but when he saw that he was determined to go out and take the pistol with him, he accompanied him, and must have been concerned about his brother-in-law's behaviour.

Just before 10 p.m. the pair went to Trustrum's Hotel in James Street where Williams had a brandy and soda water. The men went into the billiard room of the hotel and, after sitting down, Williams had again taken out the revolver and put it on the mantelpiece. Some men in the room admired the gun and one asked if he could look at it closely. Others in the room, however, were not so interested and said they would leave if he did not put it away. Williams did not drink much of his brandy and soda and the pair then left and went to another pub but did not drink any alcohol there. They then set off for their lodgings.

On the walk towards their guest house, Williams took the gun out on several occasions whenever they met someone. Goldthorpe tried to take the gun off him several times and succeeded once, but Williams soon retrieved it. The pair walked through Strand Street and into Castle Street, where they walked past a pub called the Derby Arms Hotel (now Brendan O'Donnell's). This pub was owned by a man called John Gold, who was later described in one of the local newspapers as, 'One of the most inoffensive and kindly hearted of persons. He was one of whom it could be most emphatically said he had not an enemy.'

As they passed the pub at about 10.30 p.m. Williams said to his brother-in-law, 'Come, Willy, we will go in here and have something.' The pair had then gone inside and ordered two glasses of sherry. Williams had taken the gun out of his pocket again and the barmaid who had just served him ran off on seeing it. He pointed the gun at a glass and Goldthorpe thought he was about to fire at it but he did not. John Gold had then come into the bar and stood behind the counter. He began a conversation with Williams, who said to him, 'I say old fellow, I am a good shot and would like to blow through your hat.' With Gold still on the other side of the bar, Williams then proceeded to point the pistol at the barman's head. Gold had his hat on and Williams lifted the pistol and fired. Gold fell to the ground in a sitting position, the hat still on his head. There was panic in the bar.

Goldthorpe said to Williams, 'Edward, you've shot that man! We had better be going.' Goldthorpe described Williams as looking 'very wild'.

In response to Goldthorpe accusing him of having shot Gold, Williams said, 'No I have not, Willy.'

The pair had then left the pub and Goldthorpe said to him, 'Edward you've killed him as dead as a stone,' to which he had replied, 'Oh no, you have been mistaken.'

The men had then returned to their lodgings in Castle Street. Not much was said on the short trip back and when they arrived, Williams rushed upstairs on his own. Goldthorpe told his sister that her husband had killed a man. Emma said to him, 'Then he has gone to kill himself.' The pair rushed out of the sitting room towards the bedroom where Williams had gone and at that moment they heard a pistol shot. His wife looked into the bedroom and found him dying on the bed. He had shot himself in the forehead and just before death had tried to speak and had smiled at his wife when she came into the room. They sent for a doctor and Dr Adair arrived and examined Williams, confirming that he was dead.

Meanwhile, back at the Derby Arms, John Gold had been attended by Dr Wood. The wound in his head extended from the top part of the forehead into the brain itself. Although initially he had been conscious, he had not spoken since the shooting and died shortly afterwards in the arms of two neighbours, who had carried him from the bar to his bedroom in the upper part of the house. The police had been quickly told about the shooting in the Derby Arms and had then gone to the lodgings where Williams and Goldthorpe were staying. However, they were too late and when they arrived they found that Williams was already dead.

The inquest into the two deaths was opened at 1.00 p.m. on Friday, 20 May before the High Bailiff of Douglas, Mr S. Harris. The jury first assembled at Mr Gold's house, the Derby Arms Hotel in Castle Street, where they viewed his body lying fully clothed on a bed. They then went to Castle Terrace where Williams and his wife had been staying. There they viewed the body of Williams and the inquest itself was held in the drawing room in that house. There were 11 men on the jury and the first witness was the brother-in-law of Williams, William Cliff Goldthorpe. He described how he had first met Williams before the wedding. He then went on to describe how they had arrived on the Isle of Man and the events of the previous day, culminating in the tragic shooting and suicide.

Next, Margaret Anne Cannell gave evidence. She was a barmaid in John Gold's pub and had worked there for about a year. She said that she knew Williams as he had frequently drunk in the Derby Arms Hotel when he had lived on the Island previously. She said she had often served him with brandy but had never noticed anything strange about him. She said that at about 10.40 p.m. the previous evening, Williams had come into the pub accompanied by his brother-in-law, Goldthorpe. He initially asked for two beers but had then changed his mind and asked for two sherries. Williams, however, had not drunk his. She said he produced the gun and held his coat in the other hand to cover it. She had told him that she was frightened of the gun and had run out of the bar. She then told Mrs Gold that Williams had a pistol in the bar and shortly afterwards heard the sound of the shot. She ran into the room to find that Mr Gold had been shot, but Mrs Gold initially thought it was some kind of joke. Dr Wood was then sent for and Gold was taken to a bedroom. Margaret Cannell continued, saying that Mrs Gold had then pushed Williams and his companion out of the pub, at the time still not realising what had happened. She had heard something of the conversation between Williams and Gold and remembered they were talking about a dog, but there was nothing unusual about the conversation. She told the jury that Gold had been a very quiet man when sober. She also said that to her knowledge Mr Gold and Williams were on friendly terms with each other.

Thomas Arthur Wood gave evidence. He said that he was a medical practitioner in Douglas and had been called upon about 11.00 p.m. the previous evening to see John Gold. He had found him lying on his back on the floor of the bar. At that time he was still alive but it was clear that he was mortally wounded and shortly afterwards he died. After his body had been taken to the bedroom, the doctor had looked at the wound in his head. It was at the crown of the head, a little to the right of the midline, and had penetrated his skull. In the doctor's opinion death had resulted from the gunshot causing a brain injury and the pressure effect of haemorrhage around the brain. In his opinion, Mr Gold had probably put his head down and had then received the shot at the top of the head.

The same doctor had later seen the body of Williams, at about midnight. He was also dead and had a circular wound in the centre of the forehead which again penetrated the skull.

Arthur Ingleby was the next witness. He was a barman in the pub, working for John Gold. He had heard someone cry out that Gold had been shot and had gone into the bar where he found him in a sitting position, leaning against some beer barrels. He said that his head was hanging down and his hat was still on but when Ingleby removed it he had seen the wound at the top of his head from which blood was running. He had then gone for Dr Wood.

James Jackson Adair, another doctor, also gave evidence. He had gone to see Williams at about 11.00 p.m. the previous evening. He found Williams lying across the bed with a wound in the centre of his forehead, which was bleeding, and saw that Williams was also bleeding from the nostrils and mouth. Nothing could be done to save him, the doctor said, and he died shortly after Adair had entered the room. Adair said that 'I have no doubt that he died from a gunshot wound then recently inflicted.'

Edwin Nixon told the inquest that he had been drinking in Trustrum's on the previous evening when Williams had come in. He agreed with the earlier evidence given by Goldthorpe. Nixon said that he had known Williams from when he had earlier lived on the Island and 'considered that he was a person not altogether of sound mind. He got fearfully excited when contradicted on any subject.' He went on to describe how Williams had shown him the gun and taken one of the cartridges out to show that it was loaded.

A porter in the Castle Mona Hotel, John James Sayle, addressed the jury. He said that he knew Williams and remembered him staying at the Castle Mona the previous summer. He said that Williams had been in the habit of drinking beer and a small amount would affect him. He went on to say, 'He was very excitable when in that state and if any person said anything to him, he was up in a minute, but he was very quiet when left alone. When excited he was not easily controlled. We put him to bed when he came in tipsy, which was not often, and he would be quiet.'

Elizabeth Bate was the manageress of the Castle Mona Hotel in Douglas and she described how Williams had lived there from June 1869 to January

1870. Emma, who was to become his fiancée, was working in the bar at that time and also living in the hotel, and she described how the pair had met and later married. She said that Williams was always looked upon as being 'simple-minded and eccentric in his manner'. She also agreed that he was exceedingly excitable, particularly when he'd been drinking.

John Joshua Harwood told the jury that he also knew Williams, who told him that his father was very anxious to place him 'under restraint'. He said that in his opinion Williams was 'not quite sane' and he added 'He once made an exhibition of himself which was anything but what he ought to have done. He got into a needless row with some persons who were not in the same position as himself.'

The High Bailiff then summed up at length. He gave the jury the legal definition of murder and explained that the fact that a man was drunk or under the influence of alcohol was no excuse if he committed a crime. He said, 'An offender under the influence of intoxication, can derive no privilege from madness voluntarily contracted, but is amenable to the justice of his country equally as if he had been in the full possession of his senses at the time.' He said it was the duty of the jury to consider whether Williams was, when he shot Gold, 'labouring under temporary insanity'. It was impossible, he said, that Williams could have had any malice against Gold. It was probable that in the two hours or so that Williams was separated from his wife and her brother, he would have had more to drink. He explained that on his way back to Douglas he would have had to pass four public houses and the probability was that he had called in some of them.

The jury returned two separate verdicts, one in the case of Gold and another in the case of Williams. In the former case their verdict was that 'the deceased John Gold died from a wound in the head, inflicted by Williams, and that the latter at the time had no malice against Gold, but was labouring under temporary insanity'. In Williams's case, the jury returned as their verdict that 'the deceased, when in a state of temporary insanity, shot himself in the head, inflicting a mortal wound on himself by reason of which he instantaneously died'.

16

CHARLES LEWIN (1875)

Charles Lewin was about 27 years old and lived in Castletown with his wife, Sarah. Theirs was not a happy marriage and neighbours often heard the pair arguing. It appears that both were quite heavy drinkers and the rows were often worse during the times when one or the other was drunk. Lewin's wife was later to say that in the week leading up to Christmas in 1875 there were numerous quarrels between the two. If she is to be believed, he was drunk for the greater part of that week. At 2 a.m. on the morning of Christmas Eve another quarrel resulted in Sarah leaving the house and going to a neighbour's, Mrs Teare. She had lain on the bed at Mrs Teare's for about three quarters of an hour and then returned to her own house where she went back to bed until about 9 a.m.

Sarah and her husband both got up at about 9.00 a.m. on Christmas Eve, a Friday, and he then went out, returning at about 11.00 a.m. Sarah left the house just as Charles was arriving home, fearing another argument would start if she stayed there. She went to her brother's house nearby and later went to Mrs Teare's again. It seems that Lewin was out and about that afternoon and at one point she saw him pass the house of another neighbour she was visiting. She briefly returned to her own house at about 5.00 p.m. and at that time her husband was in bed. At about 8.30 p.m. she again had gone home and after opening the front door she heard him snoring. He was lying in the hallway at that time, although in the dark she could not see him clearly. This, it appears, was not unusual and she was later to say that she often found him sleeping off the effects of an alcohol binge. It appears that the last time Sarah Lewin went back to her house on the night of Christmas Eve was between 11 p.m. and midnight and on that occasion her husband was still lying in the hallway. She told a neighbour who was with her that he would soon wake up and would make his way to bed. As a result of subsequent events that evening Sarah's movements were to be closely scrutinised. As we shall see, she was on the move quite a lot on that Christmas Eve and would be asked to account for her whereabouts until 4 a.m. on Christmas morning when she went to bed at a neighbour's house.

About 10 a.m. on Christmas morning, John Taubman was passing the front door of the Lewin house when he heard what sounded like 'a low moan'. He tried the door, found it was open and went into the hallway. There he saw Charles Lewin lying on the floor and when he asked him what was the matter he received no reply. Lewin was unconscious and fully clothed. Taubman saw that his waistcoat appeared to have been pulled up over his head and then back down again so that it was tight across his chest. He saw that there was a lot of blood, both on the floor where Lewin lay and also on the walls nearby. Also on the floor he noticed a table fork, a small piece of iron like a small poker, and a paving stone. In addition he noticed that the back door was partly open. Taubman then went to the house of William Gelling, a neighbour, who was having his breakfast at that time. The pair went back to Lewin's house and Gelling was later to say that although he was unconscious, the leg and arm on one side of Lewin's body were moving 'convulsively'. Other neighbours soon appeared on the scene and a doctor was summoned. Dr Jones then arrived and ordered that Lewin be put to bed and advised that 'his temples should be kept wet with vinegar'. Shortly after Lewin had been found unconscious, word reached his wife Sarah, who was still asleep at the neighbour's house just after 10 a.m.

Charles Lewin died at about 3 p.m. on Christmas Day and an inquest into the circumstances surrounding his death opened before J. M. Jeffcott, Coroner of Inquests for the Castletown district, the following day.

Willliam Gelling was the first witness to be heard. Gelling said he had known Charles Lewin, who lived in Queen Street in Castletown. He had seen him on the evening of 24 December on a stone bridge in the town and he was quite sober at that time. The next time he saw him was on Christmas morning when he had been summoned by John Taubman to go to Lewin's house. Gelling described the convulsive movements on one side of Lewin's body when he had seen him and said there was a large quantity of blood lying underneath him. He then helped carry the body into the kitchen just before Dr Jones arrived with a police officer. The three men subsequently carried Lewin upstairs and put him to bed, after which Dr Garrett arrived. Gelling described seeing a paving stone lying beside one of Lewin's legs and he also noticed the table fork and small piece of iron resembling a small poker, on the floor beside Lewin. He saw Lewin's wife enter the house just before he left.

Elizabeth Carr told the inquiry that she also knew Charles Lewin and had seen him on Christmas Eve about 10.30 p.m. when he was going towards the marketplace as if he was returning home. The inquiry was then adjourned until the Wednesday at 11 a.m. so the doctors could make a post-mortem examination of the body.

In order to try and ascertain the movements of Charles Lewin that night and also those of his wife, Sarah, several witnesses were called who had seen the pair at various places that evening. Wayne Carroll said he had seen Lewin on Christmas Eve in the marketplace opposite the barracks when Lewin had asked Carroll if he wanted to go for a pint of beer with him. He said he could not go as he did not have enough money and added that Lewin appeared to be sober at that time.

William Clucas also saw Lewin that same evening in Arbory Street near the Union Hotel at about 9.00 p.m. He told the inquiry that Lewin was well known as a drinker, although he was sober when he had seen him that evening. The next time he saw Lewin was on Christmas Day, about noon, when he was unconscious and lying on the kitchen floor.

George Karran also saw Lewin about 7 p.m. in New Street and in his opinion Lewin had had a few drinks by this time. He said that he 'appeared to be rolling about a good deal'.

John Taubman gave his evidence of finding Lewin lying on the floor on Christmas morning at about 10 a.m. He too told the inquiry that Lewin was known to 'like a drink' and also said he was aware that Lewin and his wife did not get on and frequently argued.

Dr Jones explained he had seen Lewin lying on the kitchen floor at his home and was unconscious at that time. He said he gave instructions that Lewin should be taken upstairs and had ordered 'warm applications to his feet and cold applications to his forehead'.

Dr Garrett told the inquiry that he was a surgeon and practised in Castletown. He described how he had been summoned on Christmas Day at about 11.30 a.m. and saw Charles Lewin lying on his bed. On the right side of his head there was a scalp wound, 1.5 in. above the right ear and approximately 1 in. behind the ear. It was a contused and lacerated wound, he said, and not a clean cut. The wound itself was just over 1 in. long and there was a lot of swelling around it. He said he had not detected any obvious fracture but had noted a bruise on the right temple and on the outer side of the left eye. He also saw a bruise just below the right elbow and noted that there was a small piece of skin missing from the back middle of the right little finger. At the post-mortem examination he later found a fracture beneath the wound and a large amount of blood in the scalp. He also found a blood clot over the left side of the brain and added that the injuries to the head were sufficient to have caused Lewin's death. The doctor said that in his opinion death had resulted from laceration and compression of the brain, caused by a fall or a blow to the head. There were no other marks or injury to the body. However, on the stone found in the hallway close to the body he had found two hair-like fibres. He also said that from the smell of Lewin's breath he believed the man had been drinking and that had the deceased fallen or been struck with the aforementioned stone, it would account for the head wound. The inquiry was then adjourned to the following Tuesday.

When it was re-opened William Corrin gave his evidence. He said he lived in School Lane near the Grammar School in Castletown and next door to Daniel Flynn. He explained that Sarah Lewin was the sister of Daniel and Hugh Flynn. At about 2.30 a.m. on Christmas morning, he had heard a knock at Flynn's door and heard a voice say, 'Here's a Christmas box' or 'I have given a Christmas box'. He said the person who had opened the door had then replied, 'Come in, they'll hear you,' adding that it was a man's voice he had heard in the street and the door had been answered by a woman.

Thomas Shimmin was a police sergeant. He described how he had spoken to Daniel Flynn, Sarah's brother, early on Christmas Eve when Flynn had complained about the abuse his sister was receiving from her husband. He told Shimmin that he had encouraged his sister to tell the police about her husband's mistreatment but she had refused to do so. Flynn told Shimmin he intended to watch Charles Lewin that night and if he saw him mistreating his sister he intended to report him to the police himself. Shimmin said that he saw Hugh Flynn, Daniel's brother, when he had come into Castletown in a car from Douglas at about 2 a.m. on Christmas Day. He got out of the car near the barracks gate and walked down the marketplace towards St Mary's Chapel.

Daniel Flynn's wife Jane said that she lived next door to William Corrin, who had earlier given evidence. She explained that Hugh had been away but had come home that night and it was about 2 a.m. when he arrived. She said her husband had been home when Hugh came in through the back door and shortly after this a man called John Kennaugh had come to the front door. She said there was no mention of a 'Christmas box' on the night of Christmas Eve or the following morning and said that Kennaugh was the only person to come to the front door after midnight. She added that her husband Daniel had come in about 10.00 p.m. and had not gone out again that night.

John Kennaugh confirmed he had gone to Daniel Flynn's house in the early hours of Christmas morning. He told the inquiry that he had been informed that Hugh was coming home from Liverpool that night and had gone to see him. He arrived about 2.30 a.m. and said there was no mention of a 'Christmas box'. He left at about 4 a.m. and went home.

Sarah Lewin then gave evidence. She said she had last seen her husband alive at about 3 p.m. on Christmas Eve. She confirmed that they had not lived on very good terms and mentioned their frequent arguments. She described their last argument in the early hours of Christmas Eve and said she had gone to Mrs Teare's house at that time before returning home and going back to her own bed. She described returning to her house at 5 p.m. when her husband was in bed and although she did not see him, she heard him snoring at that time. She had then gone to Mrs Harper's until about 7.45 p.m. when she went for a drink with James Kelly. She later went to Mrs Wilson's house for about 20 minutes and then returned to her own home, where she found her husband lying in the hallway. She said, 'I did not see him but I heard him snoring. That would be about half-past eight.' She did not go in the house but closed the door again and went into Mrs Letitia Taubman's house across the road. Mrs Taubman and Mrs Gelling were in the house at that time and Sarah Lewin told them that her husband was lying in the lobby. She explained that she had often left him sleeping in the kitchen or sometimes in the lobby or the stable when he was intoxicated. She said she then went to Mrs Harper's where she stayed until about 11.00 p.m. before returning to Queen Street again. After this she called to see Mrs Teare, where she stayed for about 15 minutes. When she left there she met Mrs Crowe and went with her to look for her husband. She later returned to Mrs Harper's house at about midnight and stayed there until about 2 a.m. when she went with Mrs Paviour to Geoff Clark's pub, the Liverpool Arms, on a message and had had a drink there. Mrs Paviour had returned to the Harper house with Sarah Lewin around 3 a.m. and had more drinks there until about 3.30 a.m. when she went to Miss Curphey's house. There Sarah Lewin lay on the sofa for a while before going to bed. She said Miss Curphey and Mrs Harper had helped her up to bed around 4 a.m. The next thing she knew it was 10 a.m. on Christmas morning and she was told that her husband was ill. She then went home and saw her husband lying on the bed unconscious. She told the inquest, 'I am quite unable to think how my husband could have come by the injuries from which he died. I cannot think of whether he met with foul play or whether it was an accident that had caused them.'

George Callister said that he remembered seeing Charles Lewin in Arbory Street, Castletown, on Christmas Eve, at about 10.15 p.m. and that Charles had been singing at that time and did not seem to be 'quite sober'. The inquest was again adjourned to the following morning, Thursday, 6 January.

Eleanor Gale, a servant to Dr Jones who had earlier given evidence, said that on the previous Friday, Christmas Eve, she had gone to Cosnahan's at about 8.30 p.m. for a jug of beer. Charles Lewin was in the hall of the pub when she arrived, in the company of William Senior and Pat Gallagher. William Senior, however, in his evidence, said he did not recall being in Cosnahan's that evening although he remembered seeing Eleanor Gale there with Sarah Lewin on the Thursday night at about 9.30 p.m.

Ann Kerruish gave some interesting evidence to the inquiry. She explained that she lived in Queen Street opposite the Lewin house where she had gone to borrow a tin between 5 and 6 p.m. on Christmas Eve. When she opened the front door she heard a noise in the entry 'like a struggle of some kind'. She said the back door was open and she saw the body of a man lying near it. She thought she heard a footstep in the yard but added that may have been the dog. She called but received no answer. She thought it was Charles Lewin lying drunk on the floor. Later, around 2.00 a.m. on Christmas morning, she claimed she heard Sarah Lewin in the street crying and saying, 'My God, what am I to do?'

Sarah Lewin was recalled to explain the presence of the stone in the hallway of her house. She said it had been there for about two months and was used to keep the door closed and sometimes for keeping it open. The fork found in the lobby had been used for fastening the front door and the small poker for fastening the back door. On Christmas Day after she had returned home to find her husband lying injured, she explained that she had asked James Kelly if he would clean up the blood in the hall and whitewash the walls, which were also blood splattered. Her brother, Hugh, had told Kelly to leave the situation as it was. She again repeated her assertion that she did not know how her husband had died. She said that she never threw the stone at him nor did she strike him with it.

Letitia Taubman, the wife of John Taubman, said that she lived in Queen Street near the Lewin house. Sarah Lewin had been in her house twice on Christmas Eve, the first time at 3 p.m. and the second just after 9 p.m. On the second occasion she was accompanied by Mrs Gelling and said that she had earlier found Charlie lying in the entry. She and Mrs Gelling had then tried to persuade Sarah to go back to her own house but she said she intended to spend the night at Mrs Harper's as she was afraid to go home and spend the night with her husband.

Ann Curphey said she lived with Mrs Harper and remembered the night of

Christmas Eve. There were several people in the house that night and amongst these were Mrs Lewin and Mrs Paviour. At around 4 a.m. she had asked Mrs Harper to help her get Sarah Lewin to bed as 'she was tipsy'.

Margaret Crellin said she had gone to Mrs Harper's on Christmas morning to tell Mrs Lewin that her husband was very ill. At that time Sarah Lewin was in the bedroom. Margaret Crellin told Sarah that her husband was dying.

The inquiry was adjourned until 11 a.m. on the following Monday.

Further information concerning the case was given in the *Manx Sun* newspaper on 15 January 1876. 'Some time during Christmas week,' the article explained,

> a sheep belonging to J.N. Jeffcott was stolen from a field near the gas works in Castletown. Parts of this sheep were found in the field, including a leg. On Thursday, 30 December some police officers accompanied by the Coroner, Mr Martin, had made a search for the rest of the sheep in some houses in Queen Street. When they were opposite the house where the Lewins lived they spoke to Mrs Teare who lived there, and it appeared to them that she was anxious that they should leave. Mr Martin suspected something was wrong and entered her house where he found nearly the whole carcass of a sheep, which had been roughly cut up. Mrs Teare was then arrested and taken to the police station and James Kelly, who lodged with her, was also arrested. The following day, New Year's Eve, they were brought before magistrates and remanded until Monday, 3 January when they were committed for trial for sheep stealing.

The article went on to say that there had been widespread disquiet about the fact that the main witnesses in the case of Charles Lewin had been allowed to listen to each other's evidence during the early stages of the hearing. The article continued:

> The result has been that one tale has been told by them all. [. . .] The only evidence that has given anything like a clue to the mystery, has been that given by Teare and Kelly, who on account of the charge against them, were kept from each other and from the rest of the witnesses. Teare from her own evidence, shows that she was a particular friend of Mrs Lewin's; and the question arises have the cases any connection with each other? Had Lewin any secret which their quarrelling would endanger?

At the resumed inquest on Monday, 10 January, Catherine Teare, a neighbour of the Lewins, gave evidence. She was aware that there was bad feeling between Charles and Sarah Lewin and said that Sarah had often sought protection in her house because of this. On Christmas Eve Mrs Lewin had been to her house several times and had also said on numerous occasions that day that she was going to the police about her husband. She had told Mrs Teare that her husband was spending all their money on drink and not giving any to herself and the children. A few weeks earlier Sarah had come to Mrs Teare's house with a stone, saying that she was going to hit her husband, Charles, with it. She had later thrown it into Mrs Teare's back yard.

On Christmas Eve, Mrs Teare called at Mrs Harper's house just after 7.00 p.m., where she saw Sarah Lewin. On Christmas Day Sarah told her that she had been in her own house, getting some clothes for the children after 11.00 p.m. the previous night – when she had found her husband asleep in the entrance. She continued that a few weeks earlier she had seen Charles Lewin unconscious and having a fit in his house. He had been drunk prior to this and she had helped to carry him into the kitchen. On Christmas afternoon at about 3.00 p.m. she said she went to the Lewin house and Sarah was in the bedroom where her husband was lying unconscious on the bed. She ended by saying that she had heard Sarah Lewin saying on several occasions that she wished her husband was dead.

James Kelly explained that he lived with Mrs Teare in Queen Street. About two weeks before Christmas he had gone to the Lewin house at about 10 p.m. one night. A few minutes later, Sarah Lewin, who had been poking the fire, suddenly threw the poker at Charles, hitting him on the side of the face. Kelly noticed the next day that Charles had a black eye as a result. He also remembered Sarah Lewin arriving at Mrs Teare's house at about 2 a.m. on Christmas Eve, saying her husband had been ill-treating her. Kelly added that he had been for a drink with Sarah later on Christmas Eve, at about 7.30 p.m. He also saw her at Mrs Harper's at about 11 p.m. He remembered Sarah asking him to whitewash the walls close to where Charles had fallen. She explained she did not want neighbours to see the blood. However, Sarah's brother, Hugh Flynn, said he was not to do this. He then recalled Charles Lewin having a fit two or three weeks earlier and told how he had also heard Sarah say she wished her husband was dead.

Elizabeth Harper then gave her evidence. She said that on Christmas Eve Sarah had left her house at about 11 p.m. saying she was going up to the station as she knew her brother was returning to Castletown by a special train. Her little girl had asked Sarah to go and get her clean clothes. Sarah returned after midnight and explained that she had gone back home, where her husband was lying drunk in the entrance. Elizabeth Harper remembered on Christmas morning that the little girl had come to her house to say that her father was very ill. Mrs Harper then went up to wake Sarah, who did not appear to take much notice. Instead she said her arm was very sore and she could hardly lift it. Mrs Crellin called at the house half an hour later and had also gone upstairs to tell Sarah that her husband was very ill.

Sarah Lewin, sister of Charles Lewin, said that she last saw her brother around 3.15 p.m. on Christmas Eve, at which time he was sober and told his sister of his wife's behaviour, adding that she had struck him with a poker and given him a black eye. He also said that his wife had hit him on the back of the head with a stone and that it was still sore. If it was not for his children, he had told her, he would have left her long ago.

Hugh Flynn, Sarah Lewin's brother, explained that he had been off the Island for a week or ten days but had returned to Castletown at about 2.00 a.m. on Christmas morning. He went straight from Douglas to his brother's house in Castletown where he sat up talking until about 4.00 a.m. He remembered Kennaugh coming in shortly after he had arrived but did not remember anything said about a 'Christmas box'. The first he heard about Charles Lewin being injured was from his brother, Daniel, at about 10.30 a.m. on Christmas morning. He at once went over to the Lewin house and saw Charles in bed, being examined by Dr Jones. He also told James Kelly not to whitewash the walls. He concluded by saying that in his opinion Charles Lewin may have been injured by falling downstairs.

Hugh Flynn's brother, Daniel, also addressed the inquiry. He remembered the conversation he had had with Sergeant Shimmin in the marketplace on Christmas Eve. He told the police officer he was concerned about his sister's ill-treatment. He had been out on the evening of Christmas Eve but got home about 10.00 p.m. and did not go out again until 11 a.m. on Christmas morning when Mrs Gelling came to say that Charles Lewin had been found unconscious. He had called upstairs to his brother Hugh, who then came down and the pair went over to Lewin's house.

Following the adjournment of the inquest until Wednesday, 19 January, Sarah Lewin was arrested on suspicion of having caused the death of her husband. On Thursday, 13 January she was brought before a court and charged with having caused the death of Charles Lewin. That case was adjourned until the following Thursday.

On 19 January the Coroner's inquest resumed. Margaret Gelling said she was in Mrs Taubman's house in Queen Street on the night of Christmas Eve, about 9 p.m., when Sarah Lewin arrived. They had a drink and Sarah said her husband would not 'have a cart and horse next week'. She did not say what she meant by this.

Dr Garrett explained the position of the waistcoat on Charles Lewin when he was found. He said he did not think it had been pulled over his head by Charles himself. His reason for saying this was that if his hands had gone up by his head, they should have had blood on them, which was not the case. He described an operation he had performed on Charles Lewin in which he had removed a small part of the skull to relieve the pressure on the brain. However, this had been unsuccessful in saving his life.

Dr Clague said that in his opinion the skull fracture could have been produced by a fall down the stairs in Lewin's house. He had witnessed the operation Dr Garrett had performed and explained that it was clearly the last chance of saving Lewin's life. Dr Clague thought that Lewin's wounds could be explained by a fall downstairs.

During this resumed inquest Sarah Lewin was in custody, Mr J. Fred Gill was watching the case on behalf of the Police Authority, and Mr Kelly and Mr Claude Cannell were watching it on behalf of Sarah Lewin.

Mr Gill summarised the case and urged the jury to return a verdict to the effect that Sarah Lewin was somehow involved in the death of her husband. Mrs Lewin's lawyers said there was not sufficient evidence for this and asked the jury to acquit her. The following day, the Coroner, Mr Jeffcott, summed up for the jury. He went through the evidence and carefully followed in detail the movements of Sarah Lewin on the night of Christmas Eve and early hours of Christmas Day. After praising the police for their work, the jury retired for an hour before returning a verdict that Charles Lewin had died from a wound in the head and they were of the opinion that such a wound was caused by violence from some person or persons to the jury unknown. The jurors were further of the opinion that the conduct of Sarah Lewin, wife of the deceased, in leaving her husband in the lobby, was censurable.

Sarah Lewin was further remanded on Thursday morning until the following Tuesday and was taken back to Castle Rushen Gaol.

On Tuesday, 25 January, Sarah Lewin was brought before magistrates on the charge of being concerned in causing the death of her husband. Mr Laughton and Mr Cannell watched the case on her behalf. The evidence heard at the inquest was repeated by the same witnesses. At the end of the hearing Mr Laughton said that there was insufficient evidence to bring the case before a jury to ask for a conviction. He added it was a waste of time to send the case for trial as there was no evidence whatsoever of a struggle between Lewin and his wife on that evening and there was no blood on her clothes. The facts of the case were consistent with an accident and he concluded by asking the court to give the prisoner the benefit of any doubt which might exist in connection with the case. After about 20 minutes of deliberation the magistrates, W. E. Stephenson, Lieutenant-Colonel Cary and Captain M.T. Quayle returned to say they felt there was insufficient evidence to justify them in sending the prisoner for trial. They then ordered Sarah Lewin's discharge and she was freed.

To this day her husband's death remains a mystery.

17

EDWIN WILMOT (1864)

Mr A. N. Laughton had been a lawyer and High Bailiff on the Isle of Man. In 1916 his son published a book about his father's memoirs entitled *High Bailiff Laughton's Reminiscences*. In Chapter 18 of that book his father describes a case in which he had acted as the advocate for the defence. That case involved a man called Patrick Gallagher, who was charged in connection with the death of Edwin Wilmot. In the book Laughton describes how he had known Gallagher when Gallagher had been an errand boy in an office where Laughton worked as a student. He describes the Gallagher he knew as 'a great favourite with us, being obliging, good tempered and thoroughly dependable. He had left the office some years before and subsequently had a hard life of it as a job car driver [. . .] he was [. . .] a sober, civil, hard working, careful chap'. It is clear from these comments that Laughton had great affection for Patrick Gallagher.

By 1864 Gallagher had long since left the office where he had earlier known Laughton and now had a horse-drawn coach and made a living taking passengers between Douglas and Ramsey. He also ran the Albert public house near the marketplace in Douglas. It seems that Gallagher had slowly built up his coach business but problems began when a rival group also started to take people on the same route. As Laughton wrote:

> This was his ruin. The opposition coach and horses were superior in every way and travelled faster; moreover by reducing the fares by one half, it was hoped to run their rival off the road in a week or two. This indeed they very soon did.

This other coach was known as 'Smyth's Coach' and was owned by a Mr Smale. Edwin Wilmot worked for Smale as a 'touter'. It appears that Wilmot's job was to encourage people to ride on Smyth's Coach. It was generally known that there was much jealousy and bad feeling between Gallagher and those working on the other coach.

On Saturday, 10 December 1864 both coaches set off from the marketplace on the quay in Douglas, bound for Ramsey. Although Smyth's Coach carried one passenger that day and quite a lot of luggage, Gallagher had no passengers and only two small parcels to take on the journey. It was later to become clear that the two men, Gallagher and Wilmot, had words before setting off on their trip and after the other coach had overtaken Gallagher's Wilmot had made gestures towards Gallagher, who had appeared unconcerned. It was evident that there was rivalry between Gallagher and the others.

The two coaches had then proceeded on their way through Douglas until the first one reached the bottom of Burnt Mill Hill, now known as Summer Hill. The first coach stopped at the bottom of the hill where Edwin Wilmot jumped off. The coach, driven by a young man called William Kinnish, then continued up the hill. It was estimated that Gallagher's coach was approximately 70 yards behind the first one and soon he approached the spot where Wilmot was waiting.

Several witnesses were later to describe the events of the next few minutes. However, what is clear is that as Gallagher's coach approached the place where Wilmot was standing, Gallagher had gone to the near side of his coach, taken hold of the whip which he was carrying, and struck out at Wilmot's head with the thick end of the whip. Whether the whip actually struck Wilmot or not was to be the subject of much discussion at the subsequent inquest and trial, but it is a fact that Wilmot had then run across to the other side of the road, a distance of approximately 15 yards, before suddenly falling heavily on to a pile of broken stones. Some witnesses were later to say that they thought he was about to pick up one of the stones to throw at Gallagher's coach. People who had seen Wilmot collapse shouted to Gallagher, who had not seen the fall and he then stopped his coach and came to see what had happened. There was blood on Wilmot's face and mouth and he was unconscious. A doctor was sent for and Wilmot was taken to a nearby pub where, after a few minutes, he died. Gallagher made a comment to the effect that he had thought he had killed Wilmot and then returned to his coach and carried on until he reached Laxey.

Whether Gallagher had actually landed a blow with the whip was to be debated at length. However, by the time he reached Laxey he did not have the whip with him. Having borrowed another one in Laxey, he had set off intending to return to Douglas and explain what had happened earlier. In the meantime however, the police had been alerted and Gallagher was taken into custody on his way out of Laxey.

The inquest into the events surrounding the death of Edwin Wilmot was opened that same day on the Saturday evening at Revitt's Hotel in The Crescent, Douglas Promenade, before His Worship the High Bailiff, and a jury of 11. The author of the book mentioned earlier, Mr Laughton, represented the defendant Gallagher. He was assisted by Mr Craigie. Just before the inquest started, Laughton had been to the scene of the incident and looked at the stones on which Wilmot had fallen. He had also looked at the body and seen that there was a wound on the left temple. This was the side on which the whip would have struck Wilmot if it had actually landed and it was also the side on which witnesses had said Wilmot had fallen. It seemed clear to Laughton that either the blow from the whip or the fall onto the stones might have been the cause of Wilmot's death and in the subsequent trial this was to become the crucial point in the case.

The first witness was Thomas Quayle, who was filling a cart with sand at the foot of Burnt Mill Hill at around 10.20 a.m. on the Saturday morning. He had seen two coaches coming along the Crescent Road, the first being driven by Kinnish, the second by Gallagher. When Kinnish's coach reached the bottom of the hill, Quayle reported, Wilmot had got off and Quayle said to Wilmot, 'That was a good team.'

'Yes and there is a good team coming,' Wilmot answered, meaning the team that Gallagher was driving.

Quayle said at this point that Wilmot was standing on the path next to a Miss Tate's house. He had seen no more until he saw Wilmot staggering across the road towards the place where he was working and as he was coming towards him, Wilmot said, 'You've seen that. You've seen that, oh!' Wilmot had then fallen at Quayle's feet but before he fell Gallagher said, 'Keep out of the road then!' Quayle had seen that Gallagher had a whip in his hand. Several people had then come to see what was happening, including Gallagher. Quayle said that Gallagher had wiped blood from Wilmot's ears and face with his handkerchief and had then asked one of the others to help carry Wilmot to the nearby Revitt's Pub. He also said that a doctor should be called. At the hotel Gallagher had asked for a half a glass of brandy, which he had poured into Wilmot's mouth. Gallagher told Quayle that Wilmot had been 'giving him impudence all the way' and added that he had struck him with the point of the whip. Kinnish, the driver of the first coach, said, 'He's done,' to which Gallagher replied, he was 'only in a slumber'. During this time Quayle said that Wilmot had neither spoken nor moved. He said that no one had called to

Gallagher to come back after the fall, as he had seen it himself and had then returned to where Wilmot had fallen. He said he had not heard any words spoken between Gallagher and Wilmot before the blow was struck. If there had been, he added, he would have heard them from where he was standing. The inquest was then adjourned until the following Monday.

It was resumed on the Monday afternoon. By this time word had spread and there were many spectators in the court. Gallagher, who was by this time in custody, was present. The High Bailiff reminded the jury that it was not for them to try Patrick Gallagher on any charge. Their duty was only to find out how Wilmot had died. The High Bailiff then said he would consider the events which had occurred before the two coaches had set off from the marketplace in Douglas.

William Berey then gave his evidence. He said he was a broker in Douglas and had an office on the north quay. He explained that on Saturday the coaches started from the quay opposite his office. He knew that there were two coaches running between Douglas and Ramsey. He said that at about 9.55 a.m. he had heard a commotion outside his office and had gone outside. The two coaches were there and he saw a man abusing Gallagher. The man was not Wilmot, he added. He heard angry words spoken between them but could not make sense of what they were saying. The coaches had then set off and the man who had been arguing with Gallagher had tried to grab hold of Gallagher's horses' heads, shouting out 'whoa, whoa' to make the horses stop. He said that Gallagher had struck at him with his whip.

William Kinnish explained that he was a coach driver employed by Mr Smale. He explained that before the coaches set off there was always a great deal of 'cadging' for passengers. He said that he had been on the quay that Saturday morning and had heard a conversation between Gallagher and Wilmot. Wilmot had said it would take Gallagher's horses a week to get to Ramsey and Gallagher told Wilmot that he had kept his wife and family from starving when he had set up his coaching business, before there was any competition from Smale's coach. Kinnish said he had one passenger when he set off but Gallagher had none. He picked up one more passenger before he reached the Crescent. Gallagher's coach had left first and he had followed immediately after this. He had passed the first coach at Bigwell Street, shortly after leaving the quay and as the coaches passed, Wilmot who was sitting next to him, had said to Gallagher, 'Ah! Ah! Old buck.' He said that nothing else was said to Gallagher and Wilmot was laughing as he said this. As the two coaches passed through Athol Street and then Finch Road, he said there was no conversation and he was not aware of any gestures Wilmot had made towards Gallagher. Just as they turned the corner of St Thomas's Church, Wilmot had again looked back and said 'Ah! Ah! Old buck' again and laughed at Gallagher. Once more Kinnish said he had not seen him make any gestures towards Gallagher and the two coaches then travelled towards the foot of Burnt Mill Hill, where Wilmot had got off the coach. Kinnish said that he had continued further up the hill but had looked back, as he fully expected Wilmot and Gallagher to have words as Gallagher's coach passed. He then described how Gallagher had moved to the near side of the box as he came to the point where Wilmot was standing. He saw Gallagher hit out at Wilmot with the whip and added that the small end of the whip was in Gallagher's hand and the butt end was the part which had struck the blow. Immediately after this he saw Wilmot running across the road with his body bent double and his head 'sideways'. He then fell down at a heap of broken stones. He added that when he saw Wilmot running he had thought he was going to pick up a stone. Kinnish described the whip as being about a yard long and said that he had got off his coach when he had seen Wilmot fall and described how Gallagher had also returned to where Wilmot was lying in the road. Kinnish said he had then sent a cart to go for a doctor and they had taken the injured man to Revitt's. He described how he checked Wilmot's pulse, initially feeling a beat, but after a short time it faded away and Wilmot died. In answer to questions from Mr Craigie, he said that he had never seen Wilmot 'make faces' at Gallagher on the trip to the bottom of Burnt Mill Hill. He said that as they were carrying the injured man to Revitt's, Gallagher told him that he had hit Wilmot with the whip.

Thomas Teare was 14 years old and worked as a guard on Smale's coach. He told the inquiry that after Wilmot had left the coach at the bottom of Burnt Mill Hill, he had sat next to Kinnish, who was driving. He described how he had looked behind and seen Gallagher hit Wilmot on the eyebrow with the whip. He also said he had seen Gallagher shift his position so that he was on the near side of the coach. He had not heard any words spoken between the two men, but after the blow had been delivered, he described how Wilmot had staggered to the other side of the road and fallen down. He had stayed with the horses while Kinnish went to see what had happened. Teare also said he thought Wilmot was about to go and pick up a stone to throw at Gallagher and could not swear that he had seen the blow actually land on Wilmot's head.

John Shimmin, a publican, said that he owned a pub on the way to Laxey called the Halfway House. He reported that on that Saturday Gallagher's coach had stopped at the pub and Gallagher had said to him that he thought he had 'hurt a man on the road'. He said that Gallagher had asked if he could borrow Shimmin's whip, so that he could continue with his journey to Laxey; Shimmin agreed.

Jane Shimmin, the wife of the previous witness, remembered Gallagher coming to their house on the Saturday morning. Gallagher asked her if they had a whip in the house and she called for her husband. She heard Gallagher say that he was afraid he had 'hurt a man coming' and that he would have to go back again. A few minutes later she had asked Gallagher what he had done with his old whip. He had answered that 'it had been broken'.

Hugh McKenna was also near the scene of the incident at the foot of the hill. He described how he had seen Gallagher lash out at Wilmot with the whip, but was unable to say whether or not the whip made contact with him. He felt at the time that it had probably missed him. McKenna described how Wilmot had stood for a few seconds until the coach had passed, before running over to the other side of the road and then falling down. He added, 'I supposed that if he had been struck he would have fallen.' He said that when Wilmot fell it was on to the left side of his face. He thought that Wilmot had had plenty of time to escape the blow.

James Barber said that he was coming down the hill at about 10.30 a.m. on that morning. He had seen the blow given by Gallagher from the box seat with the whip. He could not say for certain whether the whip had struck him or not. After the blow he saw the man put up his hand to his forehead and stagger over to the other side of the road. He too had felt that Wilmot had intended to pick up a stone to retaliate. The inquest was then adjourned to the following day.

The inquiry was resumed on Tuesday, 13 December. Again the Courthouse was crowded with spectators and Maxwell Fleming, a physician and surgeon practising in Douglas, gave his evidence. He said that he had been called to Revitt's public house on the Saturday afternoon at about 3.00 p.m. and there had seen the body of the deceased. He said that he had seen a 'slight contused wound upon the upper part of the margin of the orbit on the left side'. There was also another wound near the ear on the same side and the left ear was bleeding. He described the second wound as more of an abrasion. In the presence of Dr Ring, he described how he had opened the skull. He told how they had found blood over the surface of the brain but had found no trace of a fracture. He said he felt the cause of death was pressure on the brain stem caused by the surrounding blood. The doctor said that in his opinion the wound could have been caused by a blunt instrument such as the butt end of a whip.

Dr Ring confirmed the findings of Dr Fleming. He described how the pair had carried out a post-mortem examination at Revitt's public house. He said they had made three examinations but had been unable to find any base of skull fracture. He agreed that the most likely cause of death was a blow from a blunt instrument and added that if the injury had been caused by a fall onto stones, there would not have been as much blood round the brain.

George Finniman, also known as George Kneale, gave his evidence and described having an altercation with Gallagher before he set off that Saturday morning. He had not heard any conversation between Wilmot and Gallagher, however. As a result of their argument Gallagher had tried to hit Kneale with the butt end of his whip but he had managed to avoid the blow, Finniman explained. He told the inquiry that Wilmot was 46 years of age, had four children and was normally a very quiet, inoffensive man whom Finniman had never seen the worse for drink.

Several witnesses gave evidence of a minor altercation between Gallagher and other men that morning. However, none mentioned that anything serious had happened between Gallagher and Wilmot.

James Crowe was a driver of the coach from Ramsey to Douglas. He remembered stopping at Laxey on the Saturday and had spoken to Gallagher. When he asked him how he was Gallagher said he was 'only middling' and added that he 'had done a job today that had ruined himself forever'.

After a few other witnesses were heard the High Bailiff summarised the case for the jury. He told them he had tried to bring any witness who might be able to help in coming to a decision as to the cause of Wilmot's death. He told the jury of the difference between murder and manslaughter, reminding them that manslaughter was 'the unlawful killing of another without malice, either expressed or implied'. The High Bailiff said it was clear that if a blow had been struck, it must have been done with the butt end of the whip as the narrow end would not have caused such a severe injury. He added it was rather strange that the whip should have disappeared in such a 'mysterious manner'. He said that all efforts made to obtain possession of the whip had been unsuccessful. It was clear that Gallagher had got rid of it between the scene of the incident and arriving at Laxey.

The jury retired to consider their verdict at 5 p.m. and returned at 6.22 p.m. The jury found a verdict of wilful murder against Patrick Gallagher. The result caused a sensation in the court and the prisoner was then removed to the cells beneath the court room. The foreman of the jury said they had found that Wilmot had been killed by a blow wilfully inflicted by Patrick Gallagher and added that the jury wished to express that they could not reduce the verdict to the minor offence of manslaughter. The court was then cleared and Gallagher was later taken to Castle Rushen Gaol.

MANX MURDERS

In an article in the *Mona's Herald* the following week, 21 December 1864, the problem of increasing crime on the Isle of Man was highlighted. The story said that apart from crimes such as drunk and disorderly, petty larceny, robbery, house breaking and highway robbery, there were also the more serious crimes of manslaughter or murder. The writer said that he had known Gallagher for some time and found him to be 'a man of lively activity and energy in his small way, struggling for a livelihood in this cross-grained world'. The article went on to say that there appeared to be a degree of provocation on Wilmot's part. It was clear, said the article, that Gallagher had no intention of killing Wilmot. This was proven by his behaviour, namely that he had come back down the hill after Wilmot had fallen, wiped the blood from Wilmot's face and ear, before assisting in carrying him into the tavern. Gallagher, the article went on, had then got brandy in an attempt to revive Wilmot and had tried to despatch a messenger for a doctor. Gallagher was so distressed about the case that he could not go on to Ramsey with his coach, but had turned back towards Douglas before being arrested by police.

The next stage of the case was an inquiry before an indicting jury. The jury had to ascertain whether there was sufficient evidence to justify Gallagher's committal to stand trial at the next General Gaol Delivery for the wilful murder of Edwin Wilmot. The Acting Attorney General, Mr Adams, appeared for the prosecution and Mr Craigie and Mr Laughton for the prisoner. The court was again packed for the hearing. The evidence given was much the same as at the inquest. The hearing lasted three days and after the jury had retired for 40 minutes they returned to court, indicting the prisoner for manslaughter. Gallagher was then returned to Castle Rushen to await his trial.

It is clear from reading the chapter in Laughton's book that he was determined to win a verdict of 'not guilty' for Gallagher. In the book he writes:

> I felt for Pat as though he were my own personal friend. I had known him so long and liked him so much, and many a good and obliging turn had he done for me, without fee or reward. [. . .] I saw very clearly that to win a verdict of not guilty, I must be able to raise, in the minds of the jury, a reasonable doubt as to whether the blow of the whip was the actual cause of death. If I could do this, then the deemster would direct them to give such reasonable doubt in favour of, and not against, the prisoner.

Laughton went on to describe how he had invited several doctors to a

171

conference with a view to their giving evidence at the trial. He invited Doctors Oliver, Wise, Standhope, Templeman, Speer and Green. The men discussed the case at length and also looked at stones taken from the pile on which Wilmot had fallen. They considered whether the injury was most likely to have been from the blow of a whip or a heavy fall on broken stones. They eventually came to the conclusion that death was caused by the fall upon the stones. The doctors felt that if the whip had made contact it would have rendered Wilmot unconscious. As it was, he had crossed the road before collapsing. Several witnesses had said they felt Wilmot was about to go and pick up a stone when he crossed the road. The doctors felt that a sudden headlong fall against a protruding stone would have been more likely to cause instant death than the blow of a whip.

Gallagher's trial on the charge of manslaughter was held on Friday, 19 May 1865 at the court room in Castle Rushen before the Lieutenant Governor, Sir Henry Lock, two deemsters and the Clerk of the Rolls. Laughton commented that 'I shall not soon forget that memorable day'. He went on, 'I was in court without bite or sup, from 10 a.m. until midnight, when the verdict was given [. . .] I was weeks before I recovered from the effect of it.'

A 12-man jury was sworn in and Mr Adams the Attorney General outlined the case for the Crown. Much of the evidence was as given in the previous inquiries. However James Barber, who stated at the inquest that he had seen Gallagher strike Wilmot and was certain that the whip had struck him, now said, 'I am almost certain that the deceased was struck.'

Dr Fleming gave medical evidence for the prosecution. He said that in his opinion a severe blow on the side of the head with the butt end of a whip could have caused the injury which Wilmot had sustained. Dr Fleming said he could not conceive it possible that the injury could have arisen from a fall upon stones.

In contrast, Dr Wise said that in his opinion a heavy blow from a whip would have caused a skull fracture, which was not present. He also said that if the blow had caused the injury it would have led to unconsciousness. It was clear that this had not been the case as Wilmot had been seen to run across the road after the alleged blow.

Dr Green said that in his opinion the fall was the more likely of the two possible causes of the injury. He also felt that the blow from the whip would have rendered Wilmot unconscious.

Dr Cregeen reported that he felt the cause of death must have been the fall as a blow would have stunned Wilmot immediately. Dr Cregeen also criticised the post-mortem examination as only the head was examined and he felt that the doctors should have looked at the heart, liver and stomach, and carried out a full examination.

Mr Laughton addressed the jury. He said that of all the witnesses examined, not one had seen a blow delivered nor had one heard the sound of the blow. On the contrary, Laughton went on, several witnesses had said they believed the blow had missed. Even if he had been struck, there was no evidence that he was struck on the head. There was also the fact that there was no fracture to the skull which would have been expected if a heavy blow had occurred. There would also have been a considerable wound from the blow and it would have been expected that Wilmot would have been knocked out by the force of it. In fact however, Wilmot had actually spoken and said, 'You've seen that! You've seen that.' The defence lawyer went on to summarise the medical evidence in the case. He told the jury they should not attach any importance to the fact that Gallagher had said he had hit Wilmot and had been heard by one witness to say he had killed him. He said that Gallagher could not have actually seen Wilmot collapse but when he realised that he was unconscious, Gallagher would have assumed he had hit him. He would then have presumed that the blow was the cause of Wilmot's death, even though this may not have been the case. Laughton then went on to say that for the last six months Gallagher had been in Castle Rushen Gaol. He had been separated from his family and had suffered enough already.

One of the deemsters then summed up for the jury. He said they had to decide whether Gallagher had struck Wilmot with the whip. If they felt any reasonable doubt, then they should acquit him. If they found that he had hit him with the whip, was that blow the cause of his death? He told the jury that it was strange the whip had disappeared. If Gallagher did not strike Wilmot, then where was the whip? It was clear to everyone present that Gallagher had disposed of the whip between Douglas and Laxey. The jury retired at 10.30 p.m. They returned at 11.50 p.m. and gave a unanimous verdict of 'not guilty'.

In his book, Laughton describes the return of the jury:

> At length they returned into court, as the Castle clock was striking the hour of midnight. A death-like silence prevailed, although the court was crammed to the very doors. [. . .] [Upon hearing the verdict] There was a tremendous outburst of cheering; and I went over to The George and abundantly made up for my long and anxious fast.

Laughton concluded: 'Pat was far and away more sinned against than sinning.

He survived the trial for many a long year, living in Douglas, where he continued as formally – a sober, hard-working and well-conducted fellow.'

NOTE

It is clear that not everyone felt the same as Laughton about the acquittal of Patrick Gallagher. In an article entitled 'The Acquittal of Patrick Gallagher', the *Manx Sun* on 27 May 1865 said: 'Suspicion, regret and indignation were the feelings which rapidly succeeded each other in the public mind [. . .] [when] the jury had acquitted Patrick Gallagher.' The article continues: '[. . .] indeed it may safely be affirmed that there never was a case brought before the tribunal of this Island in which the verdict of the jury was more disparagingly criticised or more generally condemned.' The article reminded readers that the defendant had admitted 'to almost all of the witnesses' that he struck Wilmot before 'acutely attempting to palliate his conduct by the palpably untrue assertion that he had only struck the man with the point of the whip.' It went on: 'Considering all the circumstances of the case, it is extremely difficult to understand the process of hypocritical reasoning by which this jury arrived at their verdict of acquittal.'

18

SAMUEL STEWART (1869)

The case which follows gives an insight into the horrendous conditions in which some Manx people lived in parts of Douglas 130 years ago. The tragic deaths described were a direct result of the poverty, despair and hopelessness which many who lived in such conditions must have felt. It is not surprising that a lot of people in this position turned to alcohol and often became addicted to it. This certainly played a part in the extremely sad and distressing incident which follows.

In 1869 Margaret Stewart and her husband Samuel had been married for about 23 years. Samuel was often in prison for offences related to his excessive drinking and it seems that on occasion he was also violent towards his wife. The couple had three boys aged 18, 14 and 5 years, although only the youngest lived with them at the time. Their home was one room in a three-storey house in Back Strand Street, Douglas, not far from the sea front. A newspaper of the day described the area where they lived as 'one of the vilest slums in the old districts of the town'. Margaret, carrying her child, would often beg for money. During the summer Samuel would work as a car driver but he was described as a 'loafer' and for some reason often went by the nickname of 'Lucy Long'. On 6 July 1869 he was injured by a horse in an accident, again involving drink, and he was admitted to the hospital in Douglas, where he was to remain for about three weeks.

Prior to this admission he had beaten his wife and she had sworn to leave him. It seems that following this episode and her husband's subsequent hospital admission she had sold everything they owned and then spent the money on alcohol.

The rent for the one room in the house was 1s per week. From the descriptions of the house in the local newspapers of the day, it appears that there were two rooms on each of the three floors and there were several other families living in the house. Margaret and Samuel's room was on the ground floor, on the right as one entered the building. Their neighbours on the same floor were the Maxwells: Patrick, a labourer, and four other members of his family. All five lived and slept in the same small room. Jane Goodwin, separated from her husband and also a heavy drinker, had the room above the Stewarts on the first floor, sharing this with her five children. The other occupied room in the house was on the same floor and this was where Mary Kewley and her two daughters lived. The rooms on the upper floor of the house were unoccupied. Between the entrance hall and Margaret and Samuel Stewart's room there was a huge hole in the wall which was covered by a blanket or rag. Anyone entering the house could, by moving this to one side, see into their room. There was a small window containing several broken panes of glass and the floor of the Stewarts' room was full of holes. Rats would enter the room through these from the cellar below and the ceiling was unplastered, with just the bare joists visible. The walls of the room were also full of holes and by 24 July the only thing in the room was a small heap of straw, every other item including the bed and furniture having been sold. Their neighbour, Patrick Maxwell, had bought some of these. He had paid 1s each for two sheets and a quilt and had given Margaret Stewart four pennies for a small table.

It seems that the money had run out two or three days prior to 24 July and it is probable that Margaret and her son, who was also named Samuel, had nothing to eat or drink during this period. It is possible Margaret may have been suffering the effects of alcohol withdrawal, as she had begun to act quite strangely. On Thursday, 22 July she had gone into Jane Goodwin's room and told her: 'There will be murder committed in this house yet. My house is haunted. It is full of devils.' It seemed to Mrs Goodwin that Margaret was quite depressed at this time and she was quite concerned about her neighbour's mental state.

At 7.00 p.m. on Saturday, 24 July Mrs Goodwin saw Margaret and her son sitting on the straw in the Stewarts' room. Margaret had appeared to be sober at that time. Later that evening at around 10.30 p.m. she had seen the pair again in their room as she passed them on her way out to buy candles. The young boy was lying down next to his mother at this time. At 11.00 p.m. Margaret had gone into Patrick Maxwell's room and spoken to him briefly and he was later to say that she appeared sober to him. Patrick's wife had gone out for an hour or two and had left a shoemaker's knife on a table in their room, next to some bread. Shortly after this Margaret had left their room and Patrick had gone to bed. His door had been open but whilst he was in bed, he was later to say that he had not heard anyone enter the room. However, it later became clear that at some stage Margaret had taken the knife from the table in the Maxwells' room.

Jane Goodwin went to bed at about 12.15 a.m. and a few minutes after this heard what she described as 'three oaths' from Margaret Stewart in the room below her. She also heard what sounded like someone walking upstairs to one of the empty rooms. At around 12.30 a.m. she heard a child cry, 'Oh, Mamma, don't do that!' Initially she did not take much notice but shortly afterwards she heard the same cry again and also the sound of a child struggling in the room beneath her. She shouted down, 'Margaret, don't do that. You're strangling that child and I will look after you.' Mrs Goodwin got out of bed immediately, lit a candle and went to the room of Mrs Kewley who lived in the room opposite. The two women then went upstairs to the two empty rooms as they initially thought that the sound had come from there. When they realised their mistake, they went downstairs to the Stewarts' room. They then looked through the hole in the wall where they were met with an horrific sight. Margaret Stewart was not in the room but the body of her five-year-old son Samuel was lying on the floor, his head in a pool of blood. Mrs Kewley went into the room and found that he was dead. The two women looked around and noticed there was no furniture at all, but they saw Margaret Stewart's bonnet on the straw.

Patrick Maxwell was asleep but was woken up by the commotion after young Samuel's body had been discovered. He had then rushed into the Stewarts' room where he too saw the pitiful sight of the young boy lying dead on the floor, just below the window.

Meanwhile Margaret Stewart had left her house and gone to the nearby shore, taking the knife with her. Daniel Ward, a mason who lived in Strand Street, was on the shore in the early hours of that Sunday morning, about 1 a.m. tending to his boat. He saw Margaret come down to the beach and was about 20 yards away when she looked over and upon seeing him in the boat, turned her back to him. Mr Ward saw her hand moving back and forth about her throat and at that moment his daughter also came to the beach and walked towards Margaret. She then turned to her father and shouted 'Father, Father, this woman has cut her throat.' At this, Margaret ran to the sea and threw herself into the water. Daniel Ward's son then appeared on the scene and managed to drag her out of the sea after a brief struggle.

Police officers were soon at the scene and two doctors from the nearby hospital arrived and tended to Margaret's injuries. When the police found her she was unconscious and they saw that she had cut her own throat, completely severing the windpipe. Dr Weddell confirmed that her son was dead and he too had died from a cut throat. Some of the large blood vessels in her son's neck had been severed, as had his larynx.

John Daugherty lived close to the house where the Stewarts lived. He had heard a scream and ran out and gone to the shore where he found Margaret lying with her throat cut. He then returned and went to her room and saw the child. He had later returned to the beach where he stood on the knife and picked it up and later gave it to one of the police officers. The knife was later shown to Patrick Maxwell, who confirmed it was the one which had been taken from his room earlier. Margaret was then taken to the nearby hospital, the same one where her husband had been a patient for the previous three weeks or so. Later that Sunday morning her husband was released from the hospital. He promptly started drinking again, caused a disturbance and was arrested by police almost immediately and taken into custody.

On the following day, Monday at 9 a.m., the inquest into the death of Samuel Stewart was opened before the High Bailiff and a jury. After viewing the body at the house, the jury adjourned to the Courthouse and various witnesses gave evidence about the awful living conditions in the house. Dr Weddell said there was no doubt about how the young boy had died. Death was caused either by blood getting into his lungs or from blood loss from the terrible wound in his neck.

The High Bailiff summed up the case and said it was clear that alcohol had played a big part in the events of that evening but he added that it was no excuse in a case of this kind. The jury returned a verdict to the effect that the young boy had met his death by having his throat cut by his mother, Margaret Stewart, and 'did further find and say that the said Margaret Stewart did feloniously, wilfully and of her malice aforethought, kill and murder the said Samuel Stewart'.

Meanwhile, Margaret Stewart was being treated in the hospital. A silver tube had been placed into her windpipe for her to breathe through and her general condition initially had been reasonable, despite the blood loss at the time of the injury. However she later deteriorated and died one week after she cut her throat, on Sunday, 1 August. An inquest was held the following day at the hospital in front of Mr Samuel Harris, Coroner for Douglas. Much of the evidence was the same as that given at Samuel's inquest a few days earlier. Dr James Jackson Adair told the inquiry that he was a medical officer at the hospital. Margaret Stewart could not speak because of the injury to her throat and it was difficult to understand her. He said she appeared to be 'in a very low state', adding that this may have been due to blood loss. He reported that the windpipe itself had been completely severed and described the tube which had been inserted into her airway to enable her to breathe. It had been removed occasionally so that it could be cleaned and Margaret herself had sometimes taken it out. The doctor had been called to see her at midday on the previous day and said that at that time she was suffering from 'spasmodic breathing'. The doctor sent for Dr Ring and shortly afterwards Margaret Stewart died. In Adair's opinion cause of death was 'a disease of the lungs produced from the effects of the wounds in her throat'. Dr Ring confirmed Dr Adair's evidence, saying, 'I have no doubt that the deceased died from the difficulty of breathing produced by the wound in the neck and the state of the lungs resulting therefrom.'

The Coroner then summarised the case for the jury and pointed out that the main point for their consideration was the state of mind of Margaret Stewart at the time she had cut her child's throat. The jury, after a short deliberation, gave the following verdict, 'Margaret Stewart died at the hospital in Douglas, on 1st August 1869 from the effects of wounds committed on herself by cutting her own throat with a sharp knife on the night of Saturday, 24 July 1869 and we are of the opinion that at the time she inflicted the said wounds upon herself, she was labouring under temporary insanity'.

An editorial in the *Isle of Man Weekly Times* on Saturday, 31 July 1869 reminded the Manx people of the atrocious conditions in which some people were forced to live. At the time it was written Margaret Stewart was still alive; she died the following day. The article said:

> We scarcely know which feeling should predominate most –
> indignation at this fearful crime of infanticide, or pity, for the poor,
> desperate wretch, who sought vainly to atone with her own blood, for
> the sacrifice of her offspring.

It went on to say that 'it was all very well for a jury to find that she had murdered her child' but the editor of the paper felt that the verdict only 'skims the surface of a revealed depth of misery, wretchedness and woe, which we were fain to believe had no existence in Douglas'. Although Margaret Stewart was technically guilty of murder the article continued, it was clear that 'society and our laws are not free from all blame for this state of things', also adding 'We believe that the public are unaware of the real extent of local misery and wretchedness'. It ended by demanding that action be taken to address the problem of poverty, the real underlying cause of the tragic deaths of Margaret Stewart and her young son, Samuel.

MANX MURDERS

NOTE

A week after the Stewart case an article appeared in the *Isle of Man Times and General Advertiser* on Saturday, 7 August 1869 under the heading 'Horrible Suicide in Strand Street'. Although unrelated to the Stewart case, it nevertheless bears tragic similarities.

Thomas Barden was 'middle aged' and worked as a butcher and a lodging-house keeper at premises in Strand Street, Douglas. His behaviour had recently changed and he was described by several people as 'strange in his manner'. He did not answer questions appropriately, was not sleeping properly and for the previous three nights had not taken off his clothes, wearing the same ones continuously. He had been complaining of a painful arm, caused by an infection, and Dr Wood who had treated him for this was also concerned about his mental state, asking Mr Barden's family to request a doctor at the Lunatic Asylum to see him.

On Friday, 6 August he was working in the shop when he began to serve two women customers. He started by cutting up a lamb, but then, without saying anything and to the horror of the two women, he cut his own throat with the same knife.

Dr Wood was actually on his way to see Barden when, about 1.00 p.m. a police officer asked him to go quickly to the butcher's shop. When he arrived there he found the man dead – the wound had severed all the structures of the neck. He said that death must have been almost instantaneous. The verdict was 'that the deceased committed suicide while in a state of temporary insanity'.

19

JOHN KERMODE (1866)

On Wednesday, 17 January 1866 an article appeared in the *Mona's Herald* newspaper entitled 'Driver of Mail Cart Missing' which follows here as reported.

Last night the mail cart was observed coming into Castletown at the top of the Green without a driver. As the reins were dragging, a man stopped the horse and waited for quarter of an hour, when, no driver coming, he brought the cart with the English mail to the Post Office. An immediate search was made for the driver with lanterns and the wood to Ballasalla carefully examined. It appears that he arrived at the latter place at half past ten and delivered the bag, when he was asked (being a fresh hand) if he had ever been up before, to which he replied 'No', adding that he might not be again. The search was renewed again but nothing had been heard of him up to this (Wednesday) morning. His name is John Kermode and he has a wife and four children resident in Douglas, where he has been employed in driving cars. The reason of his driving on this occasion was owing to its being an extra mail.

This seemingly trivial account, hidden away in the small-print of the newspaper, was the first indication of a case which was to become one of the great Manx murder mysteries of all time.

In 1866 mail was transported around the Island by horse-drawn cart. The normal routine both for mail originating on the Island and that arriving by steamer from England, would be for it to be taken to the Post Office in Athol Street, Douglas. The mail destined for Castletown would then be taken by cart, leaving Douglas at around 5.15 p.m.

On Tuesday, 16 January 1866, the steamer from Liverpool was late and did not arrive in Douglas until around 8.30 p.m. The local mail had already been taken to Castletown and it was decided that an extra run would be made to take the English mail to Castletown that evening. The contractor for the mail cart was, at that time, a Mr William Quiggin and it would have been his responsibility to organise a driver to deliver the mail.

John Kermode was about 60 years old, married with four grown-up children and was described as a family man who worked hard, did not drink and was quiet and cheerful. For many years he had been a 'car driver' (i.e. horse-drawn cart driver) working for a man called Wesley Bell. On that Tuesday evening he was asked by Quiggin if he would deliver the late mail to Castletown and after preparing his horse and cart he collected three bags of mail from the Post Office in Athol Street. There he spoke to John Kerruish and told him that he was not familiar with the Post Office in Ballasalla, where he was to deliver mail on his way to Castletown. Later that evening he dropped off a bag of mail at Kirk Santon Post Office before travelling to Ballasalla, about a mile and a half from Castletown. The horse-drawn cart, still with the bag of mail for Castletown in it but without the driver, was later found on the road between Ballasalla and Castletown. The man who found it waited for a while and then, with no sign of the driver, he took the horse and cart to the Castletown Post Office and informed the Post Master of the incident. It was clear that something had happened to John Kermode and a search of the area began. It was not until the following afternoon that Kermode's body was found lying face down in a river about quarter of a mile to the west of the main Ballasalla to Castletown road.

Two days later, on Friday 19 January, an inquest was held in Castletown by the Coroner-General for Inquests, Mr William Christian of Andreas. A medical witness, Dr John Jones of Castletown, said that in his opinion John Kermode had died as a result of drowning. When the Coroner released the body for burial, a nephew of Kermode who came to collect it after the inquest found that there was an injury to his uncle's head and when word of this reached the High Bailiff a second inquest was arranged which commenced at 7 p.m. the following day, Saturday, 20 January, again before the Coroner-General of Castletown.

A jury of ten were sworn in and the Coroner opened the proceedings. An article had appeared in the *Manx Sun* newspaper describing the very unusual circumstances of the case, reporting the doctor's evidence at the first inquest and the subsequent finding by Kermode's nephew of the head injury. The Coroner said that this 'had created alarm in the public mind'. This, he said, was enough reason to summon the jury and open a second inquest at so late an hour. Since the first inquest on the previous day further evidence had come to light. This, he went on, had justified him in re-opening the inquiry although this was clearly 'a most unusual state of affairs'. It was clear to him that the inquest would not be concluded that evening but he hoped to have sufficient evidence to justify him issuing his warrant for the interment of the body. The Coroner said the whole affair was 'shrouded in mystery' and he hoped that at the conclusion of the second inquest they would be able to ascertain the cause of John Kermode's death.

John Kerruish was the first witness to give evidence. He was one of the Douglas letter carriers and had known Kermode for a number of years. He described how the mail had arrived late on that Tuesday evening and how Kermode had agreed to take it to Kirk Santon, Ballasalla and Castletown. He said that the steamer from Liverpool had been late and the mail had not arrived at the Athol Street Post Office until about 9 p.m. Shortly after this Kermode arrived at the Post Office and Kerruish had given him the mail bags. On the Wednesday morning Kerruish said he heard that Kermode had not arrived at his destination and it was feared that something had happened to him. He later set off for Castletown with another letter carrier and ascertained that Kermode had dropped off mail at both Kirk Santon Post Office and Ballasalla, before setting off for Castletown. When Kerruish went to Castletown he found that Kermode had still not been found and he had gone to search for him, looking round the roads and fields near King William's College on the outskirts of Castletown. Kerruish went on to describe how he had heard of the discovery of Kermode's body. He said that a Mrs Shipley formerly had the contract for the mail carts, but Quiggin was the present contractor. Quiggin continued to employ the same drivers although the usual driver for the Douglas to Castletown route was a new one, a man called John Kneen. The former driver, Hugh Flynn from Castletown, had been dismissed. On that Tuesday evening Kerruish had asked Quiggin who was going to drive and had been told that John Kermode would do the trip. He said he was not aware of any ill-feeling which had arisen from the dismissal of Flynn, neither was he aware of any ill-feeling between Flynn and John Kermode. Kerruish understood that Flynn had also put in a tender for the contract of the mail, and had heard that his estimate was next in amount to Quiggin's (it therefore seems that Flynn had just missed out on the contract). Kerruish ended his evidence by saying that he drove Kermode's cart back to Douglas and it had not been repaired or had anything done since its return.

Dr Percy Ring then gave evidence, stating he had first seen the body that morning at 10.30 a.m., when it was lying in a coffin. He had examined the body closely and the only injury he discovered was a wound approximately three quarters of an inch long on the back of the head, towards the right side. When he removed the skull he found blood around the brain on the right side. The brain itself, however, was quite healthy and there was no blood in the substance of it. The head injury might have been caused by a fall or something like a kick from a horse. The Coroner asked Dr Ring if, in his opinion, it would have been possible for Kermode to have walked some distance after receiving the head injury. The doctor replied that if the bleeding had been slow it might have been possible for him to have walked some distance before collapsing. The Coroner then asked, 'Was it a blow that killed him or was he drowned?' Dr Ring admitted that he could not be certain of the cause of death. The Coroner then said, 'Is there any way of ascertaining whether or not the deceased was put in the water alive?' Dr Ring said that without a further post-mortem examination he could not come to any positive decision but added that his current opinion was that the man had not drowned. The doctor felt that the blood around the brain was sufficient to cause the man's death. There had been blood in the scalp itself and inside the bone on the surface of the brain.

Kermode's hat was then examined and Dr Ring said there were two marks or tears on the inside which would correspond with the head wound. Dr Ring said a blow from a stick with a sharp edge to it might have caused the injury, or it could possibly have resulted from a stone which had been thrown. In answer to a juror's question, the doctor said that if it had resulted from a fall he would have to have fallen backwards to produce the wound in the position in which they found it.

Dr Samuel Laird was next in the witness box. He was present when Dr Ring had carried out the post-mortem examination and said that he found a swelling about the size of a small orange over the right side of the back of the head. He said that the 'incised wound' had penetrated the bone and he felt that it could have been caused by a fall, a blow, or the kick of a horse. He also felt that death was not due to drowning. At this point the Coroner said he felt it was necessary that a further post-mortem examination be undertaken in order to try and ascertain whether Kermode was dead or alive when he went into the water. It was agreed that Dr Ring would perform this at 10 a.m. the following morning.

Daniel Flynn was then called. He said he lived in Castletown and was there on the Tuesday. He had seen Kermode driving cars in the past and also saw Kermode's body the previous day. He explained that his son, Hugh, had tendered for the contract for the mail. He had been with Hugh on the Tuesday and they had arrived home about 6 p.m. Flynn left his son for a while but returned home later and went out and met William Quayle in the marketplace around 8 p.m. The pair had then gone to Chartres' public house where they had two half glasses of rum, after which Flynn returned home and said he did not go out again that night. He arrived home about 10.00 p.m. and his son was in the house when he got in. His son had taken off his boots and then gone to bed. The first he had heard about the mail cart arriving without the driver was the following morning.

Flynn was asked by the Coroner if there was any bad feeling between either himself or his son and Mr Quiggin. He replied 'Not that I know of.' He then went on to say that his son, Hugh, had left the Island on the previous morning, Friday 19 January. Hugh had gone to England but had returned the following day, Saturday, on the evening steamer.

Hugh Flynn then addressed the jury. He said that he lived with his father at Castletown and was the driver of the mail cart before John Kneen was appointed. He admitted he had been discharged by Mr Quiggin but said there was no bad feeling involved. He explained that Quiggin had discovered he was carrying passengers and felt this was the reason he had lost his job. He said he had seen John Kermode before but had never seen him drive the mail cart. He had seen him drive 'a sociable' for Wesley Bell. He had, he explained, tendered for the contract for the carrying of the mails but his tender had not been accepted. He was currently involved in 'pig dealing'. He left home about 10 a.m. with his father on the Tuesday morning and had been out in the fields, returning that evening. He was with his father until about 6 p.m., attended to his horse and had his tea. He then went out some time between 7 and 7.30 p.m. towards the marketplace. He returned home about 8.30 p.m. He remembered his father came in around this time and he himself went out to the house of Mrs Edwards who, he explained, lived opposite his father). He stayed there until about 10 p.m. and then returned home. He removed his boots and sat at the table for a while and had not gone out again that night The first he had heard about the missing mailman was the following morning at breakfast. He said he could throw no light on the affair and knew nothing about how John Kermode had received his wounds. Hugh Flynn told the jury he had gone to Liverpool on Friday evening. In reply to a question from a juror he said that he had driven the mail cart for about two years and enjoyed the job, adding that his wages had been about 10s a week.

After another witness gave unimportant evidence, the Coroner said he would adjourn the inquest. Before the jury sat again he said they should examine the mail cart which Kermode had driven that evening, as there was some damage to it which he wanted them to see. He told them that it seemed clear that there was an inadequate examination of Kermode's body by the doctor in Castletown after its discovery, adding that if the examination had been satisfactory there would have been no necessity for the inquiry which they were holding.

Before adjourning he took evidence from Edward Moore, the driver of the Castletown coach. Moore said he had known Kermode and had last seen him alive on the previous Monday. He had seen the body at 3.10 p.m. on the afternoon of Wednesday, after it had been discovered shortly before this by another man. The place where Kermode's body was found was called 'The Claddagh', towards the Castletown side of the College Road and he was found lying face down in the river. The water was quite shallow at that point and just about covered the body. Kermode was fully clothed, still with his cap on, and his arms were folded underneath his chest. Moore explained how the body was fully stretched out and told the court he saw no sign of any blood. He also told how Kermode's body was then placed on a gate before several men carried it to Castletown. He added that he was aware that the foot-board of the mail cart was broken and wondered whether this had been done by someone trying to get into the cart.

The Coroner then adjourned the court, urging any members of the public who had information that may assist in the inquiry to come forward. The inquiry was adjourned until the following Tuesday at 2 p.m. – the proceedings had lasted four hours and ended at 11 p.m. that night. A large crowd attended the funeral of John Kermode at Kirk Braddan cemetery the following afternoon.

The inquest resumed on Tuesday, 23 January at the Douglas Courthouse. Stephen Fargher was the first witness. He said he was coming from Castletown on that Tuesday evening on his way home to Ballasalla at around 10.30 p.m. After he had passed the College Road on the outskirts of Castletown he saw the mail cart pass by but did not take any particular notice of it. Shortly after this he heard some voices, perhaps one or two, from the other side of the road and then he saw a man. The man's legs were inside the field and he was sitting facing away from the road on the grass 'hedge'. Fargher explained that it was a stormy night and he could not get a good view of the man but he described how he had shouted to him to enquire what he was doing there at that hour of the night. The man had mumbled something to himself and then said 'It's none of your business' or 'It's no business of yours' or words to that effect. Fargher said the man 'stammered a good deal' and it was his impression that he was talking to someone in the field. Just after this he heard someone approaching and found that it was Mr William Quarrie of Ballshick. Fargher told Quarrie that he had just seen a man and felt there was something wrong. He wondered whether the man had been stealing sheep. He went across the road to the point where he had seen the man sitting and looked over the fence into the field but saw no one. He may have seen a shadowy figure going off through the field in the direction of the river but could not be certain in the dark.

Mr James Mylchreest from Castletown said that he was returning from Douglas on the Tuesday evening when he passed two men who looked like farm labourers on the west side of the Ballasalla Hill. He said he thought one of them was 'tipsy' and remarked to his companion, Mr Bradshaw, that they were rather suspicious looking. Both men were wearing caps and one was quite tall. The other was of average build and the men had said something but Mylchreest had not heard what it was.

Dr Ring said that he had made a post-mortem examination of John Kermode along with Dr Laird. As a result of this he said he had no doubt that death was due to the brain injury. The doctors found about half a pint of water in Kermode's stomach and Dr Ring said that in his opinion Kermode was probably still alive when he went into the water. He added that he did not think it possible for Kermode to have sustained the injury on the road and then walked all the way to the river, which he understood to be about quarter of a mile.

Dr Laird also gave evidence. He said they had found no water in the lungs and he agreed with Dr Ring that Kermode had been alive when he went into the water. The reason for this, he explained to the jury, was that he felt Kermode had swallowed water before dying. He added that if Kermode had not actively swallowed the water it would not have gone into his stomach.

Dr Jones of Castletown was then called to give his evidence. He said that he had previously been examined as a witness at the first inquest on the Friday and gave medical evidence then as to the cause of death. He claimed to have found the wound on the posterior part of the head before he gave his evidence. He said that in his opinion the body presented the appearance of belonging to a person who had died of drowning or suffocation. The Coroner asked him, 'Was the evidence you gave on that occasion as follows? "I have this day examined the body, and I find no marks of violence on it."' The Coroner said that this had been reported in one of the newspapers. Dr Jones said that he was not aware of what had been written in the papers and he claimed that Kermode's cap was off when he had examined him. The Coroner asked him, 'Are you quite certain the cap was off when you examined the body?' Dr Jones insisted that it was. He said he had later seen the body when Matthias Caine was there and added that in his opinion the cause of death was drowning. He told the Coroner that he had put his finger into the scalp wound and had felt the skull and could detect no fracture. Dr Jones was asked by the Coroner if he was perfectly sober that evening when he had examined the body. The doctor confirmed that he was. The Coroner insisted on getting to the truth of the matter and said, 'Now, it is stated in the public papers that you deposed at the former inquest as follows: "I have this day examined the body, and I find no marks of violence on it."' The Coroner then asked, 'Is that correct?' Dr Jones replied, 'It is incorrect.'

A newspaper article recounting the inquest in the *Mona's Herald* on 24 January stated that

> he retired from the witness box amid the suppressed laughter of the crowd. Just as he was leaving the court, the Coroner said he had better remain and hear Matthias Caine give his evidence, when he might question him if he thought fit.

Matthias Caine was called next. He explained that he had married John Kermode's niece. He went to Castletown to remove the body and bring it back to Douglas. He arrived about 2.30 p.m. and Dr Jones had told him he had examined the body. The witness said he found that John Kermode's coat was buttoned up and his cap was tied on. He had been told that Dr Jones had been to the door but had not gone inside, nor did he take off the deceased's clothes. Caine said he removed the cap and had found some blood on it. When he took off the cap he discovered the wound to the back of the head and sent for the doctor, who arrived about five or ten minutes later. When Dr Jones arrived Caine told him about the wound. The doctor said 'Where?' and looked surprised. He was then shown the wound and he put his finger into it and said it was 'merely a scratch'. Caine said at this time he had already received the certificate from the Coroner for the burial of John Kermode. He added that Dr Jones looked as if he was 'not completely sober'. Dr Jones had asked Caine if he was a medical man and Caine had answered, 'I am as much a medical man as you when I found the wound.' At this point the Coroner asked Dr Jones if he wished to question Matthias Caine on anything and he replied that he did not. The Coroner remarked on the two widely differing versions of the doctor's evidence, that would appear on record and added that one or the other must be false. Dr Jones then said, 'I suppose, Your Worship, I may go now?' The Coroner replied, 'Yes, you can go and I don't want to see you again.'

Mrs Edwards of Castletown confirmed that Hugh Flynn had been at her house on the Tuesday night until around 11 p.m.

Mr Quarrie, the man who had met Stephen Fargher on the evening in question, also gave evidence. He said that his uncle 'had heard it reported in Douglas that if a certain person came to Castletown on the mail gig that Tuesday night, they would not return again'.

Thomas Chartres an innkeeper in Castletown said that neither Daniel Flynn nor William Quayle were at his house on the Tuesday night. They had been there however on the Monday night. William Quayle confirmed the evidence of Mr Chartres.

Thomas Tyson, a police officer and the postmaster at Ballasalla, said that Kermode had arrived there at 9.40 p.m. on the Tuesday evening and had given him the mail bag. He had asked John Kermode if he had ever driven the mail gig before, to which he replied, 'No and perhaps never will again.' Tyson said he did not think there was anything wrong with the foot-board at that time and Kermode had stood on it as he passed the bag to him. He had then pulled the rug over his legs and driven off towards Castletown. Tyson had later heard that Kermode was missing and he had helped in the search for him. He had also inspected the mail cart at Castletown and found that the foot-board was broken. He had continued in the search the following day.

Thomas Corrin, a fisherman, told the inquest that he was cutting some twigs along the river bank about half a mile from Castletown when he came across the body lying face down in the river on the west side, close to the bank. He added that the river bed there consisted only of mud and there were no stones at that point.

Thomas Corrin explained how he had discovered the mail cart without a driver on the road between Ballasalla and Castletown. He waited for about 15 minutes for the driver to return before driving it into Castletown. He noted that the foot-board was broken. 'After the horse had been put up Mr Kinvig and myself went off to look for the driver. We found a rug near the Folly towards the hedge on the west side of the road. Next we found a rug on the eastward side of the road, further on a bit. The horse was a quiet one, but shied a little at the light. There are no houses between Ballasalla and the Green.'

Sergeant Hollinwraike said that on the Sunday he had gone to where the man had been seen sitting on the hedge by the witness Fargher. He went across the fields to the river where the body was discovered but found no trace of footprints. The hearing was then adjourned until the following week. At the end of a description of the inquest in the *Mona's Herald* 24 January 1866, is the following:

> In order that there might be no doubt as to the evidence given by Dr Jones at the first inquest, we applied at the Clerk of the Rolls' office and obtained a copy; it is as follows:- John Jones, of Castletown, surgeon, being sworn, sayeth: I have this day examined the body of the deceased John Kermode; I found no marks of violence, and I have no doubt that his death was caused by drowning. J JONES, surgeon.

An editorial in the same edition of the *Mona's Herald*, Wednesday, 24 January, read:

> It is a most unfortunate thing that every step taken previously to the second inquest appears to have been characterised with culpable indifference – that is the very mildest way we can put it. The body was found at three o'clock on the Wednesday afternoon; it was well known that the deputy Coroner at Castletown was absent from the Island; the Coroner-General resides remotely at Ramsey and the first he heard of the matter was by a messenger on foot between 11 and 12 o'clock on the Thursday! It was evident that the case was either a suicide or murder, but from the first, murder was suspected; and yet the foot messenger conveyed just this brief announcement – Castletown, January 17 1866 – a body found drowned in the river at Castletown this day at three o'clock.

The article goes on to say it was incredible that instead of the Coroner-General immediately going to Castletown, he had sent the foot messenger back there and ordered an inquest to be held the following afternoon. It was also unbelievable that the police had not been involved early on, so that they could begin looking for footprints and searching in the areas mentioned earlier. The first statement the police heard was Sergeant Hollinwraike's, in which he said that he had gone to make enquiries on the Sunday. The article ends:

> On the other side of the water a notion has got abroad that our insular officials hold to the doctrine of allowing great criminals to transport themselves, as it saves them all trouble, the jurors all loss of time, and

the country some expense! Certainly the proceedings in this case are not likely to cause the English public to entertain a less unfavourable opinion.

The inquest resumed the following Tuesday. The court was packed for the hearing and before witnesses were examined, the Coroner explained that he had received a letter from Daniel Flynn. Flynn told the Coroner that his evidence had been misrepresented in the press and requested that the Coroner put the record straight. He insisted that despite evidence given by other witnesses, he had gone to Chartres' on that Tuesday evening. He then went on to say that 'as you Douglas bigots thought to throw a disdain and a slur upon myself and my son, I demand of Your Worship a fair investigation'.

Dr Ring was the first witness to be called. He described how two spots of blood had been found on the mail cart on the night of the 16th, one of which was behind the seat where the driver would have sat. The doctor and Coroner had removed the two pieces of stained wood and subsequent tests by Dr Ring had proved they were human blood. Dr Thompson from Kirk Michael, had examined the marks and his letter was read out to the court by Dr Ring, in which he said he was unable to state how long the blood had been there.

Henry Wesley Bell, car proprietor, gave his evidence. He explained that Kermode had been in his employ at the time of his death. He went on to explain how he had been contacted by Mr Quiggin to ask if Kermode could deliver the mail that evening. Bell described Kermode as 'a very sober man, not at all excitable and not at all melancholy'. He said that Kermode appeared to be of the same build as Quiggin and anyone coming from behind would 'hardly tell one from the other'.

William Quiggin also gave evidence. He confirmed that he had dismissed Hugh Flynn after he found he had been taking passengers in the mail cart. He told the jury that he personally had never driven any of the mail carts since he obtained the contract. On the evening in question, he said, he never had any intention of driving the cart, nor had he told anyone that he intended to do so. Quiggin said that initially he had asked John Flynn, a cousin of Hugh Flynn, if he could drive the mail cart to Castletown that night. He initially said he would do the job for 1s but ten minutes later he came to tell Quiggin that he would only go if he gave him sixpence more. Quiggin replied that he would go and get one of Wesley Bell's men instead and went to Kermode's house and asked him if he would deliver the mail. He asked Kermode what time he expected to get home and he replied between midnight and 1 a.m. Quiggin heard nothing more of the trip until the following morning, when he was told that the extra mail cart had arrived in Castletown without a driver. He said he sat until about 4 a.m. on the Wednesday waiting for Kermode to return, but had then gone to bed.

Another witness was Henry Gale, who gave a rambling statement about some very violent threats he had heard made by Hugh Flynn against Quiggin. He said it happened about five weeks earlier when Flynn was washing a car in Quiggin's yard. He said Flynn had threatened violence against anyone going on the mail gig to Castletown. It appears that his evidence was very poorly delivered in Court and when asked to identify Hugh Flynn, he was unable to do so.

James Quarrie was again called and said he did not see Daniel Flynn in Castletown on the Tuesday night – 16 January. Daniel Flynn then made several comments regarding his movements on the night in question and requested an adjournment as he wished to call several witnesses to prove where he had been that night. Flynn added that there was a member of the jury who was not to be believed on his oath. The Coroner said he could not allow such comments in his court. Hugh Flynn said he had been told that Kermode's daughter had struck her father's head with a stool that Tuesday morning. The Coroner remarked that there were all sorts of rumours abroad and he had been doing his best to investigate some of them. The inquiry was then adjourned until the following day.

Daniel Flynn had requested that several witnesses be called. John Watterson, a school master from Castletown, said that he had gone to Chartres' public house about 9.45 p.m. on Tuesday, 16 January and had seen Daniel Flynn in the kitchen. He did not see him afterwards but had left a few minutes before 11 p.m. John Kennaugh, a farmer from Castletown, had also been in Chartres' on the Tuesday night about 9.30 p.m. He had seen Daniel Flynn at about 10.55 p.m. in the kitchen. Edward Corlett was an innkeeper in Castletown and said that Daniel Flynn was at his house on the Tuesday night about 10 p.m. and remained there until about 10.50 p.m., when he left. Several other witnesses also said that Flynn had been in the pub that evening.

The Coroner then began his summing up for the jury. He first severely criticised Daniel Flynn for his clear contempt of court the previous day, referring to his claim that one of the jurors was not to be believed. He said that such conduct deserved the strongest condemnation, adding that he would report the case 'in other quarters'.

He went on to summarise the case. Kermode, he said, had left Ballasalla about 10.20 p.m. that Tuesday evening and should have taken about 15 minutes before reaching Castletown. The second rug discovered by the men coming from Castletown was roughly halfway between the Ballasalla Post Office and the Post Office in Castletown, so he would have reached that spot in approximately seven and a half minutes after leaving Ballasalla. The mail cart finally arrived at Castletown Post Office at about 10.55 p.m. and the man who found it had waited for about quarter of an hour before taking it there. Therefore there was, he said, a very short time period unaccounted for – perhaps twelve and a half minutes and it was clear that during this time something had happened to Kermode. He went on to say that, 'His death can be accounted for in only one of three ways. He must have met with an accident; he must have committed suicide, or he must have been murdered.' An accident, he said, was out of the question. He pointed out that the wound on Kermode's head was not consistent with a fall from the cart as there were no other injuries to the body. Also, he went on, if it had been an accident, was it probable that he had 'crossed the fields and climbed two high fences before lying face down in the river and allowing himself to be drowned?' Suicide was also most improbable, he said. He went on to describe the broken left-hand side of the foot-board on the mail cart. It seemed that at Ballasalla there was no damage, but when the cart was found it had been broken. He said it may have been caused by another person other than the driver suddenly jumping on the board. A blow may have been delivered to cause unconsciousness and he may then have been carried to the river. The Coroner felt the small spot of blood behind where Kermode would have been sitting was conclusive evidence that he was struck whilst on the mail cart. He referred to Stephen Fargher's evidence about the man sitting on the hedge and wondered whether this man had been a lookout.

The Coroner referred to the evidence of Dr Jones, telling the jury that it had been given in a most unsatisfactory manner and informing them that 'You heard the utter nonsense which he stated and the foolish answers which he gave to the questions put to him. If you had read them in a novel you would not have believed that they would ever be really uttered by any person in such a position.' However he did praise the other doctors for their post-mortem examination.

The Coroner added 'The whole case is at present enveloped in mystery. Whether you can solve that mystery or not, I feel that in your hands the public are perfectly safe, and that in the terms of your oath you will present no man for hatred, malice, or ill-will, nor spare any through fear, favour or affection; but a true verdict give according to the evidence and the best of your skill and knowledge.'

The jury retired about 4.05 p.m. and after half an hour returned to give their unanimous verdict of 'wilful murder against some person or persons unknown'. 'It is the opinion of the jury that there has been great negligence on the part of those whose duty it was to attend to this case sooner, as a considerable time elapsed from the time Kermode, the deceased, was missing, before the first inquest was held.' The Coroner said that he fully agreed with their verdict and did not think it possible that they could have come to any other.

On Wednesday, 7 February the *Mona's Herald* printed a letter from John Kermode's widow:

> To the Editor of *Mona's Herald*. Sir, I most humbly beg an interest in your sympathy towards me and my bereaved family by allowing me to deny a most cruel falsehood. I refer to Hugh Flynn saying in court that he heard my daughter struck her father with a stool. The statement is false. Such behaviour never was in my family by any member from the oldest to the youngest. By so doing you will oblige your most humble and afflicted servant. Margaret Kermode, Thornhill, February 5th 1866. I trust my loss, which is a severe one, is his eternal gain.

No person was ever charged in connection with the death of John Kermode. Despite many rumours and some people writing letters to the local newspapers explaining their own theories as to how he met with his death, the mystery still remains to this day.

NOTE

On February 21 1866 the *Mona's Herald* carried an account of the finding of a baby's body under the heading 'Child Murder'. The article stated: 'No sooner has the excitement of the murder of the mail cart driver passed away than the public mind is shocked by a case of child murder.' It went on to give an account of an inquest held on Saturday, 10 February before the High Bailiff and a jury at the Quarter Bridge Inn in Douglas and the facts of the case were as follows.

A labourer called John Creer was working in a field near the Quarter Bridge when he noticed that some ground appeared to have been recently turned over. When he scraped away some soil he discovered a piece of cloth and inside this he found the body of a baby. Instead of reporting the discovery, he covered the body with soil and left it for three days before returning to the spot with three others, William Clucas, Jonas Mylchreest and his wife. They saw that the body was wrapped in a striped cloth, probably an apron.

Dr Ring gave evidence at the inquest stating that the umbilical cord had been cut with a blunt instrument but not tied. He found that the child must have died very shortly after birth and he discovered that it had not taken a breath as the lungs were not inflated. He estimated that the baby had been dead for approximately four to six days. An examination of the head revealed a mark on the skull 'as if from a blow' and blood on the surface of the brain. He explained that the pressure of this blood on the brain would have quickly caused death.

The jury returned a verdict of 'wilful murder against some person or persons unknown'. 'And we further say that there was great and unfeeling neglect on the part of the said John Creer, the person who first discovered the child, in not at once acquainting the proper authorities in order that an immediate investigation might have been made.'

As far as I can ascertain no one was ever charged in connection with the case, although the High Bailiff passed on the information he had received to the Acting Attorney General. He considered that the available evidence was 'insufficient to implicate anyone in the murder'.

20

MELVINA ANNIE KEWLEY (1859)

James Kewley was a tailor, although in 1859 illness had prevented him from working for some time. He was married but had been separated from his wife for about 18 months by September of that year. Since becoming separated he had lived mainly with his father who was a farm labourer living in Onchan. He had one child, a girl named Melvina Annie Kewley and at the end of 1859 she was two years old.

About 10 p.m. one night in June or July that year James Kewley took his young daughter to the house of Jane and John Creer in Douglas and asked Jane Creer if she would look after Melvina for him, promising to pay her the sum of 2s 9d a week. Over the next three months or so he saw very little of the girl, probably only about once every five weeks when he visited the Creers' house. John Creer felt the amount Kewley was paying was insufficient and in August Kewley promised to increase this to 3s a week. Kewley soon fell behind with his payments and Jane Creer went to James Kewley's father's house in August to ask for the money she was owed. Kewley's father said he did not have any money and instead his mother paid Jane Creer 8s. James Kewley then told John Creer that he was unable to pay them any longer for looking after Melvina and said he planned to take the child away and let her stay with some of his relatives in the north of the Island as he would not have to pay them to look after her.

On the night of Tuesday, 27 September at around 8 p.m. James Kewley called at the Creer house to collect his young daughter and carried her away. Jane Creer had assumed he was taking her to his relatives. On either the Wednesday or Thursday that same week Kewley returned to the Creers' house carrying a trunk and took away the child's clothes and other belongings. On this occasion Jane Creer asked him how Melvina was doing and he replied, 'Oh, she is quite well enough, she's quite at home.' Jane Creer then asked him if the little girl had walked when she left her house, and Kewley said, 'I put her down but she stood still and said, "Dadda carry me".' He did not tell Jane where he had taken Melvina, only that she was going 'somewhere in the north'. Kewley appeared to Jane on this second visit to be rather agitated and in a hurry. He also told her that he intended to go off the Island later that week to see a doctor about a 'gathering' in his neck.

In 1859 Howstrake Farm in Onchan had its own corn mill, powered by water from a dam known as the Mill Dam, close to St Peter's Church and the Vicarage Garden. The mill was demolished in the 1930s and the marshland which now remains is known as Onchan Wetlands. On Sunday, 9 October 1859 at around 2.30 p.m. a 13-year-old boy, Robert Killip, was playing near the Mill Dam when he noticed something in the water. When he moved the object with a stick it turned over and he was horrified to find that it was the body of a young girl. He saw that the left leg of the body was underneath a dead cat which had clearly been thrown into the water with a rope around it and a rock tied to the rope. Killip shouted for help to James Quayle, who was living nearby, and Quayle took the stick from the young boy and managed to get the body out of the water. The pair saw that the girl was fully clothed and that there was a head wound from which blood was oozing. They sent for the Coroner and the body was subsequently removed to the stable of a nearby pub, the Nursery Inn in Onchan.

An inquest was held on Wednesday, 12 October before Senhouse Wilson, the Deputy Coroner. A jury was sworn in and the body was viewed where it still lay in the stable. By this time it was in an advanced state of decomposition and the jury saw that there was a blunt wound to the left side of the head. Before he started his inquiries into the circumstances surrounding the death, the Deputy Coroner explained why an inquest had not been heard earlier. He reported that this delay was due to 'a chapter of accidents'. The Deputy Coroner said that on several occasions in the past the Coroner-General, W. W. Christian, had been blamed for delays in arranging inquests. He continued that he 'therefore thought it but right to make the circumstances attending the delay of the present inquest publicly known in order to remove any blame which, to the public, in the absence of this explanation, might seem to attach to that gentleman'. He then proceeded with the inquiry.

James Quayle was the first witness to give evidence. He told the jury that he was a tailor and lived in Onchan. On the previous Sunday, around 2.30 p.m. he was at his sister's house near the Mill Dam where the body was found when he heard Killip shouting that there was a child in the water. He said he ran as fast as he could to discover Killip trying to get the body out with a stick. Quayle managed to get the body on to the bank at the side of the water and saw it was a girl aged approximately three years. The girl was fully clothed and had a little cap on her head and wore shoes and white stockings. He saw that there was a bruise on the side of the head and explained that he then sent for help and the Coroner arrived and had the body removed to Mr Barber's stable. Quayle said there were no stones around the water on which the child might have injured her head and also added that he had often seen children playing there.

The boy who found the body, Robert Killip, then gave his evidence. He said he was 13 years of age and worked on Mr Cadman's farm looking after his cattle. On the previous Sunday afternoon, while playing near the dam, he had seen something in the water. He took a stick and saw it was the body of a young girl floating face down. He said one leg was held under a dead cat which had obviously been thrown into the water. He too had seen that the head was bruised and cut and said, 'There was a hole in the left side of the head near the eye in which we saw blood and water bubbling.' Killip said the body was fully clothed and there was a cap or hood tied tight around the head under the left ear. He went on to say that a lot of people had then arrived to see the child. The Reverend Howard sent a lad and pony to Douglas for the Coroner and later that evening, Mr Caddle, the Coroner, arrived between 6 and 7 p.m. and the body was removed to Mr Barber's stable. Killip, in answer to a juror's question, said that the hood was tied very tightly and was covering the child's eyes. He did not see how the hood could have moved while in the water.

Jane Creer was then called to give her evidence. She said she had seen the body and recognised it as that of Melvina Annie Kewley whom she had been looking after for four months or so, since the child's father brought her to the Creer house. On the evening that James Kewley had come to collect his daughter, she was dressed in the same clothes as were on the body when it was found in the water. Kewley had not told her where he had taken the child but said he planned to take her to the north of the Island later that week. She thought he may have said he was going to take her to Kirk Bride. Mrs Creer added that she had never seen the child's mother in all the time she had looked after her and did not know anything about James Kewley. She did think that he looked 'rather curious' on the night he had called for the child's clothes. He had seemed agitated and appeared to be in a hurry and she said that subsequently she had heard from her son that Kewley 'was looking for a passage to go by a Whitehaven boat'. She also added that she understood

James Kewley and his wife did not live together and she had heard that the child's mother did not live on the Island.

John Kewley, the father of James, was next called. He said his son had been separated from his wife for almost two years. His son and granddaughter had lived with him and his wife the previous spring and he told the jury that he had last seen the child in August when Jane Creer had brought her to the house to see James. At that time his wife had given Jane Creer 8s towards the money owed by her son. John Kewley said his son was very fond of Melvina. The last time he had seen James was on the morning of 30 September and on the previous evening he had seen him bringing a box downstairs and assumed that he was getting his clothes ready and planned to leave soon. James told his father some time in August that he planned to go to sea. John said he did not know anything about his taking the child away from Mrs Creer's and James had not brought the child to their house over the previous few weeks. John Kewley said he had several brothers in the north of the Island but none were living at Kirk Bride and added that he had not heard from his son since he left. He also said that sometimes he felt his son was 'not right in his mind', adding that 'he always seemed in trouble about something; I and my wife thought it was on account of his unfortunate marriage'.

Dr Cornelius Percy Ring then gave his evidence. He explained that he was a doctor who worked in Douglas and had made a post-mortem examination of the child's body. He described a cut on the left side of the head, which he felt had been produced by an instrument with a sharp edge. On removing the scalp he had discovered a skull fracture which was depressed and he said that he felt this fracture would be sufficient to have caused the child's death. In the girl's stomach he had found the remains of some bread and a liquid, such as milk or tea. He estimated the body had been in the water from ten to fourteen days and he also felt the child must have died within three hours of eating her last meal. The doctor said, 'I found the heart quite free from coagulated blood in both cavities, which is generally found in cases where death has been occasioned merely by drowning.' He went on, 'I should say also, from the state of the tongue that life had not become entirely extinct when the child was immersed in the water.' He added that her injuries may have been produced by a fall but this would have to have been from a good height to cause such a fracture.

Mrs Creer was then recalled and confirmed that the last meal the child had at her house was 'some sop composed of bread, milk and some tea and she had this about quarter of an hour before her father came to take her away'. A juror asked her if James Kewley was fond of the child and she replied in her opinion he seemed very distant towards Melvina.

The jury then visited the spot where the body had been found and looked at the various ways a child could have got to the Mill Dam. They thought it improbable that a three year old child could have made her own way there.

After about ten minutes of deliberation the jury gave their verdict as one of 'wilful murder against James Kewley'.

An article describing the case in the *Mona's Herald* on 12 October 1859 ended with the following paragraph:

> It is generally stated that no formal steps have been taken for the apprehension of the convicted murderer, there being no funds, it is stated in the hands of the authorities for applying to purposes of this kind. If this report is incorrect, it will no doubt be a matter of course on the part of those holding power, in connection with criminal cases of the sort, publicly to make a statement to that effect, in order to relieve the public minds and apprehension which will otherwise tend to be a stigma upon our local laws.

In a letter to the editor of the *Mona's Herald* on 9 November 1859 which appeared under the heading 'The Onchan Murder' and was signed 'The Father of a Family', the author stated:

> If there has ever been perpetrated a murder more atrociously cruel and hellish than any other, that of the poor innocent child by her fiendish father, in the case above named, is unquestionably of that foul character; and if there ever was an occasion upon which the astonishment and indignation of a civilised (not to say Christianised) community should be more vehemently aroused and expressed than another, it is when they are given to understand that no efficient effort has been made to arrest the wretch by whose hand the poor innocent evidently was butchered. Shall we, Sir, be told in the middle of the nineteenth century that there are no funds available for the pursuit and punishment of a cold blooded assassin whose victim was his own inoffending child?

The writer of the letter urges the Governor, deemsters and high bailiffs to inform the Queen, saying,

> Why, a dozen telegraphic words from them of this fearful tragedy borne to the ear of Her Majesty, would result in the publication of

such a hue and cry throughout and beyond Europe as would place the
miscreant in the hands of Justice (if alive) in a very short time.

NOTE

I have been unable to discover what happened to James Kewley. He certainly never stood
trial on the Isle of Man for the murder of his young daughter.

21

MARGARET E.N. KELLY (1889)

In 1889, William Kelly was 55 years old and, like his father before him, a plasterer by trade. By all accounts he was an excellent workman and many thought of him as the best plasterer in Douglas, where he lived with his wife and three of his children. Although the couple, who had been married for 37 years, had 13 children, only 6 were still living at this time and the three who lived with them were his sons, Charles, aged 13 and Louis, aged 18, and daughter, Christina, aged 16.

Their home was two rooms in a building which was formerly a hotel in James Street, Douglas. This was known as Redfern's Hotel and in the 1840s and 1850s the hotel was known as 'one of the town's leading hostelries'. With the building of new hotels on Loch Promenade and Victoria Street, its popularity waned and it later became a pub and after this a lodging house where many families lived. It provided cheap accommodation for families and it is clear that those who lived there were poor.

William Kelly appears to have been quite an interesting character. His father had been known as 'Bully Kelly' and William seems to have inherited the same nickname – not because he was a bully but simply because his father was known by that name. It appears that he was very widely read and was particularly interested in Shakespeare and Robert Burns. As the *Isle of Man Examiner* reported on 30 November 1889, however, 'his great failing . . . was his indulgence in drink'. The article also described how 'he would occasionally go on a spree of several weeks' duration'. When sober, Kelly was a quiet, unassuming, inoffensive man. When drunk he was a completely different character and would love to argue with anyone about almost any subject. During these discussions he would often tightly clasp the hand of the person to whom he was speaking. What seems clear is that even when drunk he was never violent or offensive. His wife Margaret Elizabeth Nicholson

Kelly was also an alcoholic and when one or the other was drunk there would be frequent rows but all who knew Kelly agreed that William Kelly was a good family man who cared deeply about his wife and children. The family lived in two rooms, one on the third floor and one directly above it on the fourth floor of the building. The lower room was used as a living room and the upper as a bedroom.

On the morning of Tuesday, 26 November 1889, at about 7.40 a.m., a neighbour of the Kellys, Thomas William Corlett, 24, had gone into their living room. He spoke to the couple while Margaret was preparing breakfast and it was clear to him that William had been drinking. Kelly had gone out for a while before returning and Corlett stayed in the room until about 11.40 a.m. Corlett was later to say that William Kelly did not look any different when he returned than when he had gone out. He did not feel he had any more to drink while he was out of the room. Shortly after this Margaret Kelly and her daughter, Christina, were getting lunch ready. Corlett left the Kellys' living room to return to his own and was followed out by Christina. The pair walked down one flight of stairs and stood talking for a few minutes before they heard William Kelly call to his daughter, shouting, 'Bella! Bella! Come; I have murdered your mother!' Corlett and Christina then went back to the room to find Margaret seated in a chair with her throat cut and blood pouring from the wound. Corlett ran out to look for a doctor and returned soon afterwards with Dr Woods and Police Constable Corkish but Margaret Kelly was dead. From that moment on William Kelly never denied that he had killed his wife. He claimed that he killed her under extreme provocation.

At 1.30 p.m. that same day an inquest was held by Mr Samuel Harris, Coroner of Inquests for Douglas, in front of a hastily assembled jury of 13 men. They first viewed the body in the room where the death occurred and it was still in the sitting position in which it had been found. After what must have been a horrific ordeal for all concerned, the jury adjourned to the nearby courthouse. A large crowd had gathered by this time and the courtroom was packed. Kelly was brought into court and said to the jury in a loud voice: 'Good morning, gentlemen.' The Coroner told him in a firm voice to 'keep quiet please'.

Kelly's youngest daughter, Christina, was called as the first witness. She was crying and too upset to give evidence. As she was being taken to a nearby room she cried out, 'Father, Father, poor Father!' At this, Kelly bowed his head and began to weep.

Thomas William Corlett related the events of that morning, explaining that he had spent some time with the Kellys in their room. The pair had been quite friendly towards each other he said, although it was clear that William had been drinking. Mrs Kelly had asked him if he would have a meal with them but Corlett told her he would go to his own room and have it there. He had gone down one flight of stairs talking to Christina for five or ten minutes. It was then they heard William cry to Bella that he had murdered Margaret. Bella, Corlett explained, was Kelly's married daughter Bella Tyman, who was at the time in the upstairs room.

When Corlett and Christina entered the room they saw Margaret sitting in the chair bleeding profusely from a neck wound. Christina took hold of her mother around the neck and said, 'Oh, Father, you should not have done this.'

Corlett reported that Kelly replied, 'She was too bad tempered.' Corlett told the jury that he then went for a doctor and returned shortly afterwards to find Margaret still in the same position, covered with blood and unconscious. He denied hearing any noises that would have suggested there had been a struggle or argument while he was talking to Christina.

Jane Loughlin, a close neighbour of the Kellys, was next called. She lived with her husband in a room on the same landing. She told the jury that she had heard Mr and Mrs Kelly the previous evening and it was clear that by midnight to 1 a.m. they were both drunk. She added that there were others in the room including the Kellys' son-in-law, Thomas William Corlett, their daughters and James Ellison. She said William Kelly got up early and went to work, before returning about 8 a.m. She had heard no more until he called to his daughter, telling her to come down as he had cut her mother's throat. Jane Loughlin entered the Kellys' room just after Bella and she had seen Mrs Kelly sitting with a 'pool of blood in her lap and running on to the floor'. She said William Kelly was 'drunk' and added that Margaret was almost dead when she first saw her. She described William as a 'nice man' but admitted that she 'did not think his head is right when he has drink in him'.

Christina Kelly was then able to give evidence at the inquiry. She told the jury: 'They were very good parents indeed. If sober, a better father could not be wished for.' She went on, 'My mother was bad for tantalising him.' There had been an argument the previous evening between her parents and Christina had taken her mother to the bedroom she shared with her sister. Margaret had slept there, getting up around 6.15 a.m. The parents had seemed happy together and later the pair had breakfast. At 8 a.m. when Christina got up they were having a drink and her father had gone out for a 'noggin' of rum, giving half of it to his wife. She went on to describe how her mother used 'some aggravating language' around 10.30 a.m. and her father had again gone out, later returning with another 'noggin' of rum which they again shared. The couple were having lunch when she and Corlett left the room. A few minutes later she heard her father calling for Bella. She had rushed to the room to find her mother bleeding profusely from her mouth, nose and neck.

Isabella Tyman, Christina's sister, explained that her husband John was away at sea and she had lived with her parents since March. She described an argument between her parents around midnight and how the following morning, she had heard her father calling to her saying he had cut her mother's throat. She had not entered the room immediately but had screamed for help and run out of the building and found two police constables before returning. She fainted shortly after this but added that earlier in the morning her parents were 'slightly tipsy'.

Dr Black told the jury he was a medical practitioner in Douglas. He was in the marketplace when he was told about the injured woman in Redfern's Hotel. He said Margaret's head was thrown back and her throat was covered with cloths. On removing these he saw that her windpipe was almost completely severed, as was the main artery on the right side of the neck. The wound was 7.5 in. long and gaped 2.5 in. but was only about 0.75 in. deep. The left end was slightly lower than the right. Blood had spurted about 9 ft across the room and a large quantity lay on and around the body. The doctor said it was clear that this wound had caused the woman's death. He said he felt a more detailed post-mortem examination of the body was required and the Coroner, although he considered this was unnecessary, granted the request. The inquest was then adjourned until the following day.

On the following Wednesday morning, Dr T. A. Woods explained that he and Dr Black had carried out a post-mortem examination. The cause of death was haemorrhage from the right carotid artery and death would have occurred within seconds.

Superintendent Fayle said that William Kelly admitted he had cut his wife's throat and had then produced two knives from his pocket saying he used one to inflict the injury. When asked why he had done it he said, 'She has always been tantalising me, accusing me of going with other women and also with my youngest daughter.' Kelly had told him how his wife had, when seated, put her head back and told him to 'come and do it now'. Kelly had then cut his wife's throat. It was clear, added the superintendent, that Kelly was under the influence of drink.

The Coroner then summed up for the jury. He said it was clear that alcohol played a big part in the tragedy of the previous day and told them, 'Although you may take it in small quantities unharmed, in large quantities it is as deadly a poison as anything you can take to drink, no matter what other poison you may select'.

The jury retired to consider their verdict, returning after 16 minutes. The foreman said 'We find that Margaret Elizabeth Nicholson Kelly died from exhaustion and loss of blood caused by her husband, William Kelly, cutting her throat under considerable provocation'.

Kelly was removed from the court but returned a few minutes later. Several witnesses were again called and repeated their earlier evidence. Kelly's daughters cried bitterly during the hearing and he was committed for trial. The Coroner again talked of the evils of alcohol, saying he hoped others in court would 'take warning by the unfortunate position of this man'. Kelly was then removed to Castle Rushen Gaol. His wife was buried two days later on the Friday afternoon.

Kelly was brought before Deemster Drinkwater and a special jury on Friday, 6 December to decide if there was sufficient evidence to send him for trial at a Court of General Gaol Delivery, on either a charge of murder or manslaughter. There was applause in court when they found that he should be tried for manslaughter instead of murder.

At the subsequent trial on Friday, 17 January 1890 Kelly pleaded guilty to manslaughter. Several witnesses gave excellent character references, including Assistant Police Superintendent Fayle, who told the judges that the defendant had always been kind-hearted, inoffensive and, to his knowledge, never violent in the past.

Mr Ring pleaded with the court to take a lenient view of the offence. He reminded the court that Kelly had never tried to deny the crime and said, 'The prisoner seems to have been a man of kind-hearted and amiable disposition. He was subject to one fault, that was of taking, on occasion, too much drink, but irrespective of that he seems to be a man of blameless character. He was a man particularly affectionate to his wife and daughters.' Ring went on to criticise the behaviour of Margaret Kelly, saying, 'It seemed that she exerted all her powers to cause him distraction and misery in the house. She was addicted to drink and she was habitually making charges against the prisoner-at-the-bar of the most abominable character. The charges were that he was having illicit intimacy with his own daughter. We are told, Your Excellency, by the evidence called for the prosecution, that this man was on occasions driven to the very brink of madness by the conduct of his wife.'

He went on to tell them that this behaviour had continued for years but

Kelly had never resorted to violence prior to the incident which resulted in his wife's death.

The court retired at 11.24 and the jury returned after 30 minutes to deliver their verdict. They reminded Kelly that the indicting jury had felt that manslaughter was the appropriate charge for the offence, although in their view they would have been justified in recommending that he be charged with murder. He was told that they accepted there were mitigating circumstances and took into consideration the fact that he had never used violence until provoked on this occasion. He was then sentenced to ten years' imprisonment.

The moment of sentencing is described in the *Mona's Herald*:

> The conclusion of His Honour's remarks were lost in the piercing shrieks and groans which rent the court and which proceeded from three of the prisoner's daughters . . . Mrs Tyman, after one piercing shriek on hearing the sentence pronounced, dropped to the floor as if dead . . . [she] was carried into the corridor and laid upon her back, and in about five minutes recovered sufficiently to be able to leave the court, but during this time her sisters kept up a most distressing wail and excited the pity of many of those who were present.

Of Kelly's reaction to the sentence, the report went on 'the poor fellow seemed utterly prostrated with the severity of the sentence and buried his head on the front of the dock, and gave way to a flood of tears'. Finally, the reporter commented: 'The whole scene was, perhaps, the most painful that has ever been witnessed in the court, and will not soon be forgotten by many who were present.'

After spending several weeks in the gaol in Douglas, Kelly was transferred to Wormwood Scrubs in London to start serving his sentence.